TYBURN
TALES

THE CRIMINAL
CHRONOLOGY OF
YORK CASTLE

CRIMINAL CHRONOLOGY

OF

YORK CASTLE;

WITH

A REGISTER OF THE CRIMINALS CAPITALLY CONVICTED
AND EXECUTED AT THE COUNTY ASSIZES,

COMMENCING MARCH 1ST, 1379, TO THE PRESENT TIME:

*An interesting Record to those who trace the Progress of Crime through the
Change of Manners, the Increase of Population, and the Raised
Complexion of the Penal Code.*

CAREFULLY COMPILED FROM PRISON DOCUMENTS, ANCIENT
PAPERS, AND OTHER AUTHENTIC SOURCES,

MATERIALLY ASSISTED BY

WILLIAM KNIPE, ANTIQUARIAN, OF CLEMENTHORPE, YORK.

Entered at Stationers' Hall.

YORK:
PUBLISHED BY C. L. BURDEKIN,
No. 2, PARLIAMENT STREET;
LONDON: SIMPKIN, MARSHALL, & CO.
1867.

First published 1867
This edition 2010

The History Press
The Mill, Brimscombe Port
Stroud, Gloucestershire, GL5 2QG
www.thehistorypress.co.uk

British Library Cataloguing in Publication Data.
A catalogue record for this book is available from the British Library.

ISBN 978 0 7524 5537 2

Typesetting and origination by The History Press
Printed in India by Nutech Print Services

PREFACE.

---◆◇◆---

THE universal consent of every stage of society has proved
the necessity of laws to restrain, by punishment, the
licentious and cruel dispositions of bad men ; indeed, but for
these regulations, however severe and partial they may have
sometimes been, society would have missed its first great
object, namely, the better security of men's persons and
property.

The several systems of criminal jurisprudence which have,
at various periods, been adopted by different nations, though
dissimilar in their specific regulations, all agree in one fun-
damental principle,—*that the proper end of human punishment is the prevention of crime.*

This grand principle is the basis of the English criminal
code, and fully justifies it from the character of cruelty with
which it is in the present day too commonly branded.   This
odious charge is best answered by observing that the criminal
laws were never intended to be carried into indiscriminate

execution ; that the Legislature, when it establishes its last and severest penalties, trusts to the benignity of the Crown to relax their severity, as often as circumstances appear to palliate the offence, or even as often as those circumstances of aggravation are wanting which render this vigorous interposition necessary.

It is true, that by the great number of statutes creating capital offences, it sweeps into the net every crime which, under any possible circumstances, may merit the punishment of death ; but when the execution of the sentence comes to be deliberated upon, a small proportion of offenders are singled out, whose general bad character, or the peculiar aggravation of whose crimes, renders them fit examples of public justice. By this expedient few actually suffer death, whilst the dread and danger of it hang over the crimes of many. Thus the weakness of the law cannot be taken advantage of—the life of the subject is spared as far as the necessity of making public examples will permit, yet no one will venture upon the commission of any enormous crime, from a knowledge that the laws have not provided for its punishment.

The criminal jurisprudence of England may further be defended from the imputation of cruelty, by considering that though it be strict in its enactments, and visits many minor offences with severe punishment, yet in its administration, jealousy of the criminating, and compassion for the offender, temper its firmness, and soften the rigour of its decisions. It requires no one to criminate himself, and in dubious cases leans invariably to the side of mercy. It is ever ready to allow the previous good character of the criminal to lighten his punishment, and never wantonly aggravates, by protracted sufferings, the awful penalty it assigns to the most enormous crimes; it ever extends its compassion beyond the present life, and by the consolations of religion which it provides, often calms and alleviates the last moments of its unhappy victims. In this respect, all denominations of religion can be supplied with their own minister, pastor, or priest.

The numerous and melancholy examples which our pages record of persons hurrying on from one crime to another, till the awful hand of justice has required their lives, will, we trust, alarm and deter the young and inexperienced from an indulgence in those pursuits or company which tend to weaken their ideas of justice and morality, the sure and certain prognostic of future ruin.

At once to perpetrate the more atrocious crimes is unusual; but the commission of one vice leads to another; frequent repetitions stifle the voice of conscience; the distance to the next degree of criminality is lessened, till at length the unhappy victim of self-delusion is awakened from his perturbed dream to the more awful scenery of real guilt and retribution.

To avoid, and as much as possible to lessen the great and increasing number of offences against the salutary restrictions of justice, is the duty of every well-wisher to society and civilization. This purpose will be best effected by supporting and countenancing those institutions which have for their object the instruction of youth, by endeavours to excite habits of content and industry, and above all, by the constant practice and inculcation of the principles of that religion which enjoins us to "love our neighbour as ourself."

RECORD OF EXECUTIONS IN YORK.

Tuesday, March 1st, A.D. 1379.—A special meeting of the bailiffs of the city of York and county of the said city, with the magistrates and gentlemen of the late Grand Jury, assembled for the purpose of considering the propriety of appointing a place to erect a gallows, was held in the Castle of York, on Tuesday, the 1st day of March, 1379. The Mayor of York occupied the chair, and addressed the meeting, when several gentlemen spoke and explained the circumstances relating to the insubordination and rising of the monks at the late execution which took place at the gallows of the Abbot of St. Mary's. It was then proposed and seconded by two of the city bailiffs, that a gallows be erected upon the ground where the gibbet-post now stands, and that it be taken down and a gallows re-built and erected there upon Knavesmire, on the south side, opposite the York Moor, about one mile from the Castle, and that Master Joseph Penny, joiner, of Blake-street, in the city of York, do build the said gallows forthwith, at the cost of £10. 15s. This resolution was unanimously adopted, and the meeting, after complimenting the chairman, separated. On Wednesday, the 7th day of the said month, the new gallows was erected for the public execution of the criminals capitally convicted in the city of York, and county of the said city, to be called the York Tyburn.

EDWARD HEWISON.

At the Spring Assizes of 1379, Edward Hewison, aged 20, a native of Stockton, near York, and a private soldier in the

Earl of Northumberland's Light Horse, was tried and capitally convicted for committing a rape upon Louisa Bentley, 22 years of age, of Sheriff Hutton, a servant belonging to that Castle, as she was coming to York, in a field where she was walking, about three miles from Sheriff Hutton. When Hewison saw her alone in the field on the foot-path, he got off his horse and tied it to a tree. He then went into the field, threw the young woman down, and ravished her. Having violated her person against her consent, on Monday, the 28th day of February, at two o'clock in the afternoon, next day Hewison was taken at his quarters in the Pavement, and committed to the Castle. On Tuesday, March 31st, 1379, he was executed at the new gallows, without Micklegate Bar. Hewison being the first man that suffered at the new Tyburn, caused a great number of people from the neighbouring towns and villages, to assemble to witness his untimely end. After the execution his body was hanged upon a gibbet in the field where he had committed the crime, in Sheriff Hutton Road. This happened in the second year of the reign of King Richard the Second.

John Chambers and Others.

Monday, November 27th, A.D. 1488.—John Chambers and several others, who were concerned in an insurrection in the North, and murdered the Earl of Northumberland and some of his servants, at Maiden Bower, Topcliffe, the seat of the Earl, were executed at the Tyburn without Micklegate Bar. During this year a tax of a tenth penny was laid on men's goods and lands to aid the Duke of Bretagne against the French King, which caused an insurrection amongst the people of the North.

Sir Robert Aske.

Wednesday, August 13th, A.D. 1537.—In the reign of Henry VIII., Sir Robert Aske, aged 58, of Aughton, in this county, was beheaded in the Pavement, and next day hanged in chains upon Heworth Moor, near York, for being the leader of the unsuccessful insurrection called "Pilgrimage of

Grace." He was drawn upon a sledge from the Castle of York, at eight o'clock in the morning, guarded by the sheriff officers, and a troop of Light Horse, where a scaffold was erected in the Pavement 25 feet by 12 feet, and 13 feet high, at the east end of All-Hallows Church. This unfortunate man mounted the scaffold with a firm step, and with a smile upon his countenance kneeled down to pray, which he did fervently and aloud for the space of fifteen minutes, warning all that were within the hearing of his voice to attend to their rights and privileges as true-born Englishmen, and not to mind his death, as he considered he had done no more than his duty. After the execution his body was taken to Master Robert Pyements, the sign of the Eagle and Child, in the Pavement, and there the chains were fixed upon his lifeless remains. Next morning, at five o'clock, the Sheriff and his officers, with a troop of Light Horse, and a large number of citizens took the body to Heworth Moor, east of the Wind-mills, then standing, where a gibbet-post had been erected 35 feet high. The body having been hung at the top of the gibbet, and all things cleared away, the Sheriff read his proclamation, stating that any person or persons found taking down the body or damaging the post would be imprisoned for twenty years. In about ten minutes the Sheriff and his officers left the moor amidst a large concourse of spectators who were going to and coming from the city.

Lord Hussey.

Wednesday, August 27th, A.D. 1537.—In the reign of Henry VIII., Lord Hussey, aged 62, of Duffield, in this county, was hanged and quartered at the Tyburn, without Micklegate Bar, for being concerned in the late insurrection called the "Pilgrimage of Grace." He was drawn upon a sledge from the Castle of York to the place of execution, at half-past eleven o'clock in the forenoon, and arrived at the scaffold a few minutes past twelve. After a short time spent in prayer, he addressed the spectators for a length of time, and hoped that the period was not far distant when every Englishman would have the rights and privileges which they now required and were contending for, as he had only done his duty, and was about to seal his testimony with his blood.

After so saying, he gave himself up to his executioner, and in a few moments had ceased to exist. After hanging twenty minutes, he was cut down, stripped, and laid upon a stage built for that purpose, close to the gallows, where his head was cut off, his body quartered, and his mutilated remains put into a coffin and given to his friends for interment, in the presence of a large number of spectators.

N.B.—Duffield Castle was the seat of Lord Hussey.

WILLIAM WODE, PRIOR OF BRIDLINGTON.

Saturday, September 21st, A.D. 1537.—William Wode, Prior of Bridlington, aged 67, was executed for high treason, at the Tyburn gallows on Knavesmire, without Micklegate Bar, near the city of York. He was drawn from the Castle upon a hurdle, to the place of execution, and there beheaded and quartered, upon the charge of being concerned in a rebellion of the same nature as that denominated the " Pilgrimage of Grace." After the execution his mutilated remains were given to his friends for interment.

SIR JOHN NEVILL AND OTHERS.

Tuesday, March 31st, A.D. 1541.—Sir John Nevill and ten of his associates, for creating a disturbance and insurrection in the North, were executed at the Tyburn without Micklegate Bar. The Lord Mayor, Robert Hall, was present, and was most deeply affected at Sir John's untimely end.

WILLIAM OMBLER, THOMAS DALE, AND JOHN STEPHENSON.

September 21st, A.D. 1549.—William Ombler, Thomas Dale, and John Stephenson, were executed at the Tyburn without Micklegate Bar, for raising a rebellion in the North. George Gayle was Lord Mayor that year, and James Harrington and Edward Greenberry were Sheriffs.

SIMON DIGBY AND OTHERS.

Good Friday, March 27th, A.D. 1570.—Simon Digby,

aged 42, of Asknew ; John Fulthorpe, aged 39, of Iselbeck, in this county, Esqrs. ; Robert Pennyman, aged 37, of Stokesly ; Thomas Bishop, the younger, aged 29, of Pocklington, gentlemen, were drawn from the Castle of York to the place of execution on Knavesmire, and there hanged, headed, and quartered. Their four heads were set on the four principal gates of the city, with four of their quarters. The other quarters were set up in divers places in the county, as a warning to rebels to avoid a similar fate.

THOMAS WILSON, *alias* MOUNTAIN.

July 30*th*, A.D. 1570.—At Peter's Prison, York, in the Hall of Pleas, Thomas Wilson, *alias* Mountain, was tried on an indictment, wherein he was charged with having been guilty of the wilful murder of George de Walton, Abbot of St. Mary's, on the 13th day of July, 1570, in the Cathedral Church of St. Peter's, York ; also charged for that he on the said 13th day of July, did feloniously stab the Right Reverend Father in God, Edmund Grindall, Lord Archbishop of York, with intent to do him some grievous bodily harm, in the said Cathedral Church of St. Peter, York. He was found guilty after a trial which lasted four days, and ordered to be executed on the 18th of August following. On Monday morning, being the day fixed for the execution of the said Thomas Wilson, *alias* Mountain, he was taken from the dungeon of Peter's Prison, at eight o'clock in the morning, to the gallows of the Abbey of St. Mary, Clifton. Since his confinement, he had several times attempted to break the prison, and, after his condemnation, he made a hole through a brick-and-a-half partition, large enough for him to pass into the chapel gallery, from which he astonishingly ascended into another ten feet above, with fetters weighing nearly fifty pounds, and so formed as not to permit one foot to step six inches before the other. Here he broke through a plaster partition, and thus got over the brick ceiling of all the cells, and immediately under the roof of all the building, where he was overheard and soon secured. On searching him, a hooked nail and a bit of tin plate were found. The bit of plate he had whetted to a very keen edge, as a knife, to cut up the stout canvass cover of his bed into long strips. These he had twisted and strongly tied together, so as to form a very stout rope, nearly forty feet long, whereby he intended to make his descent from the roof into the surrounding yard. He was afterwards confined in a dungeon on the ground floor, and so chained that he could not reach any of the walls, and a guard was constantly kept with him. Since then his conduct had been a mixture of rage and disappointment, very unbecoming his situation. He was brought under the gallows at nine o'clock in the morning, where he spent some time in addressing the crowd, after which he twice called out, "God save the Queen," threw aside his book, and was launched into eternity. After the execution his body was hung in chains on Clifton Ings.

BARNHARD SIEGFRED.

Tuesday, March 30th, A.D. 1571.—Barnard Siegfred, aged 49, a native of Dover, was executed at the gallows of St. Leonard's, Green Dykes, without Walmgate Bar, for highway robbery and attempt to murder one Master John Dolland, in Stockton Forest, in December, 1570. He expiated his crime on the gallows, and was next day hung in chains upon Stockton Forest.

THE EARL OF NORTHUMBERLAND.

Wednesday, August 22nd, A.D. 1572.—The unfortunate Earl of Northumberland was executed at York for high treason. He was drawn from the Castle upon a sledge to the Pavement, the place appointed for his execution, where a scaffold was erected at the east end of All-Hallows Church, 25 feet long by 15 feet broad, and 12 feet in height. The noble Earl mounted the scaffold with a firm step, looked about him for a short time, then spoke to the Sheriff and Chaplain of the Castle, and to the spectators for the space of fifteen minutes. After addressing the people, he kneeled down and prayed for a short time, then rose and shook hands with those that were on the scaffold, but did not speak to them. After this he went to the fatal spot, knelt down with his face to the east, laid his head upon the block, and gave the signal to the executioner, who struck off his head at one blow. After his execution, his head was set up on a very high pole at the top of Micklegate Bar, and his body was buried in the Church of St. Crux, in this city, by two of his servants and three women.

GEORGE RUTBY, ESQ., AND OTHERS.

Wednesday, April 3rd, A.D. 1573.—George Rutby, Esq., aged 45, a native of Scarborough ; Robert de Scheele, Knight, aged 56, a native of Hull ; Edward de Lavoiffier, aged 58, a native of Hull ; Thomas de Berthollet, aged 49, a native of Driffield ; William Diequemare, aged 63, a native of Knaresborough ; Robert de Rosier, aged 57, a native of Knaresborough ; Robert de Alcock, Esq., aged 50, a native of Hull ; William de Alembert, aged 59, a native of Pocklington ; Robert Charles de Aleym, aged 54, a native of Wakefield ; and George Richard de Allestry, aged 59, a native of Wetherby, were executed at the Tyburn without Micklegate Bar, for high treason. They were drawn to the place of execution upon sledges, and there hanged and quartered. Three of their heads were set upon Micklegate Bar, two upon Bootham Bar, two upon Monk Bar, two upon Walm gate Bar, and one over the Castle gates, with their quarters.

ROBERT DE FLEURY AND OTHERS.

Saturday, June 27th, A.D. 1574.—Robert de Fleury, aged 50, a native of Wakefield ; George de Abbot, aged 48, a native of Kirkham ; and William de Abbot, aged 58, a native of Leyburn, were executed at the Tyburn without Micklegate Bar, for wounding Baron de Cavallo, in the Forest of Galtres, near the village of Shipton, with intent to murder him as he was returning from Penrith, on the night of the 29th day of May, 1574. After the execution, their bodies were given to the surgeons of the city to be dissected and anatomized.

FREDERICK GOTTFRIED AND THOMAS CONRAT.

Friday, March 27th, A.D. 1575.—Frederick Gottfried aged 37, a native of Hull ; and Thomas Conrat, aged 27, a native of Keswick, in the county of Cumberland, were executed at the gallows of St. Leonard's, Green Dykes, without Walmgate Bar, for coining guineas in Thursday market, in the city of York. After the execution their bodies were buried in St. Giles's Churchyard, Gillygate, York.

EDWARD DE SATRE AND SARAH HOUSLAY.

Saturday, August 8th, A.D. 1576.—Edward de Satre, aged 36, a native of Selby, and Sarah Houslay, aged 27, a native of Shipton, in this county, were executed at the Tyburn without Micklegate Bar, for uttering forged promissary notes of the value of fifty guineas, at Leeds, belonging to Mr. John Learoyd, innkeeper. After the execution, their bodies were buried behind the Castle walls, near the river Foss.

ROBERT SCHEVEREL, JOHN DE TRADESCANT, AND HENRY GEORGE MASSON.

Tuesday, March 30th, A.D. 1577.—Robert Scheverel, aged 43, a native of Goldsbro' ; John de Tradescant, aged 38, a native of Cottingham ; and Henry George Masson, aged 42, a native of Badsworth, were executed at the gallows of St. Leonard's, Green Dykes, without Walmgate Bar, for breaking into the dwelling-house, with intent to rob and murder Mr. John Pascal and his family, on the night or morning of the 20th of January, 1577. After the execution their bodies were given to the surgeons of the city to be dissected and anatomized.

WILLIAM HENRY DE BOYLE.

Monday, April 2nd, A.D. 1578.—William Henry de Boyle, aged 57, a native of Bentham, was executed at the Tyburn without Micklegate Bar, for the wilful murder of his servant maid, Sarah Robson, of Wakefield, by strangling her with his whiplash in his bed-room, on the morning of the 5th of February of the said year. The cruel tragedy was performed in the presence of his wife and two daughters. After the execution his body was conveyed to Wakefield Common and hung in chains.

CHARLES DE PASCAL AND OTHERS.

Wednesday, July 30th, A.D. 1579.—Charles de Pascal, aged 38, a native of Sheffield; Thomas de Warltire, aged 29, a native of South Kirby; George Edward de Priestley, aged 40, a native of Kildwick, along with Charlotte Morrett, aged 27, a native of Hambleton, and Hannah Fourcroy, aged 25, a native of Yeadingham, were executed at the gallows of St. Leonard's, Green Dykes, without Walmgate Bar, for breaking into the warehouse of Mr. Robert Kirwan, in Stonegate, York, and stealing a quantity of silks and drapery goods of the value of one hundred guineas. After the executions, the bodies of Pascal and Warltire were buried in St. George's Churchyard, Bean Hill, without Fishergate Postern, in this city; and the bodies of Morrett, Fourcroy, and Priestley were interred in St. Wilfred's Churchyard, in Blake-street, York.

JAMES RICHARDSON.

Saturday, July 30th, A.D. 1581.—James Richardson, aged 27, was executed at the gallows of St. Leonard's, Green Dykes, without Walmgate Bar, for the wilful murder of Thomas Miller, Esq., at Knaresborough, on the 5th day of April, 1581. After the murder he took from his victim the sum of twenty pounds in silver coins of this realm.

GEORGE FOSTER.

Monday, April 8th, A.D. 1582.—George Foster, aged 25, of Tadcaster, was executed at the Tyburn without Micklegate Bar, for coining. There were supposed to be about ten thousand people present to witness his untimely end.

PETER CLARK.

Tuesday, March 31st, A.D. 1583.—Peter Clark, aged 28, was executed at the gallows of St. Leonard's, Green Dykes, without Walmgate Bar, for the wilful murder of Hannah Thompson, at Pocklington.

RINION FOSTER.

Tuesday, March 31st, A.D. 1583.—Rinion Foster, aged 32, a native of York, was executed at the gallows of St. Leonard's, Green Dykes, without Walmgate Bar, for horse-stealing and committing a rape upon Mary Thompson, servant to Mr. William Johnson, at Dunnington, near York.

HENRY WILLIAM GENYEMBRE.

Saturday, August 8th, A.D. 1584.—Henry William Genyembre, aged 60, a native of Knaresborough, was executed at the gallows of St. Leonard's, Green Dykes, without Walmgate Bar, for robbery on the king's highway, and horse-stealing at Stokesley, in the county of York. After the execution his body was buried at St. Helen's Church, in Fishergate.

GEORGE DE KIRWAN AND THOMAS DE ALASCO.

Wednesday, August 3rd, A.D. 1585.—George de Kirwan, aged 34, a native of Ripon, and Thomas de Alasco, aged 39, a native of Penistone, were executed at the Tyburn without Micklegate Bar, for coining guineas, at the house of Simon Pontius, in Jubbergate, silversmith, of York. They were drawn on a sledge to the place of execution, when they both seemed firm but resigned to their fate. They both died penitent, and were buried at the Church of St. Helen, Fishergate, in this city.

FREDERICK DE ALCYONIUS, RICHARD DE ALDRICH, AND WILLIAM DE MALCOLM.

Saturday, March 28th, A.D. 1587.—Frederick de Alcyonius, aged 47, a native of Pontefract ; Richard de Aldrich, aged 37, a native of Rotherham ; and William de Malcolm, aged 28, a native of Richmond, were executed at the gallows of St. Leonard's, Green Dykes, without Walmgate Bar. These three unfortunate culprits were drawn from the Castle of York upon a sledge to the fatal spot, where they suffered the severe penalty of the law. Since their condemnation their behaviour had been such as became their unhappy situation, and they acknowledged the justice of their sentence. After their execution they were beheaded and quartered ; their heads were set up on Micklegate Bar, with their quarters. This execution took place at three o'clock in the afternoon, in the presence of not less than eight thousand spectators.

ANDREW TURNER.

Monday, August 10th, A.D. 1588.—Andrew Turner was executed at the gallows of St. Leonard's, Green Dykes, without Walmgate Bar, for coining.

HENRY ASHE.

Monday, August 10th, A.D. 1588.—Henry Ashe was executed at the gallows of St. Leonard's, Green Dykes, without Walmgate Bar, for a rape committed on Jane Furnish, on the highway road leading from York to Hull.

GEORGE WYNCH AND PETER DE RAMUS.

Monday, April 23rd, A.D. 1590.—George Wynch, aged 24, a native of Stamford Bridge, and Peter de Ramus, aged 34, a native of Slaidburn, were executed at the gallows of St. Leonard's, Green Dykes, without Walmgate Bar, for highway robbery on the Hull road, near Kexby, on the night of the first of February, 1590. Their bodies were buried at St. George's Church, Bean-hill, without Fishergate Postern, in this city.

JOSEPH DE HAMEL, RICHARD DE BOURBOULOM, AND ANTHONY HODSON.

Monday, July 28th, A.D. 1592.—Joseph de Hamel, aged 43, a native of Manchester; Richard de Bourboulom, aged 53, a native of Blackburn ; and Anthony Hodson, aged 37, a native of Burnley, in the county of Lancashire, were executed at the Tyburn without Micklegate Bar, for house-breaking and highway robbery on the night of the 5th of May, 1592. Their bodies were buried at Holy Trinity Curia Regis, in this city.

RICHARD CRAW.

Monday, March 30th, A.D. 1594.—Richard Craw, aged 28, was executed at the Tyburn without Micklegate Bar, and the next day hung in chains in Knaresborough Forest, for the wilful murder of Mr. James Giles, of Knaresborough.

WILLIAM DE ALLESTRY, ROBERT DE HAMMOND, AND THOMAS DE ALLIX.

Saturday, March 24th, A.D. 1595, William de Allestry, aged 37, a native of York ; Robert de Hammond, aged 34, a native of York ; and Thomas de Allix, aged 38, a native of York, all of Walmgate, were executed at the Tyburn without Micklegate Bar, for coining and paying bad money. After the execution they were all buried in St. George's Churchyard, Bean Hill, without Fishergate Postern.

HENRY DE ALMS.

Saturday, July 7th, A.D. 1596.—Henry de Alms, aged 58, a native of Darlington, in the county of Durham, was executed at the Tyburn without Micklegate Bar, for paying bad guineas in the York Fair, and at Hull. After the execution he was buried in St. Andrew's Churchyard, in St. Andrew-gate, in this city.

JOHN THOMAS DE NELME.

Saturday, March 27th, A.D. 1597.—John Thomas de Nelme, aged 36, a native of North Driffield, was executed at the gallows of St. Leonard's, Green Dykes, without Walmgate Bar, for robbing Eugene Petit with intent to murder him, on Heworth Moor, near York, on the 8th day of January, 1597. After his execution his body was conveyed to Heworth Moor, and there hung in chains.

THOMAS HENRY DE ALTING AND ROBERT THOMAS SWEDIER.

Monday, July 27th, A.D. 1598.—Thomas Henry de Alting, aged 45, a native of Beverley, and Robert Thomas Swedier, aged 33, a native of Sheffield, were executed at the Tyburn without Micklegate Bar, for housebreaking and taking twenty-four guineas from Mr. William de Boucham, with intent to murder him and his wife at Knaresborough. After the execution their bodies were conveyed to Knaresborough Forest, and there hung in chains.

JOHN TAYLOR.

Saturday, August 10th, A.D. 1599.—John Taylor, of Doncaster, was executed at the Tyburn without Micklegate Bar, for horse-stealing. After the execution his body was buried in the Church of St. Mary, Castlegate, York.

JOHN MILBURN.

Saturday, August 10th, A.D. 1599.—John Milburn was executed at the Tyburn without Micklegate Bar, for coining. His remains were interred in the churchyard of St. Mary's, Castlegate, in this city.

GEORGE WOLSTENHOLME, ESQ., THOMAS WILSON, ESQ., AND OTHERS.

Monday, April 2nd, A.D. 1600.—George Wolstenholme, Esq., aged 59 ; Thomas Wilson, Esq., aged 48 ; Richard Thomas, aged 60 ; James Norrison, aged 39 ; Robert Noke, aged 43 ; Francis Mitchel, aged 46 ; and Henry Hutchinson, aged 29, all natives of Hull, were executed at the gallows of St. Leonard's, Green Dykes, without Walmgate Bar, for smuggling and the wilful murder of Captain Thomas Fletcher, of the ship *Nancy*, of Hull ; Guy Foster, mate of the same ship, *Nancy;* William Forest and George Fowler, seamen of the said ship. The murderers perpetrated their bloody work while the ship was lying in the port of Hull, on the 6th day of January, 1600, about four o'clock in the morning. The next day they were apprehended, and committed to the Castle of York, and on the 20th of March in the said year they were tried and convicted of the above murders, and sentenced to be executed on Monday, the 2nd day of April following. When the culprits appeared at the place of execution they seemed firm but resigned to their fate, and, after a short time spent in devotional exercises, they gave themselves up into the hands of the executioners, and in a few seconds had ceased to exist. It was computed that not less than six thousand spectators were present to witness their dying struggles. After the executions their bodies were given to the surgeons of York and Hull to be dissected and anatomized.

CHARLES BEAUMOND, THOMAS BENNINGTON, MARY BLAKEY, AND EMMA BROWN.

Thursday, July 28th, A.D. 1602.—Charles Beaumond, aged 35, a native of Sheffield ; Thomas Bennington, aged 37, a native of Doncaster ; Mary Blakey, aged 23, and Emma Brown, aged 25, both natives of Bradford, in this county, were executed at the gallows of St. Leonard's, Green Dykes, without Walmgate Bar, for counterfeiting the gold coin of this realm called guineas. They were drawn from the Castle of York to the place of execution upon sledges. Since their condemnation they all evinced striking marks of penitence, and their conduct was such as became their unhappy situation. After their execution, the bodies of Beaumont and Bennington were buried in the churchyard of St. Helen's, Fishergate, in this city ; and the bodies of Blakey and Brown were buried in the churchyard of St. John's, Hungate, York, at ten o'clock at night, in the presence of the constables of each parish.

WILLIAM PENALTON.

Saturday, March 30th, A.D. 1603.—William Penalton, aged 34, a native of Barnby, in this county, was executed at eight o'clock in the morning at the Tyburn without Micklegate Bar, for the wilful murder of John Young at Pocklington, on the night of the 7th of December, 1602. After his execution, the body was conveyed to Barnby Moor, and there hung in chains.

John de Viner and Harris Rosenberg.

Saturday, March 30th, A.D. 1603.—Harris Rosenberg, aged 56, a native of Florence ; and John de Viner, aged 32, servant to the above, a native of Paris, were executed at the Tyburn, without Micklegate Bar, for the atrocious murder of Mr. Millington, an innkeeper at Leeds, on the night of the 8th day of November last. These unfortunate men suffered death in the presence of a large concourse of spectators. Their bodies on being taken down from the scaffold were given to the surgeons for dissection, in accordance with the sentence passed upon them.

Richard Cullingworth, Elizabeth Bradwith, Hannah Bulmer, and Jane Buckle.

Tuesday, April 6th, A.D. 1604.—Richard Cullingworth, aged 43, a native of York; Elizabeth Bradwith, aged 30, Hannah Bulmer, aged 28, and Jane Buckle, aged 34, all of Walmgate in this city, were executed at the Tyburn without Micklegate Bar, for coining and paying money, well knowing it to be counterfeit and bad. The execution of the unfortunate transgressors was witnessed by a large concourse of spectators.

Elizabeth Cook.

Monday, March 29th, A.D. 1605.—Elizabeth Cook, aged 48, a native of Kexby, was hanged and burnt at the gallows of St. Leonard's, Green Dykes, without Walmgate Bar, for the cruel and wilful murder of her own mother, aged 82, by burning her to death, at Heworth, near York. The heartless murderess was executed amidst the hisses, groans, and execrations of the crowd of spectators.

Stephen Dobson, Esq.

Friday, April 3rd, A.D. 1607.—Stephen Dobson, Esq.,

aged 50, a native of London, was executed at the Tyburn without Micklegate Bar, for the wilful and deliberate murder of his servant, Michael Penrose, a native of Barton, in the county of Lancashire, at his lodgings in Coney Street, in this city, on the 18th day of January, 1607. After the execution, his body was given to the surgeons of the city to be anatomized.

FREDERICK WRIGHTSON.

Wednesday, July 29th, A.D. 1608.—Frederick Wrightson, aged 37, a native of Keswick, in the county of Cumberland, labourer, was executed at York, for the wilful murder of Mary Ann Coupland, at Wakefield, in the county of York, on the 4th day of May, 1608. This culprit had been transported for seven years, and had only just returned when he committed this horrid murder. After the execution his body was conveyed to Wakefield Common, and there hung in chains.

ROBERT BLACKLEY.

Monday, July 28th, A.D. 1610.—Robert Blackley, aged 45, was executed at the Tyburn without Micklegate Bar, for high treason. He was drawn upon a hurdle from the Castle of York to the place of execution, and after hanging fifteen minutes, he was cut down, headed, and quartered, and his head along with his quarters were placed on the top of Micklegate Bar.

RICHARD CARSON AND THOMAS ARMSTRONG.

Wednesday, September 5th, A.D. 1612.—Richard Carson, aged 26, and Thomas Armstrong, aged 24, both natives of Leeds, were executed at the Tyburn without Micklegate Bar, for coining and paying bad money, in order to deceive and rob the public. Both were buried at the Church of St. George, Bean Hill, in this city.

WILLIAM GRAME.

Monday, March 27th, A.D. 1613.—William Grame, aged

22, a native of York, was executed at the Tyburn without Micklegate Bar, for robbery, and the murder of Mr. Robert Gott, flax-dresser, of High Ousegate, in this city, as he was returning from Knaresborough, on the 4th day of February of the same year. After the execution, his body was given for dissection.

MARK BARNARD, MARY ROBINSON, THOMAS BARKER, PHILIP DARLING, THOMAS EASINGWOLD, ROSE DUTTON, EMMA FOUNTAIN, AND MARIA FOWLER.

Monday, February 6th, A.D. 1614.—Mark Barnard, aged 34, a native of Pocklington ; Mary Robinson, aged 20 ; Thomas Barker, aged 29, a native of Mirfield, in this county ; Philip Darling, aged 42 ; and Thomas Easingwold, aged 48 ; with Rose Dutton, aged 25, and Emma Fountain, aged 23 ; also Maria Fowler, aged 22, all natives of York, were executed at the Tyburn without Micklegate Bar, for coining and paying bad money at Malton. After the several executions, the body of Barnard was buried in the churchyard of St. George's, Bean Hill, in this city ; the body of Robinson was taken to be buried at Pocklington by her relations ; that of Easingwold was buried in St. Sampson's Churchyard, in this city ; and the bodies of Dutton, Fountain, and Fowler, were buried in the churchyard of St. John's, in Hungate, of the above city.

MARK TRUMBLE AND ROBERT MARTINSON.

Saturday, March 29th, A.D. 1615.—Mark Trumble, aged 25, a native of Ripon ; and Robert Martinson, aged 26, a native of Haxby, near York, were executed at the Tyburn without Micklegate Bar, for highway robbery near Shipton, in the Forest of Galtres. After the executions, their bodies were buried in the churchyard of St. Olave's, in Mary Gate, city of York.

THOMAS PINDHAM.

Monday, March 23rd, A.D. 1616.—Thomas Pindham was executed at the Tyburn without Micklegate Bar, for rape, and the murder of Miss E. D. Johnson at Marston. After execution, his body was given to the surgeons of the city for dissection.

HENRY MUSGRAVE AND GEORGE RIDLEY.

Thursday, September 23rd, A.D. 1616.—Henry Musgrave, for coining bad money, and George Ridley, for burglary at Naburn, near York, were both executed at the gallows of St. Leonard's, Green Dykes, without Walmgate Bar.

SIMON ROUTLEDGE.

Saturday, July 27th, A.D. 1617.—Simon Routledge was executed at the Tyburn without Micklegate Bar, for stealing a mare from Mr. John Potts, of Huntington, near York, in the month of May, 1615. After the execution, his body was buried in the churchyard of St. John's, Hungate, in this city.

MARK ADDISON.

Monday, March 25th, A.D. 1618.—Mark Addison was executed at the gallows of St. Leonard's, Green Dykes, without Walmgate Bar, for the wilful murder of Elizabeth Robinson, at Kexby. After the execution, his body was given to the surgeons of this city for dissection.

ROBERT HALL.

Saturday, April 20th, A.D. 1620.—Robert Hall was executed at the Tyburn without Micklegate Bar, for coining and paying bad money at Easingwold. After the execution, his body was buried in the churchyard of St. George's, Bean Hill, without Fishergate Postern.

GEORGE BELL, ESQ.

Tuesday, March 31st, A.D. 1622.—George Bell, Esq., aged 32, attorney-at-law, of Leeds, was executed at the

Tyburn without Micklegate Bar, for forging a will belonging to Ralph Dalton, Esq., of Halifax. After the execution, his friends took his body to be buried at Leeds the next day.

RALPH RAYNARD, MARK DUNN, AND MRS. FLETCHER.

Saturday, July 28th, A.D. 1623.—Ralph Raynard, of the White House, near Easingwold ; Mark Dunn, of Huby ; and Mrs. Fletcher, of Raskelfe, were executed at the Tyburn without Micklegate Bar, and their bodies afterwards hung in chains near the place where the murder had been committed.

There is something very curious in connection with this murder, and in the manner in which it was discovered. A yeoman of good estate of the name of Fletcher, who resided at Raskelfe, formerly called Rascal, married a young lusty woman from Thornton Bridge, who had been formerly too kind with one Ralph Raynard, who kept an inn betwixt Raskelfe and Easingwold, his sister living with him. This Raynard continued an unlawful lust with the said Fletcher's wife, who, not content therewith, conspired the death of Fletcher, one Mark Dunn, of Huby, being made privy thereto, and hired to assist in the murder, which they, with the assistance of his own wife, accomplished on May-day of the said year, by drowning Fletcher as they came together from a town called Huby, where Mark Dunn resided. The murder was committed at Dawnay Bridge, whence a road at that time left the main line, and, crossing the shires, led over the Lund to Raskelfe. Fletcher's wife was laid in ambush at the place where the murder had previously been arranged to take place, and had brought a sack wherein to convey the dead body of her husband, which they did, and buried it in Raynard's garden or croft, where an old oak root had been stubbed up, and they sowed mustard-seed upon the place, thereby to hide it. So they continued their wicked course of lust and drunkenness, and the neighbours did much wonder at Fletcher's absence ; but his wife, in excuse, said that he was but gone aside for fear of some writ being served upon him.

It appears, however, that Fletcher had some previous

suspicion that the two confederates, along with his wife, had contemplated his death in some way or other, from the following doggerel rhyme addressed to his sister a short time before the event :—

> " If I should be in missing or suddenly in wanting be,
> Mark Ralph Raynard, Mark Dunn, and my own wife for me."

Thus matters went on till about the 7th day of July, when Raynard going to Topcliffe Fair, and setting up his horse in the stable, the spirit of Fletcher, in his usual shape and habit, did appear unto him, and said, "Oh, Ralph, repent, repent, for my vengeance is at hand ;" and ever after, till he was put into the gaol, it seemed to stand before him, whereby he became sad and restless. And his own sister overhearing his confession and relation of it to another person, did, through fear of her own life, imme· diately reveal it to Sir William Sheffield, a justice of the peace, who resided at Raskelfe Park. Whereupon they were all three apprehended and sent to the gaol at York, where they were all condemned and executed accordingly. After the executions, the guilty parties were hung up in irons on the roadside not far from the place where the murder had been committed, and only a short distance from the " White House " where Raynard lived, and where the body of the murdered man had been buried, and where it was found. After hanging upon the gibbet for a considerable time, their shattered fragments were taken down and buried under the gallows. The place has gone by the name of Gibbet Hill ever since. About fifty years ago, a quantity of human bones were found on the spot, supposed to have been the bones of the three murderers who committed this terrible tragedy.

JOSEPH HETHERINGTON.

Monday, August 2nd, A.D. 1623.—Joseph Hetherington, aged 35, was executed at the Tyburn without Micklegate Bar, for stealing four horses in Tadcaster, at the "Hand and Whip" public-house, on the night of the 4th of March, 1623. After the execution, his body was buried in the churchyard of St. George's, Bean Hill, without Fishergate Postern, in this city.

RICHARD BELL.

Monday, April 23rd, A.D. 1624.— Richard Bell, aged 52, a native of York, was executed at the Tyburn without Micklegate Bar, for coining bad money in Thursday market, in this city, and paying it at Kexby, Pocklington, Market Weighton, and at Hull. After the execution, his body was buried in St. Dyonis's Churchyard, in this city.

RICHARD RIDLEY AND AMOS ARMSTRONG.

Saturday, August 25th, A.D. 1625.—Richard Ridley, aged 24, and Amos Armstrong, aged 28, were executed at the gallows of St. Leonard's, Green Dykes, without Walmgate Bar, for horse-stealing from Mr. William Rooks, of Deighton, near York, on the 2nd of February, 1625. After the execution the two culprits were buried at St. Dyonis's Churchyard, in this city.

WILLIAM CAWAN AND WILLIAM HALL.

Monday, March 30th, A.D. 1627.—William Cawan, aged 25, a native of Stockton, near York, and William Hall, aged 26, a native of Dunnington, near York, were executed at the Tyburn without Micklegate Bar, for housebreaking, and attempt to murder one John Williamson, his wife Ellen, and two children, at Halifax, on the night of the 10th of December, 1626. Their bodies were afterwards buried in the churchyard of St. George's, Bean Hill, without Fishergate Postern, in this city.

ROBERT STORIE.

Tuesday, April 2nd, A.D. 1628.—Robert Storie, aged 28 a native of Clifton, near York, was executed at the Tyburn without Micklegate Bar, for setting fire to Mr. R. Wilson's dwelling-house and outbuildings at Malton, which were consumed to the ground in the month of January of the above year. The culprit died very hardly, in the presence of between eight and nine thousand people. His body was buried in the churchyard of St. Mary's, Castlegate, in this city.

CHARLES ROCHESTER, GEORGE ROCLIFFE, CHRISTOPHER SINGLETON, AND HENRY SMELT.

Saturday, March 31st, A.D. 1630.—Charles Rochester, aged 28, a native of Leeds; George Rocliffe, aged 33, a native of Doncaster; Christopher Singleton, aged 37; and Henry Smelt, aged 25, both natives of Halifax, in this county, were executed at the Tyburn without Micklegate Bar, for coining base money in Walmgate, in this city. Their bodies were afterwards buried in St. Sampson's Churchyard, in this city.

ROBERT NIXON AND JOHN NEWTON.

Saturday, May 2nd, A.D. 1632.—Robert Nixon, aged 42, a native of Hull, and John Newton, aged 35, a native of Hunslet, near York, were executed at the Tyburn without Micklegate Bar, for coining and circulating bad money at Leeds, in January, 1632. Their bodies were buried in St. Helen's Churchyard, in this city.

EXECUTION OF TEN CULPRITS FOR RIOTING.

Thursday, February 4th, A.D. 1634. — Thomas Wardle, aged 48, a native of Bradford; William Hornby, aged 50, a native of Huddersfield; Benjamin Hornsey, aged 39, a native of Dewsbury; Charles Hopkinson, aged 27, a native of Aldburgh; Thomas Jefferson, aged 28, a native of Bradfield; Peter Kibblewhite, aged 32, a native of Helmsley; George Henry Kilvington, aged 46, a native of Keighley; William Kitching, aged 39, a native of Little Driffield; Thomas Lazenby, aged 35, a native of Pontefract; and Thomas Langdale, aged 27, a native of Scarborough. The above ten unfortunate culprits were executed at the gallows of St. Leonard's, Green Dykes, without Walmgate Bar, for rioting about corn at Hull, and demolishing the dwelling-house of Edward Cooper, Esq., and taking therefrom and stealing a quantity of wearing apparel. After hanging the usual time upon the gallows, their bodies were taken and given to their several friends for interment.

JOHN BARTENDALE.

In the reign of King Charles I., and on the 27th day of March, 1634, John Bartendale was executed on the York gallows, without Micklegate Bar, for felony. When he had hung three-quarters of an hour, he was cut down and buried near the place of execution. A short time after, a gentleman of the ancient family of the Vavasours, of Hesselwood, while riding by, thought he saw the earth move, upon which, ordering his man to alight, and dismounting from his own horse, both of them charitably assisted to throw off the mould, and to help the buried convict from his grave. He was then conveyed again to York Castle, and through the intercession of his deliverer, at the next Assizes, he obtained a reprieve. When the case was brought a second time before the judge, who seemed amazed at so signal a Providence, the resurrectionist obtained a free and full pardon. Bartendale was a piper, or strolling musician, and is noticed by Drunken Barnaby in his Book of Travels into the northern parts. Paraphrased from the Latin, it runs thus :—

> " Here a piper apprehended,
>   Was found guilty and suspended ;
>   Being led to fatal gallows,
>   Boys did cry, ' Where is thy bellows ?
>   Ever must thou cease thy tuning.'
>   Answered he, ' For all your cunning,
>   You may fail in your prediction.'
>   Which did happen without fiction,
>   For, cut down and quick interred,
>   Earth rejected what was buried ;
>   Half alive or dead he rises,
>   Got a pardon next assizes,
>   And in York continued blowing,
>   Yet a sense of goodness showing."

After this wonderful deliverance the poor fellow turned hostler, and lived honestly afterwards. On being asked to describe his feelings and sensations while undergoing the process of hanging and entering the trap-door of death, he replied, that when he was turned off, flashes of fire seemed to dart into his eyes, from which he fell into a state of darkness and insensibility.

Owen Thompson and Elizabeth Mary Harrison.

Monday, March 29th, A.D. 1636.—Owen Thompson, aged 32, a native of Snaith, was convicted and condemned to suffer death for horse-stealing ; and Elizabeth Mary Harrison, aged 25, was found guilty and condemned to suffer death for poisoning Jacob Jackson, at Stockton, near York, on the 5th day of January, 1636. They were both executed at the gallows of St. Leonard's, Green Dykes, without Walmgate Bar, and their bodies were buried in St. Sampson's Churchyard, in this city.

Henry Aske.

Monday, May 8th, A.D. 1638.—Henry Aske, aged 23, a native of Middleham, was executed at the Tyburn without Micklegate Bar, for stabbing with intent to murder one George Wilson, of Wakefield. The prisoner was tried at the March Assizes, but received a respite until the above date, when the sentence of the law was inflicted upon him. After the execution, his body was buried in the churchyard of St. Helen's, in Fishergate, York.

Robert Skelton.

Saturday, August 1st, 1639.—Robert Skelton, aged 32, a native of Hull, was executed at the gallows of St. Leonard's, Green Dykes, without Walmgate Bar, for forging a will belonging to Thomas Bell, Esq., of Hull. After the execution, his body was buried in St. George's Churchyard, Bean Hill, without Fishergate Postern.

John Taylor.

Monday, April 23rd, A.D. 1641. — John Taylor, aged 21, a native of York, was executed at the gallows of St. Leonard's, Green Dykes, without Walmgate Bar, for setting fire to Mr. William Hodgson's farm-house, between Stamford Bridge and York, on the night of the 13th day of January, 1641. His body was buried in the churchyard of St. Crux, in this city.

Amos Lawson.

Wednesday, July 30th, A.D. 1644.—Amos Lawson, aged 34, a native of Huddersfield, was executed at Tyburn without Micklegate Bar, for highway robbery. Lawson was a noted daring highwayman, who had carried on his dangerous exploits for some length of time, but was at last taken in the forest of Galtres, on the night of the 3rd of April, 1644, by William Taylor, Esq., who was then sheriff of the city of York, and whom he intended to rob. Thousands attended to witness his dying struggles, and Knavesmire resembled more a fair for business and pleasure than a place of execution. His body was buried at St. George's Churchyard, Bean Hill, without Fishergate Postern.

Thomas Empson, John Dove, Joseph Dunning, Thomas Robinson, and John Robinson.

Tuesday, March 31st, A.D. 1646.—Thomas Empson, aged 27, a native of Sheffield ; John Dove, aged 23, a native of Halifax ; Joseph Dunning, aged 31, a native of Leeds ; Thomas Robinson, aged 22, a native of Bradford ; and John Robinson, aged 30, a native of Bradford, were executed at the Tyburn without Micklegate Bar, for highway robbery, near Huddersfield, on the night of the 10th of February, 1646. After the execution, their bodies were received for interment by their friends.

Elizabeth Drysdale and Helen Drysdale.

Saturday, April 10th, A.D. 1647.—Elizabeth Drysdale, aged 26, and Helen Drysdale, aged 24, sisters, and natives of Tadcaster, were executed at the gallows of St. Leonard's, Green Dykes, without Walmgate Bar, for the wilful and deliberate murder of Robert Boss, of Heslington, near York, joiner, and Robert Blanchard, of Walmgate, in this city, woolcomber, by poisoning them at the house of Dame Robinson, the sign of the " Maypole," at Clifton, on the 16th day of February, 1647. It appeared on the trial that these two young men were paying their addresses to the prisoners, and had been doing so for some time, so that they were unconscious of receiving any poison from the hands of the prisoners at the period when it was administered. It was proved that the prisoners had bought some oxalic acid on the morning of that day, at the shop of Mr. William Brooks, chemist, in Stonegate, in this city. The two young men only lived about an hour and a half after taking the poison, although every means were adopted by the surgeons which their skill and judgment could think of, but all to no use. Before these young men expired, they said that they freely forgave the young women for what they had done, and left the rest in the hands of God. After sentence of death was passed upon these two unfortunate young women, they both behaved with becoming resignation, and met their fate with more than womanly fortitude. They left behind them a father and mother, four brothers, and two sisters. After the execution their bodies were given to the surgeons of the city to be dissected and anatomized.

EBENEZER MOOR.

Saturday, August 13th, A.D. 1648.—Ebenezer Moor, aged 39, a native of Boroughbridge, one of the most notorious highwaymen that ever existed for his intrepid courage in robberies, was executed at the gallows of St. Leonard's, Green Dykes, without Walmgate Bar, for shooting one Thomas Kent, farmer, upon Barnby Moor. His body was buried in the churchyard of All Hallows, in Fishergate, York.

GEORGE FREDERICK MERRINGTON AND MARIA MERRINGTON.

Tuesday, April 13th, A.D. 1649. — George Frederick Merrington, and Maria Merrington, his wife, were executed at the gallows of St. Leonard's, Green Dykes, without Walmgate Bar, for the murder of William Rex, Esq., of Dunnington, near York. This dreadful murder was committed in their own house, at Fulford, in the evening, just before dinner, on the 9th day of March, 1649. Mr. Rex's body was found by a piece of cord that led to his grave in the kitchen, where they had buried his body, near the fire-place, on the 13th of March, by Thomas Radge, constable of that village.

These two unfortunate malefactors were taken in a cart from the Castle of York, guarded by the sheriff officers and a troop of dragoons, at half-past seven o'clock in the morning. It was with great difficulty that they could pass down Castlegate by reason of the great multitude of people with whom that street was crowded from top to bottom, so that nothing could be seen but a forest of hats, and in the Pavement the people had to form a passage for the cart to pass through, the crowd pulling off their hats as the solemn cavalcade passed by. In turning to Fossgate, the street was one mass of human beings. One woman had her leg broken in the crowd, and a young man had his thigh broken : both were removed to a doctor. On entering Walmgate, the same scene presented itself, but no accident occurred. The two culprits here fainted, and stopped before the house of Mr. James Addinale, the sign of the " Golden Barrel," when the good sheriff ordered Dame Addinale to give them some mint-water, and, after their recovery, each had a glass of wine, and then proceeded to the place of execution, where they arrived at twenty minutes past nine o'clock, in the presence of thousands of spectators. Their bodies, after the execution, were given to the surgeons for dissection.

Execution of Fourteen Men and Seven Women.

Saturday, April 30th, A.D. 1649.—At the Lent March Assizes, fourteen men and seven women were condemned and received sentence of death, in a very solemn manner by Judge Thorpe, who informed them that they would be executed on this day. The following are the names of the culprits, with their crimes and the places of their nativity :—

John Hollins, aged 35, a native of Otley, for rebellion.

William Askwith, aged 45, a native of Leeds, for rebellion.

Joseph Baines, aged 30, a native of Ripon, for rebellion.

Thomas Barker, aged 54, a native of York, for rebellion.

Edward Calvert, aged 43, a native of York, for rebellion.

Thomas Darley, aged 47, a native of York, for rebellion.

Henry Cave, aged 39, a native of Hull, for rebellion.

William Cropper, aged 40, a native of Hull, for rebellion.

James Dallin, aged 57, a native of Otley, for rebellion.

John Danby, aged 58, a native of Ripon, for rebellion.

James Eastwood, aged 44, a native of York, for rebellion.

William Ellison, aged 48, a native of Leeds, for rebellion.

Thomas Exley, aged 30, a native of Bedale, for rebellion.

George Frankish, aged 59, a native of Bedale, for rebellion.

Also at the same time and place of execution, the following seven poor unfortunate females, with their crimes and places of their nativity, viz. :—

Elizabeth Thomlinson, aged 27, a native of Selby, for the wilful murder of her bastard child, at Blackburton. She was hanged, and burned close to the gallows. She died penitent.

Grace Bland, aged 29, for setting fire to the house of her mistress, known by the sign of the " Maypole," in Clifton, near York, which was burnt to the ground on the 5th day of November, 1648. She was a native of Easingwold, and wept bitterly at the place of execution. She died very penitent.

Emma Robinson, aged 25, a fine-looking young woman, better known by the name of "Fair Emma," a native of Masham, in this county, for poisoning her fellow-servant, Mary Wood, through jealousy. She was hanged, and burnt close to the gallows, according to her sentence.

Jane Lickiss, aged 43, for the wilful murder of her servant maid, Mary Lumley, by strangling her while in her bed, at Wetherby, on the 5th day of December last. This unfortunate woman was a native of Shipton, near York. She was hanged and burnt close to the gallows, but appeared firm and resigned to her fate.

Hannah Meynell, aged 53, for wounding George Myers, at Marston, with intent to murder him. She was a very stout woman, weighing sixteen stones. After her execution her body was given to the surgeons of this city, to be dissected and anatomized, according to her sentence. She was a native of York, and belonged to highly respectable parents in the Pavement.

Ellen Nicholson, aged 28, for wilfully setting fire to her master's house and destroying the whole of the furniture belonging to the said house, also the outbuildings thereto belonging, with four valuable horses, three cows, and two calves, three stacks of wheat, two of barley, four of hay, and two of straw, which were all consumed by the said fire. This unfortunate woman was a native of Selby, and at the time of her execution made a full confession of her guilt to the sheriff. She died very penitent, and was buried in St. Andrew's Churchyard, in St. Andrew-gate, in this city.

Isabella Billington, aged 32, for crucifying her mother at Pocklington, on the 5th day of January, 1649, and offering a calf and a cock for a burnt sacrifice; and her husband was hanged for being a participator in the crime.

The above culprits were drawn from the Castle of York, upon sledges, to the place of execution on Knavesmire, and there hanged and quartered, according to their sentences. They left the Castle at a quarter past nine o'clock in the morning in the following order :—

In two sledges, with seven men on each, guarded by the sheriff officers and twenty-four dragoons. The unfortunate women were conveyed in two carts, four in the first and three in the second, guarded by thirty dragoons, fifteen on each side of the carts. On entering Castlegate, that street appeared one mass of human beings, and the solemn procession was stopped for some time before it could proceed, the people were so closely jammed together. The whole of the twenty-one culprits joined as one voice in singing psalms from this street to the gallows. They were stopped several times in Micklegate by reason of the great number of spectators that thronged the road to the Tyburn, but this did not take the attention of the culprits from their devotions in singing. They arrived at the place of execution at ten minutes past ten o'clock. Since their condemnation they all evinced striking marks of penitence, and their conduct had been becoming their awful situation. All seemed firm but resigned to their fate, and after being engaged for a short time in devotional exercises, they all gave themselves up to the hands of the executioner, and in about five minutes, twenty-one lifeless corpses were hanging suspended between earth and heaven. It was a most awful scene—a terrible day, and thousands witnessed the dreadful catastrophe.

COLONEL JOHN MORRICE AND CORNET BLACKBURN.

Saturday, August 22nd, A.D. 1649. — Colonel John Morrice, aged 53, and Cornet Blackburn, aged 52, were executed at the Tyburn without Micklegate Bar, for the wilful murder of Colonel Robert Rainsborough.

The former was Governor of Pontefract Castle, which he
had taken with great difficulty, and maintained in the midst
of extreme hardships. The latter was one of that gallant
party sent out of the Castle in that memorable expedition
to Doncaster, and the very man that killed Rainsborough.
After the rendition of the Castle they were both taken
prisoners as they were attempting to escape and go abroad,
and were brought prisoners to York. They had once an opportunity to make their escape, and one of them had slid
down the Castle walls by a rope, which his partner endeavouring to do after him, either by haste or inadvertency, fell and
broke his leg. This misfortune cost them both their lives,
for the Colonel would not leave his unhappy companion, but,
out of a noble spirit of generosity, stayed by him till they were
both retaken. After twenty-two weeks' imprisonment they
were sentenced to death by the Judges Thorpe and Puleston,
who were purposely sent down to try them, and both testified
at their death that steady loyalty which had made their lives
so remarkable. After execution, their bodies were buried in
St. John's Churchyard, Hungate, in this city.

RICHARD THOMAS, GEORGE HARRISON, AND MARY POPE.

Wednesday, April 22nd, A.D. 1650.—Richard Thomas,
aged 23 ; George Harrison, aged 27 ; and Mary Pope,
aged 25, were executed at the Tyburn without Micklegate
Bar, for paying bad money. They all died penitent, and their
bodies were buried in the churchyard of St. Dyonis, in this
city.

GEORGE JOHNSON, LUKE HINDERSON, ELIZABETH ANDERSON, AND MARY ELLISON.

Saturday, April 2nd, A.D. 1652.—George Johnson,
aged 56, a native of Thirsk ; Luke Hinderson, aged 45, a
native of Stamford Bridge ; Elizabeth Anderson, aged 26 ;
and Mary Ellison, aged 30, natives of this city, were executed
at the gallows of St. Leonard's, Green Dykes, without
Walmgate Bar, for robbing Peter Ellison, butcher of York,
upon Barnby Moor, and leaving him for dead. After the
execution their bodies were buried in St. Wilfred's Churchyard, in this city.

MARMADUKE HOLMES.

Thursday, July 27th, A.D. 1654.—Marmaduke Holmes, aged 40, was executed at the Tyburn without Micklegate Bar, for stealing fifteen sheep, from John Wright, farmer, at Aldborough. He had sold part of them in the York market. His body was buried in St. Dyonis's Churchyard, in this city.

JONATHAN BRAMMALL.

Monday, April 21st, A.D. 1656.—Jonathan Bramall, aged 29, was executed at the Tyburn without Micklegate Bar, for uttering and paying counterfeit coin, at Doncaster, on the 5th day of February, 1656. He was buried in St. John's Churchyard, Hungate, in this city.

CHARLES SPOONER.

Saturday, March 29th, A.D., 1659.—Charles Spooner, aged 23, a native of Bradford, was executed at the gallows of St. Leonard's, Green Dykes, without Walmgate Bar, for the robbery and wilful murder of Francis Groves, on Barnby Moor, on the night of the 15th of December, 1659. On the day after the execution his body was hung in chains on Barnby Moor.

MICHAEL REYNARD, R. LINDOP, O. WILLIAMS, AND T. P. REYNOLDS.

Monday, April 2nd, A.D. 1660.—Michael Reynard, R. Lindop, O. Williams, and T. P. Reynolds, were executed at the gallows of St. Leonard's, Green Dykes, without Walmgate Bar, for highway robbery, near Whitby, in the month of November, 1659. Their bodies were buried in the churchyard of St. George's, Bean Hill, in this city.

PETER HALL AND R. GARDENER.

Thursday, March 30th, A.D. 1661.—Peter Hall and R. Gardener were executed at the Tyburn without Micklegate Bar, for coining. The body of Hall was buried in St.

George's Churchyard, Bean Hill, and that of R. Gardener was buried in the churchyard of St. Michael-le-Belfrey, close to the Minster, where some of his relatives are laid.

JEREMIAH BALDERSON AND RICHARD SOULY.

Saturday, August 19th, A.D. 1661.—Jeremiah Balderson, aged 32, and Richard Souly, aged 25, two notorious highwaymen, were executed at the Tyburn without Micklegate Bar, for robbing one George Melrose, and cutting off his nose, on the night of the 3rd of February, 1661, in the Forest of Galtres. Their bodies were buried in the churchyard of Holy Trinity, Curia Regis, in this city.

ANTHONY BEEDAM.

Monday, March 25th, A.D. 1662.—Anthony Beedam, aged 26, was executed at the Tyburn without Micklegate Bar, for the wilful murder of Elizabeth Beedam, his wife, aged 24, at Ripon, in this county, on the 25th day of December, 1661. His body was given to the surgeons for dissection.

EXECUTION OF EIGHTEEN REBELS.

Wednesday, January 25th, A.D. 1663, was the day fixed for the execution of the eighteen unfortunate men who were tried on the 4th and 5th of this month, and were convicted, when sentence of death was passed upon them. The following is a list of their names, ages, and places of abode :—

Robert Archbell, aged 41, a native of Ripon.

William Amber, aged 41, a native of Ripon.

Matthew Champney, aged 43, a native of Thorparch.

George Campion, aged 48, a native of Tadcaster.

Thomas Carbutt, aged 47, a native of Poppleton, near York.

Christopher Simpson, aged 29, a native of Poppleton, near York.

George Slater, aged 34, a native of Rufforth.

George Mouncer, aged 49, a native of Rufforth.

Joseph Morley, aged 51, a native of Rufforth.

Timothy Mosley, aged 45, a native of Otley.

John Hutchinson, aged 48, a native of Otley
David Jackson, aged 49, a native of Otley.
Henry Richardson, aged 45, a native of Ripley.
Cornelius Thompson, aged 44, a native of Otley.
Thomas Fox, aged 45, a native of Leeds.
Benjamin Hornby, aged 29, a native of Leeds.
Francis Holmes, sen., aged 56, a native of Leeds.
William Holmes, jun., aged 25, a native of Leeds.

They were all executed at the Tyburn without Mickle-gate Bar, for an insurrection in Yorkshire. These men were all of them conventional preachers, and the old Parliamentarian soldiers. Their pretence for this rebellion was to redeem themselves from the excise and all subsidies, to establish a Gospel magistracy and ministry, to restore the Long Parliament, and to reform all orders and degrees of men, especially the lawyers and clergy. In order to this, they printed a declaration, calling upon the people to rise up, come forward, join the noble band of staunch patriots, and defend their rights against injustice and oppression. The declaration commenced thus :—" If there be any city, town, or country, in the three nations that will begin this righteous and glorious strife," &c.,—words evidently of a treasonable character. Accordingly, a great number of them appeared in arms at Farnley Wood, near Otley, in this county. But the time and place of rendezvous being known, a body of regular troops, with some of the county militia, was sent against them, who seized upon several and prevented the execution of their design. A commission was sent down to York in the depth of winter to try the principal leaders of the gang, and the above eighteen culprits suffered death on the day mentioned above.

Two of them were quartered, and their heads and quarters set up on the several gates of the city ; four of their heads were placed over Micklegate Bar, three at Bootham Bar, one at Walmgate Bar, one at Monk Bar, and three over the Castle gates. Thus ended the executions of this day.

RUBEN BEVERAGE.

Tuesday, July 30*th*, A.D. 1664.—Ruben Beverage, aged 28, was executed at the gallows of St. Leonard's, Green Dykes, without Walmgate Bar, for robbery and cutting and maim-ing one Robert Kyle, in Stockton Forest, on the night of the 8th of March last. His body was buried in the church-yard of Holy Trinity, Curia Regis, in this city.

GEORGE DAGNELL AND ROBERT SNOWDON.

Saturday, April 24th, A.D. 1665.—George Dagnell, aged 21, and Robert Snowdon, aged 28, were executed at the gallows of St. Leonard's, Green Dykes, without Walmgate Bar, for horse-stealing, at Bradford, in the month of March, 1663. After the execution, their bodies were buried in the churchyard of St. Sampson's, in this city.

GEORGE HABBISHAW AND BENJAMIN AMBROSE.

Friday, May 13th, A.D. 1668.—George Habbishaw, aged 37, and Benjamin Ambrose, aged 29, were executed at the Tyburn without Micklegate Bar, for the wilful murder of George Lumley, Esq., at Knaresborough, on the 10th day of January, 1666. The body of Habbishaw was hung in chains early next morning in Knaresborough Forest, and the body of Ambrose was given to the surgeons of this city for dissection.

EDWARD ROCLIFFE, PETER B. SHARP, AND RICHARD WADKINS.

Wednesday, March 29th, A.D. 1670.—Edward Rocliffe, aged 24 ; Peter B. Sharp, aged 27 ; and Richard Wadkins, aged 29, were executed at the gallows of St. Leonard's, Green Dykes, without Walmgate Bar, for robbing Mr. John Leng, butcher, of York, on Strensal Moor, on the 20th of December, 1669. Their bodies were all interred in the churchyard of St. Andrew's, in St. Andrew-gate, in this city.

WILLIAM VASEY.

August 18th, A.D. 1670.—William Vasey was executed at the Tyburn without Micklegate Bar, for the wilful and deliberate murder of Marian, the housekeeper of Mr. Earle, of Beningbrough Hall, and for the attempted murder of Martin Giles, Mr. Earle's head gamekeeper.

Beningbrough Hall, at the time alluded to (1670), was occupied by a gentleman of the name of Earle, who left a large number of servants in the house, and among the rest was his steward, named Philip Laurie, and a housekeeper, named Marian. He also had a gamekeeper, named Martin Giles. Beningbrough Hall at the time alluded to was an ancient structure of the Elizabethan style of architecture, which since then has been taken down, and the new and elegant mansion as it now exists was erected on the site thereof. It happened that while the family were from home in London, two gentlemen who were strangers to the steward made their appearance at the Hall, and summoned all the servants together, and gave orders for the removal of the plate, pictures, and all other valuables. There was a great deal of mystery in this affair, but the housekeeper told the steward that the two gentlemen were duly authorized by Mr. Earle so to do. The steward set watch to see where the property was removed to, and discovered that it was taken to the house of Martin Giles, the gamekeeper, where it was considered for the time to be in a place of safety. It appeared that Mr. Earle was in embarrassed circumstances, and Laurie, the steward, was jealous of Marian, the housekeeper, whom he blamed for losing the favour and confidence of his master, Mr. Earle, and also in not being made acquainted with the particulars of this mysterious affair. Besides he owed her an old grudge, and sought for an opportunity to wreak his vengeance on the innocent cause of the disgrace which his vile conduct had brought upon himself. Chance had recently thrown in his way a person of the name of William Vasey, who at that time resided at a convenient distance from Beningbrough Hall, who was a reputed thief and a very base and notorious character. With this miscreant Laurie, the steward, now hoped to accomplish the murder of his intended victim, Marian, and plotted and arranged the perpetration of the foul deed accordingly. Vasey laid wait for Marian, near to the Hall, and one evening he saw her going along the pathway, when he brutally seized her by the throat, and, stifling her cries, dragged her to the brink of the river Ouse, close by, and with a shriek and a struggle she sank lifeless in its waves. Laurie, with his accomplice Vasey, then agreed to possess themselves of the valuables that were concealed in the house of the gamekeeper. The country people blamed Martin Giles for the murder of the house-keeper, and it was thought by the two villains, Laurie and Vasey, that the present time offered a good opportunity for committing the burglary, as the tide of popular prejudice ran very strong against Giles. Vasey was accordingly to enter the gamekeeper's house, and Laurie was to watch out-side and be ready to assist if Martin, the gamekeeper, should be awake ; for it was their design to accomplish the bloody deed in the midnight hour of darkness. The chamber in which he slept was in the back part of the house. Poor Martin Giles, instead of being asleep as Vasey imagined, was labouring under severe anguish of mind for the loss of his Marian, and on hearing the sound of the latch of his room door, he immediately jumped upon the floor, but fell instantly from the effects of a severe blow, by the midnight assassin. The gamekeeper on raising himself up was again knocked down, but, becoming a little more conscious, jumped up again, and, being a daring, powerful, and persevering man, seized Vasey by the throat, threw him down, took his bludgeon from him and entangled him in the meshes of a sheep net. The gamekeeper then had his assassin secure, and opening his window, fired off a double-barrelled gun, purposely to alarm the inmates of the Hall, which had the desired effect, for the servants soon made their appearance. Vasey was taken into custody, and the following day was removed to York Castle, to which place he was committed for burglary with the intent to commit murder. He was tried and executed for the latter charge. Previous to his execution, he made a confession of many depredations he had been guilty of, and among the rest was the murder of poor Marian. If Martin Giles had known when he seized Vasey by the throat, that he (Vasey) was the murderer of her who was his only earthly hope, there is little doubt but the villain, with all his energies, would have become a fatal prey in the hands of the gamekeeper. Soon after Mrs. Earle, on hearing of Laurie's bad character, determined on parting with him. Laurie tried all ways and means to retain his situation, but

finding his entreaties of no avail, he swore he would be revenged, and immediately pointed and pulled the trigger of a
pistol with intent to shoot her, but by some means, she
parried the pistol off, and the shot missed her.   Laurie
directly made his exit to his lodgings, and on the beadles of
the parish going to apprehend him, he was discovered a
lifeless corpse, having shot himself.   The body of poor
Marian had been discovered floating in the river Ouse, and
being taken out it was conveyed to the Hall, after which it
was interred in the churchyard of Newton-upon-Ouse, which
is almost contiguous to Beningbrough Hall.   She was to
have been married to the gamekeeper, Martin Giles.   Some
parties imagined that she had committed suicide, as, previous
to the death of Vasey, there was no clue to the mysterious
affair; others thought that the innocent and much distressed
gamekeeper had been guilty of the foul deed, but Vasey's
confession removed all doubts and supposition.   It was
always considered that one of the two gentlemen before
mentioned was the owner of Beningbrough Hall, Mr. Earle,
but he was in disguise, and none of his servants were aware
of it except the unfortunate Marian, for the affair was
guarded with the utmost secrecy.   It has been already stated
that Mr. Earle was in embarrassed circumstances. 'How he
had acted or what he had done is involved in mystery, but
he was accused of being a traitor to his country, and was
going to be tried by the Government for sedition ; and Mr.
Earle, being of opinion that his property would be seized, gave
orders for its secret removal, he himself having purposed to
flee his country.

ROBERT DRIFFIELD AND MARK EDMUND.

Wednesday, August 2nd, A.D. 1672.—Robert Driffield,
aged 24, and Mark Edmund, aged 22, were executed at the
Tyburn without Micklegate Bar, for setting fire to six corn
stacks belonging to Mr. George Robson, at Skelton, near
York, on the 1st day of May, 1672.   A very large concourse
of people assembled to witness the execution, after which
their bodies were interred in the churchyard of St. Mary,
Bishophill, Senior, in this city.

Miles Beckett, Jane Thompson, and Thomas Thomlinson.

Monday, July 23rd, A.D. 1673.—Miles Beckett, aged 21, a native of Heslington, near York ; Jane Thompson, aged 23, a native of Fulford, near York ; and Thomas Thomlinson, aged 22, a native of Clifton, near York, were executed at the Tyburn without Micklegate Bar, for coining guineas at Sheffield. The body of Jane Thompson was buried in St. George's churchyard, Bean Hill, without Fishergate Postern, and the bodies of Beckett and Thomlinson were interred behind the Castle-walls near the river Foss.

Amos Cropper.

Friday, April 3rd, A.D. 1674.—Amos Cropper, aged 25, a native of Hull, was executed at the Tyburn without Micklegate Bar, for the wilful murder of Mr. Joseph Beck, of Dewsbury, on the king's highway, near Huddersfield. He was taken by John Hall, an old man 84 years of age, on the said road, on the 16th day of February of the said year. After the execution, his body was given to the surgeons of York to be dissected.

Leonard Gaskill and Peter Rook.

Saturday, May 1st, A.D. 1676.—Leonard Gaskill, aged 27, and Peter Rook, aged 25, both natives of Beverley, in this county, were executed at the gallows of St. Leonard's, Green Dykes, without Walmgate Bar, for stealing thirteen sheep from Mr. John Brown, of Driffield, on the 10th day of March last. Their bodies were buried in the churchyard of St. John's, Hungate, in this city.

Mark Dovenor.

Thursday, March 20th, A.D. 1678.—Mark Dovenor, aged 40, a native of Mirfield, in this county, wool-comber, was executed at the Tyburn without Micklegate Bar, for setting fire to his employer's workshops in Dewsbury, belonging to Mr. John Tate, on the night of the 6th of January last.

His body was taken by his shopmates to Mirfield to be interred at their own expense.

ANDREW TUCKER.

Saturday, July 28th, A.D. 1680.— Andrew Tucker, aged 29, a native of Halifax, a most notorious highwayman, and a dread to the surrounding country, was executed at the Tyburn without Micklegate Bar, for stopping and robbing the London mail post, as it was passing through Knaresborough, on the night of the 28th of March. He was taken at Simon Knowles's, the Bull inn, in Barnsley, on the 1st day of April, 1680. After the execution, his body was buried in the churchyard of Holy Trinity, Curia Regis, in this city.

ELI HYDES.

Saturday, March 31st, A.D. 1682.—Eli Hydes, aged 21, a native of Fartown, in the parish of Huddersfield, was executed at the Tyburn without Micklegate Bar, for committing a rape upon Miss Mary Elizabeth Brown, aged 20, in a field one mile from Huddersfield, as she was returning from that market, on the evening of the 12th of May, 1681. After the execution, the body was buried in the churchyard of St. Wilfred, Blake-street, in this city.

WILLIAM NEVISON.

May 4th, A.D. 1684, in the reign of King James II., William Nevison, aged 43, was executed at the Tyburn gallows without Micklegate Bar, for robbery. He was a notorious highwayman, and the story of Turpin's ride from London to York (so beautifully and graphically described by Mr. Harrison Ainsworth in his "Rookwood"), on his mare "Black Bess," is all fabulous, no such account appearing in his life, but is taken from the circumstance of Nevison's escape from the gallows on one occasion, a fact authenticated in the "History of York," in which there is the following account :—

"In this year was tried William Nevison, a notorious

highwayman, who had committed a robbery in London, about sunrise, and, finding he was known, fled to York, which place he reached by sunset the same evening, on one mare (Charles II. called him 'Swift Nick'). On his trial he proved himself to have been at the Bowling-green at York the same evening the robbery was committed. A number of witnesses swore positively to him, but neither judge nor jury would believe them, and he consequently was acquitted.

" He was afterwards arrested near Wakefield (probably at an old road-side inn at Sandal Magna, which he used to frequent, called the 'Sandal Three Houses,' on the road from Barnsley to Wakefield), for a series of crimes, and hung as above. The scenes of this most extraordinary man's robberies and exploits were principally in the midland counties, betwixt London and York, at which chief market-towns he was well known. It was said that he often robbed the rich and gave to the poor, was a man of large stature, of gentlemanly manners, and unparalleled courage. If he robbed (or borrowed, as he called it) at any time from the poor in his exigency, he would return it them again when better supplied by the rich ; and so terrible a man was he to the carriers and drovers in these northern parts, that they paid him a quarterly contribution, which then engaged him so far, not only to spare them himself, but to be their protector from other highwaymen. There is but one account of his shedding blood, which was in the case of a butcher who attempted to arrest him ; and finding some half-dozen persons bent on his capture, Nevison fired at the butcher with a pistol, a number of which weapons he was always well provided with. The others deemed it most prudent to beat a retreat, and ever afterwards allowed him to pursue his own course unmolested. He used to frequent a house at Gleadless, occupied by the late Mr. Joseph Barker. There is a room which still bears the name of ' Nevison's Room.' On one occasion, at a small village public-house, where he was staying, hearing the conversation about a small farmer with a large family being sold up, and finding the bailiff to be one of the company, with the cash (the proceeds of the sale) upon him, he resolved to rob him of it. He called for a candle, it being evening, and being shown to bed by the landlord, soon arranged his plan. He got out of the window, and had not long to wait before the object of his night's exploit appeared. At a very short distance he presented his pistol, and demanded the man's money in a tone and manner which the poor bailiff well understood. He begged for his life, and very submissively gave up every farthing of the money. Returning to his lodgings by the same way as he came, Nevison passed a good night, congratulating himself on the pleasure he should have in restoring back to the poor farmer and his family the money for which their little all had been sold, which he did the next day, not stopping a single penny. Nevison frequently visited the farmer afterwards on his journeys, and ultimately acquainted him with the whole affair."

At last, being taken, he was ordered for transportation, but getting his liberty, he fell to his old employment till he was taken by Captain Hardcastle, who, on riding to Wakefield, perceived Nevison at a town called Milford. He was then sent to York Castle, and soon after executed.

Nathaniel Pickett.

Wednesday, July 30th, A.D. 1684.—Nathaniel Pickett, aged 28, a native of Hull, was executed at the Tyburn without Micklegate Bar, for scuttling a brig lying in the Humber, called the *Ararinah*, on the 5th day of May last. His body was buried in St. Helen's Churchyard, Stonegate, in this city.

John Mortimer.

Saturday, April 10th, A.D. 1685.—John Mortimer, aged 27, a native of Thirsk, was executed at the Tyburn without Micklegate Bar, for breaking into the house of Mr. William Knowles, at Flaxton, and stealing therefrom 150 guineas, on the 10th of January, 1685. After the execution, his body was buried in the churchyard of St. Olave's, Marygate, York.

Mary Cotnam.

Friday, August 2nd, A.D. 1686.—Mary Cotnam, aged 29, was executed at the Tyburn without Micklegate Bar, for the wilful murder of her own daughter at Bentham, on the 3rd of July last. She died penitent, and her body was given to the surgeons of the city for dissection.

QUINTON HURWORTH, WILLIAM PASHLEY, AND ROBERT MYERS.

Thursday, March 28th, A.D. 1688.—Quinton Hurworth, aged 34 ; William Pashley, aged 28 ; and Robert Myers, aged 25, were executed at the Tyburn without Micklegate Bar, for the wilful murder of George Marsland, Esq., at Kirk Burton, on the 28th of December, 1687. After the execution, their bodies were given to the surgeons of the city for dissection.

HENRY KILVINGTON.

Saturday, March 31st, A.D. 1690.—Henry Kilvington, aged 25, a native of Dunnington, near York, was executed at the Tyburn without Micklegate Bar, for cutting and robbing one Thomas Kyle, as he was returning from the York market, on the night of the 16th of January, 1689. His body was buried in St. Andrew's Churchyard, in St. Andrewgate, in this city.

WILLIAM BORWICK AND EDWARD MANGALL.

William Borwick, aged 45, was tried and convicted before the Honourable Sir John Powel, Knight, at the Summer Assizes, held at York, on the 18th of September, 1690, for the wilful murder of his wife, being at the time with child. The murder was perpetrated near Cawood, on the 14th of April, 1690, and the apparition or spiritual appearance of the poor woman who had been murdered revealed the fact, and led to the discovery and apprehension of the murderer. When Borwick ascended the gallows to be hung, he told the hangman that he hoped the rope was strong enough, as, if it should break with the stretch put upon it, and he should unfortunately fall to the ground, he might be so seriously injured as to become a cripple for life. His apprehensions, however, were soon quieted, when the hangman assured him that he might venture upon it with perfect safety.

Edward Mangall, aged 39, suffered at the same time the severe penalty of the law, for the wilful murder of Elizabeth Rose and her child, on the 4th of September, 1690, who said that he was tempted by the devil to accomplish this diabolical act, which no doubt was true, for it was the devil in human shape that perpetrated the foul deed.

They were both executed at the White Cross Hill, Haxby-lane end, on Monday, September 19th, 1690, and next day hung in chains near to the place where the crimes were committed.

MARK GRAYSTON AND THOMAS DARNBROUGH.

Thursday, August 5th, A.D. 1691.—Mark Grayston, aged 24, a native of Bishopthorpe, near York, was executed at the Tyburn without Micklegate Bar, for highway robbery, between Ripley and Leeds; and Thomas Darnbrough, aged 26, a native of Pontefract, for attempted murder of one Eli Brown, at Pateley Bridge, was also executed at the same time and place. The body of Grayston was buried in the churchyard of St. Andrew's, in St. Andrew-gate, in this city; and the body of Darnbrough was given to the surgeons for dissection.

CHARLES DIMMEY AND HANNAH WILKINSON.

Monday, July 29th, A.D. 1692.—Charles Dimmey, aged 27, a native of Huddersfield, was executed for the forgery of a will belonging to William Robinson, Esq., of Halifax, in this county; and Hannah Wilkinson, aged 24, a native of Richmond, suffered a similar penalty for the wilful murder of her own daughter, a bastard child, at Rotherham, in this county, on the 30th of April, 1692. They both were executed at the Tyburn without Micklegate Bar. The body of Dimmey was buried in the churchyard of St. Olave's, Marygate, York; and the body of Hannah Wilkinson was given to the surgeons of the city for dissection.

JOHN COLLENS.

Saturday, March 30th, A.D. 1694.—John Collens, aged 17, a native of York, was executed at the Tyburn without Micklegate Bar, for stealing lead and a quantity of copper from Scarborough Church, on the 23rd of December, 1683. After the execution, his body was interred in the churchyard of All Hallows, Ousegate, in this city.

NELSON CAMPION.

Wednesday, August 5th, A.D. 1695.—Nelson Campion, aged 39, a native of Northallerton, was executed at the Tyburn without Micklegate Bar, for highway robbery of Mr. William Jones, cooper, in Jubbergate, York, upon Heworth Moor, on the night of the 4th of June last. After the execution, his body was buried in the churchyard of St. George's, Bean Hill, without Fishergate Postern, in this city.

ARTHUR MANGEY.

Saturday, March 30th, A.D. 1696.—Arthur Mangey, aged 68, goldsmith, of Leeds, was executed at the Tyburn without Micklegate Bar, for counterfeiting the current coin of the realm. He was drawn on a hurdle to the place of execution in the presence of a large concourse of spectators. After the execution, his body was given to his friends to be interred at Leeds.

MARTIN BURRELL.

Saturday, March 25th, A.D. 1697.—Martin Burrell, aged 22, a native of Richmond, in this county, was executed at the Tyburn without Micklegate Bar, for stealing a mare from Mr. Thomas Richardson, of Darlington, on the 19th of December, 1696. After the execution, his body was buried in the churchyard of St. Giles, in Gillygate, York.

JOHN BLACKBURN.

Thursday, August 10th, A.D. 1698.—John Blackburn,

aged 19, a native of Dunnington, near York, was executed at the Tyburn without Micklegate Bar, for coining and issuing base money. After the execution, his body was buried in the churchyard of St. Giles, Gillygate, in this city.

PETER ARUNDEL.

Saturday, July 30th, A.D. 1699.—Peter Arundel, aged 35, a native of Heslington, near York, butcher, was executed at the Tyburn without Micklegate Bar, for cutting and maiming one Anthony Wilson, at Tollerton, in the month of May last. His body was buried in the churchyard of St. Andrew's, in St. Andrew-gate, in this city.

June 3rd, A.D. 1700.—This year was remarkable for the removal of the old gallows of St. Leonard's, Green Dykes, without Walmgate Bar, the grand jury having petitioned the judges at the Lent March Assizes for its removal. The judge told them that he would mention it in its proper quarter, and on the 1st of June the sheriff of the county received an order from the Secretary of State for the Home Department, to remove the said gallows of St. Leonard's. It was accordingly taken down and demolished on the 3rd day of June, 1700, to the great joy of the citizens of York. Leonard Gaskill and Peter Rook, who were executed for sheep-stealing, were the two last victims that suffered the extreme penalty of the law on the gallows of St. Leonard's, in the year 1676.

WILLIAM BRYANT AND ROBERT WHEAT.

Saturday, April 7th, A.D. 1729.—William Bryant and Robert Wheat were executed at the Tyburn without Micklegate Bar, for horse-stealing.

WILLIAM PARKINSON.

July 28th, A.D. 1729.—William Parkinson was condemned for the murder of Archibald Noble, a Scotch drover,

in a close near Brouton, in Cleveland, in the North Riding
of this county. He was sent from York to the above-named
place, and was executed on Friday, August 15th, 1729, and
afterwards hung in chains.

JOHN CHAPELLO AND ABRAHAM POWELL.

Saturday, July 25th, A.D. 1730.—John Chapello was
executed at the Tyburn without Micklegate Bar, for horse-
stealing ; and Abraham Powell was sentenced to suffer the
severe penalty of the law for cutting cloth off the tenters
at Leeds. He was conveyed there, and executed on Wednesday, July 29th, 1730.

JAMES LAMBERT.

Saturday, August 21st, A.D. 1730.—James Lambert was
executed at the Tyburn without Micklegate Bar, for stealing
cattle.

JOSEPH ASKWITH, RICHARD FREEMAN, AND JOHN
FREEMAN.

Saturday, December 19th, A.D. 1730.—Joseph Askwith,
alias Sherling, Richard Freeman and John Freeman, brothers,
were executed at the Tyburn without Micklegate Bar, for
the robbery of Matthew Wilks. With their last breath
every one of them denied being guilty of the crime for
which they suffered, and declared that they never either
robbed Matthew Wilks or offered him the least violence.
They all died very penitent.

BENJAMIN ARMITT, JOHN WARD, AND JAMES WOOD.

Monday, March 29th, A.D. 1731.—Benjamin Armitt, a
miller, from Cliff; John Ward ; and James Wood, were
executed at the Tyburn without Micklegate Bar, for wilful
murder. They all died very penitent. John Ward and
James Wood confessed their being guilty of the crime for
which they suffered ; but Benjamin Armitt denied to the
last his being guilty of the murder of his boy, but that the

correction he gave him was only in a friendly way, and without any intention to murder or hurt him.

John Stead.

Saturday, April 7th, A.D. 1739.—John Stead, aged 38, was executed at the Tyburn without Micklegate Bar, for horse-stealing. He was a native of Pontefract, in Yorkshire, and died very penitent.

Richard Turpin.

April 17th, A.D. 1739.—Richard Turpin, highwayman, horse-stealer, and murderer. This notorious character was, for a long time, the dread of travellers on the Essex road, on account of the daring robberies which he daily committed ; he was also a noted housebreaker, and was for a considerable time remarkably successful in his desperate course, but was at length brought to an ignominious end, in consequence of circumstances which, in themselves, may appear trifling. He was apprehended in consequence of shooting a fowl, and his brother, refusing to pay sixpence for the postage of his letter, occasioned his conviction.

He was the son of a farmer at Thackstead, in Essex, and, having received a common school education, was apprenticed to a butcher in Whitechapel, but was distinguished from his early youth for the impropriety of his behaviour and the brutality of his manners. On the expiration of his apprenticeship he married a young woman of East Ham, in Essex, named Palmer ; but he had not been long married when he took to the practice of stealing his neighbour's cattle, which he used to kill and cut up for sale.

Having stolen two oxen belonging to Mr. Giles, of Plaistow, he drove them to his own house ; but two of Giles's servants, suspecting who was the robber, went to Turpin's, where they saw two beasts of such size as had been lost, but as the hides were stripped from them it was impossible to say that they were the same ; but learning that Turpin used to dispose of his hides at Waltham Abbey, they went thither, and saw the hides of the individual beasts that had been stolen.

No doubt now remaining who was the robber, a warrant was procured for the apprehension of Turpin ; but, learning that the peace officers were in search of him, he made his escape from the back window of his house at the very moment that the others were entering at the door.

Having retreated to a place of security, he found means to inform his wife where he was concealed ; on which she furnished him with money, with which he travelled into the hundreds of Essex, where he joined a gang of smugglers, with whom he was for some time successful, till a set of the Custom-house officers, by one successful stroke, deprived him of all his ill-acquired gains.

Thrown out of this kind of business he connected himself with a gang of deer-stealers, the principal part of whose depredations were committed on Epping Forest and the parks in its neighbourhood ; but this business not succeeding to the expectation of the robbers, they determined to commence house-breaking.

Their plan was to fix on houses that they presumed contained any valuable property, and while one of them knocked at the door, the others were to rush in and seize whatever they might deem worthy of their notice.

The first attack of this kind was at the house of Mr. Stripe, an old man who kept a chandler's shop at Watford, whom they robbed of all the money in his possession, but did not offer him any personal abuse.

Turpin now acquainted his associates that there was an old woman at Loughton who was in possession of seven or eight hundred pounds ; whereupon they agreed to rob her, and when they came to the door one of them knocked, and the rest forcing their way into the house, tied handkerchiefs over the eyes of the old woman and her maid.

This being done, Turpin demanded what money was in the house, and the owner hesitating to tell him, he threatened to set her on the fire if she did not make an immediate discovery. Still, however, she declined to give the desired information, on which the villains actually placed her on the fire, where she sat till the tormenting pains compelled her to discover her hidden treasure, so that the robbers possessed themselves of above four hundred pounds, and decamped with the booty.

Some little time after this they agreed to rob the house of a farmer near Barking, and knocking at the door, the people declined to open it; on which they broke it open, and having bound the farmer, his wife, his son-in-law, and the servant-maid, they robbed the house of above seven hundred pounds, which delighted Turpin so much that he exclaimed, " Ay, this will do if it would always be so !" and the robbers retired with their prize, which amounted to above eighty pounds for each of them.

This desperate gang, now flushed with success, determined to attack the house of Mr. Mason, the keeper of Epping Forest, and the time was fixed when the plan was to be carried into execution; but Turpin, having gone to London to spend his share of the former booty, intoxicated himself to such a degree that he totally forgot the appointment.

Nevertheless, the rest of the gang resolved that the absence of their companion should not frustrate the proposed design, and having taken a solemn oath to break every article of furniture in Mason's house, they set out on their expedition.

Having gained admission, they beat and kicked the unhappy man with great severity. Finding an old man sitting by the fireside, they permitted him to remain uninjured, and Mr. Mason's daughter escaped their fury by running out of the house and taking shelter in a hogsty.

After ransacking the lower part of the house and doing much mischief, they went upstairs, where they broke everything that fell in their way, and among the rest a China punchbowl, from which dropped one hundred and twenty guineas, which they made prey of, and effected their escape. They now went to London in search of Turpin, with whom they shared the booty, though he had not taken any part in the execution of the villany.

On the 11th of January, 1735, Turpin and five of his companions went to the house of Mr. Saunders, a rich farmer at Charlton, in Kent, between seven and eight in the evening, and having knocked at the door, asked if Mr. Saunders was at home. Being answered in the affirmative, they rushed into the house, and found Mr. Saunders, with his wife and friends, playing at cards in the parlour. They told the company that they should remain uninjured if they made no disturbance. Having made prize of a silver snuff-box which lay on the table, a part of the gang stood guard over the rest of the company, while the others attended Mr. Saunders through the house, and breaking open his escrutoires and closets, stole above one hundred pounds, exclusive of plate.

During these transactions the servant-maid ran up-stairs, barring the door of her room, and called out—"Thieves!" with a view of alarming the neighbourhood; but the robbers broke open the door of her room, secured her, and then robbed the house of all the valuable property they had not before taken. Finding some minced pies and some bottles of wine, they sat down to regale themselves, and meeting with a bottle of brandy, they compelled each of the company to drink a glass of it.

Mrs. Saunders fainting through terror, they administered some drops in water to her, and recovered her to the use of her senses. Having stayed in the house a considerable time, they packed up their booty and departed, having first declared that if any of the family gave the least alarm within two hours, or advertised the marks of the stolen plate, they would return and murder them at a future time.

The division of the plunder having taken place, they, on the 18th of the same month, went to the house of Mr. Sheldon, near Croydon, in Surrey, where they arrived about seven in the evening. Having got into the yard, they perceived a light in the stable, and going into it, found the coachman attending his horses. Having immediately bound him, they quitted the stable, and meeting Mr. Sheldon in the yard, they seized him, and compelling him to conduct them into the house, they stole eleven guineas, with the jewels, plate, and other things of value, to a large amount. Having committed this robbery, they returned Mr. Sheldon two guineas, and apologized for their conduct.

This being done, they hastened to the "Black Horse," in the Broadway, Westminster, where they concerted the robbery of Mr. Lawrence, of Edgware, near Stanmore, in Middlesex, for which place they set out on the 4th of February, and arrived at a public-house in that village about five o'clock in the evening. From this place they went to Mr. Lawrence's house, where they arrived about seven o'clock, just as he had discharged some people who had worked for him.

Having quitted their horses at the outer gate, one of the robbers, going forwards, found a boy who had just returned from folding his sheep ; the rest of the gang following, a pistol was presented, and instant death threatened if he made any noise. They then took off his garters and tied his hands, and told him to direct them to the door, and when they knocked to answer and bid the servants open it, in which case they would not hurt him ; but when the boy came to the door he was so terrified that he could not speak, on which one of the gang knocked, and a man-servant, imagining it was one of the neighbours, opened the door, whereupon they all rushed in, armed with pistols.

Having seized Mr. Lawrence and his servant, they threw a cloth over their faces, and taking the boy into another room, demanded what firearms were within the house ; to which he replied, only an old gun, which they broke in pieces. They then bound Mr. Lawrence and his man, and made them sit by the boy, and Turpin, searching the old gentleman, took from him a guinea, a Portugal piece, and some silver ; but not being satisfied with this booty, they forced him to conduct them upstairs, where they broke open a closet, and stole some money and plate. This not being sufficient to satisfy them, they threatened to murder Mr. Lawrence, each of them destining him to a different death, as the savageness of his own nature prompted him. At length one of them took a kettle of water from the fire, and threw it over him, but it providentially happened not to be hot enough to scald him.

In the interim, the maid-servant, who was churning butter in the dairy, hearing a noise in the house, apprehended some mischief, on which she blew out her candle to screen herself ; but being found in the course of their search, one of the miscreants compelled her to go upstairs, where he gratified his brutal passion by force. They then robbed the house of all the valuable effects they could find, locked the family in the parlour, threw the key into the garden, and took their ill-gotten plunder to London.

The particulars of this atrocious robbery being represented to the King, a proclamation was issued for the apprehension of the offenders, promising a pardon to any one of them who would impeach his accomplices, and a reward of £50 was offered, to be paid on conviction. This, however, had no effect. The robbers continued their depredations as before, and flushed with the success they had met with, seemed to bid defiance to the laws.

On the 7th of February, six of them assembled at the " White Bear " inn, in Drury Lane, where they agreed to rob the house of Mr. Francis, a farmer near Mary-le-bone. Arriving at the place, they found a servant in the cow-house, whom they bound fast, and threatened to murder him, if he was not perfectly silent. This being done, they led him into the stable, where finding another of the servants, they bound him in the same manner.

In the interim Mr. Francis happening to come home, they presented their pistols to his breast and threatened to murder him immediately, if he made the least noise or opposition.

Having bound the master in the stable with his servants, they rushed into the house, tied Mrs. Francis, her daughter, and the maid-servant, and beat them in a most cruel manner. One of the thieves stood as a sentry, while the rest rifled the house, in which they found a silver tankard, a medal of Charles the First, a gold watch, several gold rings, a considerable sum of money, and a variety of valuable linen and other effects, which they conveyed to London.

Hereupon a reward of £100 was offered for the apprehension of the offenders; in consequence of which two of them were taken into custody, tried, convicted on the evidence of an accomplice, and hanged in chains; and the whole gang being dispersed, Turpin went into the country to renew his depredations on the public.

On a journey towards Cambridge, he met a man genteelly dressed and well mounted, and, expecting a good booty, he presented a pistol to the supposed gentleman and demanded his money. The party thus stopped happened to be one King, a famous highwayman, who knew Turpin; and when the latter threatened destruction if he did not deliver his money, King burst into a fit of laughter, and said, " What ! Dog eat dog?—Come, come, brother Turpin; if you don't know me, I know you, and shall be glad of your company."

These brethren in inquity soon struck the bargain, and immediately entering on business, committed a number of robberies, till at length they were so well known that no public house would receive them as guests. Thus situated, they fixed on a spot between the King's Oak and the Loughton road, on Epping Forest, where they made a cave, which was large enough to receive them and their horses.

This cave was inclosed within a sort of thicket of bushes and brambles, through which they could look and see passengers on the road, while themselves remained unobserved.

From this station they used to issue, and robbed such a number of persons, that at length the very pedlars who travelled the road carried firearms for their defence ; and while they were in this retreat, Turpin's wife used to supply them with necessaries, and frequently remained in the cave during the night.

Having taken a ride as far as Bungay, in Suffolk, they observed two young women receive fourteen pounds for corn, on which Turpin resolved to rob them of the money. King objected, saying it was a pity to rob such pretty girls ; but Turpin was obstinate, and obtained the booty.

Upon their return home on the following day, they stopped a Mr. Bradell, of London, who was riding in his chariot with his children. The gentleman seeing only one robber, was preparing to make resistance, when King called to Turpin to hold the horses. They took from the gentleman his watch, money, and an old mourning ring ; but returned the latter, as he declared that its intrinsic value was trifling, yet he was very unwilling to part with it.

Finding that they readily parted with the ring, he asked them what he must give for the watch : on which King said to Turpin, " What say ye, Jack ? Here seems to be a good honest fellow ; shall we let him have the watch ? "— " Do as you please." On which King said to the gentleman, " You must pay six guineas for it ; we never sell for more, though the watch should be worth six-and-thirty." The gentleman promised that the money should be left at the " Dial," in Birchin-lane.

On the 4th of May, 1737, Turpin was guilty of murder, which arose from the following circumstance. A reward of £100 having been offered for apprehending him, one Thomas

Morris, a servant of Mr. Thompson, one of the keepers of Epping Forest, accompanied by a higgler, set out in order to apprehend them. Turpin seeing them approach near his dwelling, Mr. Thompson's man having a gun, he mistook them for poachers, on which he said, there were no hares near the thicket : " No," said Morris, " but I have found a Turpin ; " and presenting his gun, required him to surrender.

Hereupon Turpin spoke to him as in a friendly manner, and gradually retreated at the same time, till, having seized his own gun, he shot him dead on the spot, and the higgler ran off with the utmost precipitation.

This murder being represented to the Secretary of State, the following proclamation was issued by Government, which we give a place to, from its describing the person of this notorious depredator.

" It having been represented to the King that Richard Turpin did, on Wednesday, the 4th of May last, barbarously murder Thomas Morris, servant to Henry Thompson, one of the keepers of Epping Forest, and commit other notorious felonies and robberies near London, his Majesty is pleased to promise his most gracious pardon to any of his accomplices, and a reward of £200 to any person or persons that shall discover him, so that he may be apprehended and convicted. Turpin was born at Thackstead, in Essex, is about thirty, by trade a butcher, about five feet nine inches high, very much marked with the small-pox, his cheek-bones broad, his face thinner towards the bottom, his visage short, pretty upright, and broad about the shoulders."

Turpin, to avoid the proclamation, went further into the country in search of his old companion King ; and in the mean time sent a letter to his wife to meet him at a public house at Hertford. The woman attended according to his direction ; and her husband coming into the house soon after she arrived, a butcher, to whom he owed five pounds, happened to see him, on which he said, " Come, Dick, I know you have money now, and if you will pay me, it will be of great service."

Turpin told him that his wife was in the next room, that she had the money, and that he should be paid immediately ; but while the butcher was hinting to some of his acquaintance that the person present was Turpin, and that they might take him into custody after he had received his debt, the highwayman made his escape through a window, and rode off with great expedition.

Turpin having found King, and a man named Potter, who had lately connected himself with them, they set off towards London in the dusk of the evening ; but when they came near the "Green Man," on Epping Forest, they overtook a Mr. Major, who riding on a very fine horse, and Turpin's beast being jaded, he obliged the rider to dismount and exchange horses.

The robbers now pursued their journey towards London, and Mr. Major going to the "Green Man," gave an account of the affair ; on which it was conjectured that Turpin had been the robber, and that the horse which he exchanged must have been stolen.

It was on a Saturday evening that this robbery was committed, but Mr. Major being advised to print hand-bills immediately, notice was given to the landlord of the "Green Man," that such a horse as Mr. Major had lost had been left at the "Red Lion," in Whitechapel. The landlord going thither, determined to wait till some persons came for it, and at about eleven o'clock at night, King's brother came to pay for the horse and take it away, on which he was immediately seized and conducted into the house.

Being asked what right he had to the horse, he said he had bought it ; but the landlord examining a whip which he had in his hand, found a button at the end of the handle half broken off, and the name of Major on the remaining half. Hereupon he was given into the custody of a constable ; but as it was supposed that he was not the actual robber, he was told that he should have his liberty if he would discover his employer.

Hereupon he said, that a stout man in a white duffel coat was waiting for the horse in Red-Lion-street, on which the company going thither saw King, who drew a pistol and attempted to fire it, but it flashed in the pan. He then endeavoured to draw out another pistol, but he could not, as it got entangled in his pocket.

At this time Turpin was watching at a small distance, and riding towards the spot, King cried out, "Shoot him, or we are taken;" on which Turpin fired, and shot his companion, who called out, "Dick, you have killed me," which the other hearing, rode off at full speed.

King lived a week after this affair, and gave information that Turpin might be found at a house near Hackney marsh ; and on inquiry it was discovered that Turpin had been there on the night that he rode off, lamenting that he had killed King, who was his most faithful associate.

For a considerable time did Turpin skulk about the forest, having been deprived of his retreat in the cave since he shot the servant of Mr. Thompson. On the examination of this cave, there were found two shirts, two pairs of stockings, a piece of ham, and part of a bottle of wine.

Some vain attempts were made to take this notorious offender into custody, and among the rest the huntsman of a gentleman in the neighbourhood went in search of him with blood-hounds. Turpin perceiving them, and recollecting that King Charles II. evaded his pursuers under covert of the friendly branches of the oak, mounted one of those trees, under which the hounds passed, to his inexpressible terror, so that he determined to make a retreat into Yorkshire.

Going first to Long Sutton, in Lincolnshire, he stole some horses, for which he was taken into custody ; but he escaped from the constable as he was conducting him before a magistrate, and hastened to Welton, in Yorkshire, where he went by the name of John Palmer, and assumed the character of a gentleman.

He now frequently went into Lincolnshire, where he stole horses, which he brought into Yorkshire, and either sold or exchanged them.

He often accompanied the neighbouring gentlemen on their parties of hunting and shooting ; and one evening, on a return of an expedition of the latter kind, he wantonly shot a cock belonging to his landlord. On this, Mr. Hall, a neighbour, said, "You have done wrong in shooting your landlord's cock;" to which Turpin replied, that if he would stay till he loaded his gun he would shoot him also.

Irritated by this insult, Mr. Hall informed the landlord of what had passed, and application being made to some magistrates, a warrant was granted for the apprehension of the offender, who being taken into custody, and carried before a bench of Justices then assembled at the Quarter Sessions at Beverley, they demanded security for his good behaviour, which he being unable or unwilling to give, he was committed to Bridewell.

On inquiry, it was found that he made frequent journeys into Lincolnshire, and on his return always abounded in money, and was likewise in possession of several horses, so that it was conjectured he was a horse-stealer and highwayman.

On this the magistrates went to him on the following day, and demanded who he was, where he lived, and what was his employment? He replied in substance, "that about two years ago he had lived at Long Sutton, in Lincolnshire, and was by trade a butcher, but that having contracted several debts for sheep that proved rotten,' he was obliged to abscond, and come to live in Yorkshire."

The magistrates not being satisfied with this tale, commissioned the Clerk of the Peace to write into Lincolnshire, to make the necessary inquiries respecting the supposed John Palmer. The letter was carried by a special messenger, who brought an answer from a magistrate in the neighbourhood, importing that John Palmer was well known, though he had never carried on trade there; that he being accused of sheep-stealing, for which he had been in custody, had made his escape from the peace officers; and that there were several informations lodged against him for horse-stealing.

Hereupon the magistrates thought it prudent to remove him to York Castle, where he had not been more than a month, when two persons from Lincolnshire came and claimed a mare and foal, and likewise a horse, which he had stolen in that county.

After he had been about four months in prison, he wrote the following letter to his brother in Essex :—

York, Feb. 6, 1739.

DEAR BROTHER,

I am sorry to acquaint you that I am now in York Castle for horse-stealing. If I could procure an evidence from London to give me a character, that would go a great way towards my being acquitted. I had not been long in this county before my being appre-

hended, so that it would pass off the readier.   For Heaven's sake, dear
brother, do not neglect me ; you will know what I mean when I say,

I am yours,

JOHN PALMER.

This letter being returned unopened to the Post Office in
Essex, because the brother would not pay the postage of it,
was accidentally seen by Mr. Smith, a schoolmaster, who
having taught Turpin to write, immediately knew his hand ;
on which he carried the letter to a magistrate, who broke
it open, by which it appeared that the supposed John Palmer
was the real Richard Turpin.

Hereupon the magistrates of Essex despatched Mr. Smith
to York, who immediately selected him from all the other
prisoners in the Castle.   This Mr. Smith and another
gentleman afterwards proved his identity on his trial.

On the rumour that the noted Turpin was a prisoner in
York Castle, persons flocked from all parts of the country
to take a view of him, and debates ran very high whether he
was the real person or not. Among others who visited him was
a young fellow who pretended to know the famous Turpin,
and having regarded him a considerable time with looks of
great attention, he told the keeper he would bet him half a
guinea that he was not Turpin ; on which the prisoner,
whispering the keeper, said, " Lay him the wager, and I'll
go you halves."

When this notorious malefactor was brought to trial, he
was convicted on two indictments, and received sentence of
death.

After conviction, he wrote to his father, imploring him to
intercede with a gentleman and lady of rank, to make
interest that his sentence might be remitted, and that he
might be transported.   The father did what was in his
power, but the notoriety of his character was such that no
persons would exert themselves in his favour.

This man lived in the most gay and thoughtless manner
after conviction, regardless of all considerations of futurity,
and affecting to make a jest of the dreadful fate that awaited
him.

Not many days before his execution, he purchased a new
fustian frock and a pair of pumps, in order to wear them at
the time of his death ; and on the day before he hired five

poor men, at ten shillings each, to follow the cart as mourners. He also gave hatbands and gloves to several other persons, and left a ring and some other articles to a married woman in Lincolnshire, with whom he had been acquainted.

On the morning of his death he was put into a cart, and being followed by his mourners, as above mentioned, he was drawn to the place of execution, in his way to which he bowed to the spectators with an air of the most astonishing indifference and intrepidity.

When he came to the fatal tree, he ascended the ladder with firmness, but his right leg trembling, he stamped it down with an air of assumed courage, as if he was ashamed of discovering any signs of fear. Having conversed with the executioner about half an hour, he threw himself off the ladder, and expired in a few minutes.

The spectators of the execution were affected by his fate, as he was distinguished by the comeliness of his appearance. The corpse was brought to the " Blue Boar," in Castlegate, York, where it remained till the next morning, when it was interred in the churchyard of St. George's parish, with an inscription on the coffin, the initials of his name and his age. The grave was dug remarkably deep ; but notwithstanding the people who acted as mourners took such measures as they thought would secure the body, it was carried off about three o'clock on the following morning. The populace, however, got information where it was conveyed, and found it in a garden belonging to one of the surgeons of the city.

Having got possession of it, they laid it on a board, and carried it through the streets in a kind of triumphant manner ; they then filled the coffin with unslacked lime, and buried it in the grave where it had been before deposited. The irons which Turpin wore in York Castle weighed upwards of twenty-eight pounds.

WILLIAM SPINK, JUN.

Saturday, March 27th, A.D. 1740.—William Spink, aged 26, was executed at the Tyburn without Micklegate Bar, for horse-stealing. The following is an account of the confession he made in the Castle the day before his execution, to the Rev. Mr. Barker ; viz.—

I was born at Sawley, in the parish of Ripon. From thence my father and mother removed to Wharsdale, where I continued till I was six years of age. From thence my parents removed to Bishop Thornton, where I lived till 1 was fit to go to service, in which capacity of life I served duly and honestly as a farm servant, till I married Frances Mawson, of Park Hay, and was advised to rob the barn of my honest master (Mr. Haire) of corn, which I did. After that I broke into Bilton Hall with the assistance of a relation, and took from thence bedding and other goods. At another time I stole a quantity of linen from a hedge, the property of William Long, of Whip Moor. After that I stole Uncle Mawson's colt and fled the country. On returning, I stole a horse belonging to William Waddington, and another from Francis Buck, of Burthate, near Ripley, where I broke a lock off the stable. These two robberies were committed in one night. Last of all, I stole a black mare, the property of James Rickaby, in the parish of Upper Dunsley, in the Bishopric of Durham, which mare was found in my possession at Ascough, and for which robbery I received sentence of death. This is a true confession.

Signed the 26th day of March, 1740.

WILLIAM SPINK.   +   His mark.

GEORGE BAINTON, ATTORNEY; JOHN WRIGHT, JOSEPH TYSON, AND JOHN BARKER.

Saturday, April 11th, A.D. 1741.—George Bainton, attorney, for forging a will ; John Wright, for the murder of Upkin Stirling ; Joseph Tyson and John Barker, for burglary, were all executed at the Tyburn without Micklegate Bar. Bainton had, to the very last, flattered himself with the hope and almost certain expectation of a reprieve ; but unexpectedly he had to suffer like the rest.

EXECUTION OF TEN REBELS.

Saturday, November 1st, A.D. 1746.—The following rebels were executed at the Tyburn without Micklegate Bar; viz.,—George Hamilton, Edward Clevering, James Spark, Charles Gordon, Angus McDonald, James Mayne, Benjamin Mason, William Dempsey, and two others, who were ordered for execution this day (William Crosby, an Irishman, of Colonel Townley's regiment, and William Barclay, of Colonel Grant's regiment, having been reprieved), were brought from the Castle in three sledges. But as they were coming down Castlegate, Mr. Duct, one of his Majesty's messengers, brought a reprieve for John James Fellens, who was immediately taken out of the sledge and conveyed back to the Castle. Hamilton, Clevering, Frazier, and Gordon were in the first sledge ; Mason, Mayne, Conolly, and Dempsey in the second ; McDonald and Spark in the last. When they had hung ten minutes, the executioner cut them down, laid their bodies on a stage built for that purpose, and stripped them naked. Captain Hamilton was the first whose heart was taken out, which the executioner threw into the fire, crying out, " Gentlemen, behold the heart of a traitor." When he came to the last man, which was Frazier, he said, " Gentlemen, behold the heart of the last traitor. God save King George." Upon which the spectators gave a loud huzza. Then he scored each of their arms and legs, but did not cut them off, crying, " Good people, behold the four quarters of a traitor," and when he had finished that part of the operation, he chopped off their heads, beginning with Frazier, and ending with Hamilton, which finished the execution. The whole of the proceedings was conducted throughout with the utmost decency and good order. Two hearses were ready to receive the bodies of Captain Hamilton, Clevering, and Gordon, and coffins for the rest. The heads of Conolly and Mayne were set up at Micklegate Bar, and the head of Hamilton was put into a box, in order to be sent to Carlisle; but the rest were put into coffins with their bodies, and were buried behind the Castle.

Saturday, November 8th, A.D. 1746.—The remainder of the rebels were executed at the gallows without Micklegate Bar. Their execution was performed after the same manner as the others last week, viz. :—David Row, who was taken in the skirmish at Clifton. He was a volunteer in the Pretender's army, and entered immediately after the battle of Preston Pans. He had formerly been an officer in the Customs. William Hunter, of Newcastle-upon-Tyne, of Colonel Townley's regiment ; John Endsworth, of Knottesford, in Cheshire, of Colonel Grant's regiment ; John McClean, a Highlander; and John McGreggor, of Perthshire ; both of the Duke of Perth's regiment ; Simon McKensie, of Inverness ; and Alexander Parker, of the shire of Murray,

of Colonel Stuart's regiment; Thomas McGennis, of the
shire of Banff, and Archibald Kennedy, of Ayrshire, both
of Glenbucket's regiment, the latter a servant to Colonel
Grant; James Thompson, of Lord Oglevie's regiment; and
Michael Brady, an Irishman, of Glengarry's regiment.
They all behaved with great decency, and good order was
maintained throughout.

In 1754, one William Arundel, a tailor, in York, assisted
by an Irish journeyman of his, stole from Micklegate Bar
the heads of the two rebel chiefs viz.,—Conolly and Mayne,
which had been placed there in 1746. The Irishman
betrayed his master, and he was fined and imprisoned for
two years, in the old gaol on Ouse Bridge. The following
account respecting these Scotch rebels has lately appeared in
the newspapers :—

DISCOVERY OF THE REMAINS OF SCOTTISH REBELS.—Within the
last few days a curious discovery has been made behind York Castle.
A number of excavators were employed there to dig a drain, when they
turned up the remains of about twenty human bodies; but the skulls
of three or four of them were wanting, and the bones appeared mixed
together in such an unusual manner as to excite the curiosity of all
who saw the positions in which they were found. The conclusion
formed respecting them is, that they are the remains of twenty-one
Scottish rebels, who were executed near York, ten of them on Saturday,
the 1st, and the remainder on Saturday, the 8th of November, 1746,
when they were hanged, drawn, and quartered.

JOSIAH FEARN, THOMAS BROWN, AND ROBERT FAWTHORP.

Saturday, March 26th, A.D. 1749.—Josiah Fearn, Thomas
Brown, and Robert Fawthorp were executed at the Tyburn
without Micklegate Bar for the following crimes :—Josiah
Fearn for wilful murder; Thomas Brown, *alias* Clark, *alias*
Sanderson, on suspicion of stealing a black mare ; and Robert
Fawthorp for the murder of Elizabeth Ferrand and Mary
Parker, grocers, of Church Fenton. He committed the
bloody deed in broad daylight, on the 3rd day of October,
1748, and was married on the 4th. He was apprehended
on the 6th, and committed to York Castle for trial. After
the perpetration of this cruel and bloody deed, he robbed
the house of all the money and valuables it contained, and
decamped with his booty. Afterwards the barking of a

dog attracted the attention of some of the neighbours, who then broke into the house, and discovered the two lifeless bodies, mangled in a most awful and shocking manner. The bloody deed had been done with a cooper's adze, or some other blunt instrument.

JOSEPH GARBUTT, ABRAHAM SCOTT, AND JOHN TIPLADY.

Saturday, March 31st, A.D. 1750.—Joseph Garbutt and Abraham Scott were executed at the Tyburn without Micklegate Bar, for sheep-stealing; and John Tiplady was executed at the same time and place for horse-stealing. To the last he bitterly denied the fact for which he suffered on the gallows.

ROBERT LOVEDAY AND BENJAMIN FARMERY.

Saturday, April 11th, A.D. 1752.—Robert Loveday and Benjamin Farmery were executed at the Tyburn without Micklegate Bar, for housebreaking.

EDWARD WELLS AND BEZALIEL KNOWLES.

Monday, April 28th, A.D. 1753.—Edward Wells, of Northallerton, in this county, bricklayer, aged 40, was executed at the Tyburn without Micklegate Bar, for forgery. At the gallows he took off his hat, wig, and handkerchief, unbuttoned his shirt, then turned about, opened the noose of the rope, kissed it, put it under his chin, and would have thrown it over his head if his being pinioned had not withheld him. When the executioner had put the rope about his neck, he fixed the knot under his left ear, and when the cart was drawn away, he threw himself off it with the greatest resolution.

Bezaliel Knowles, aged 17, was executed at the same time and place, for the wilful murder of Dorothy Gibson. He behaved with much decency and contrition, and prayed with the greatest fervency. As he endeavoured to step upon the board for the executioner to fix the halter round his neck, he fell back in the cart. He made a very ample confession, and died penitent.

David Harkness.

Saturday, April 7th, A.D. 1753.—David Harkness was executed at the Tyburn without Micklegate Bar, for horse-stealing.

Thomas Downing and John Wentworth.

Saturday, August 2nd, A.D. 1753.—Thomas Downing, of Howbrook, in the parish of Tankersley, labourer, aged 22, was executed at the Tyburn without Micklegate Bar, on suspicion of sheep-stealing from James Bincliff. John Wentworth, *alias* Thomlinson, gardener, aged 29, was executed at the same time and place, on suspicion of breaking open a box, and taking out of it seventeen guineas, the property of Mr. James Taylor, of Selby.

William Smith.

Wednesday, August 22nd, 1753.—William Smith was executed at the Tyburn without Micklegate Bar, for the wilful and diabolical murder of Thomas Harper, William Harper, and Ann Harper, his wife, the father, scn, and daughter-in-law. The culprit behaved to the very last in the most unconcerned and insensible manner. His body was sent to the county hospital to be dissected and anatomized, according to the direction of the late Act of Parliament against murder.

Joseph Riddell and Francis Jefferson.

Saturday, August 17th, A.D. 1754.—Joseph Riddell was executed at the Tyburn without Micklegate Bar, for the nrurder of Richard Marsden; and Francis Jefferson, for house-breaking at South Cliff, in the East Riding, was executed at the same time and place.

David Evans, Richard Varley, and John Holdsworth.

Saturday, August 28th, A.D. 1756.—David Evans was executed at the Tyburn without Micklegate Bar, for highway robbery and horse-stealing. Richard Varley also was executed at the same time and place for highway robbery ; and John Holdsworih shared the same fate for house-breaking with violence.

ELIJAH OAKS.

Saturday, August 28th, A.D. 1756.—Elijah Oaks, aged 27, was executed at the Tyburn without Micklegate Bar, for burglary. He died very penitent.

MARY ELLAH.

*Saturday, March 30th,*A.D. 1757.—Mary Ellah, of Brom-fleet, near Cave, was executed at the Tyburn without Micklegate Bar, for the wilful murder of her husband, by strangling him while in a fit of jealous excitement. She was hanged, and her body was burnt when taken down.

GEORGE TROTTER.

Monday, April 3rd, A.D. 1757.—George Trotter, aged 27, was executed at the Tyburn without Micklegate Bar, for the wilful murder of his sweetheart, Hannah Wilson, at the town feast of Todwick, near Rotherham, on the 6th day of July, 1756. It appeared that he intended to marry the girl, but, fancying she had a regard for another person, he became furiously jealous, whereupon he called her out into the yard, and, on pretence of speaking to her, stabbed her in the belly with a penknife, which caused her death. Though he behaved remarkably insolent at his trial, he became penitent before his execution. His body was sent to the county hospital for dissection.

THOMAS COOPER AND STEPHEN TUDEAR.

Saturday, July 30th, A.D. 1757.—Thomas Cooper was executed at the Tyburn without Micklegate Bar, for horse-stealing ; and Stephen Tudear was executed at the same time and place, for the wilful murder of Ellen Applegarth, of

Wetherby. He was afterwards hung in chains on Clifford Moor, near Wetherby, the place near to the spot where the brutal murder was committed.

MATTHEW BILTON, WILLIAM WATSON, RICHARD FORD, ROBERT COLE, AND GEORGE BERRY.

Monday, May 1st, A.D. 1758.—The above rioters were executed at the Tyburn without Micklegate Bar, pursuant to their sentence. Bilton, Watson, and Ford were convicted of high treason, and were not only hanged, but drawn and quartered. In their rioting wantonness they proceeded from market-town to market-town demanding money from the inhabitants, and using violent threats, by which they obtained seven guineas from the servants of Mr. Osbaldeston; also money from the Hon. and Rev. Henry Egerton. They died remarkably penitent, confessed to their being concerned in the said riots, and exhorted their countrymen to take warning from their untimely fate. Cole, in addition to the crime of rioting, was convicted for obstructing the execution of the Militia Act. They were called the " Wensleydale rioters," and originated in consequence of the high price of corn.

BENJAMIN WINDLE AND HENRY NELSON.

Saturday, March 24th, A.D. 1759.—Benjamin Windle was executed at the Tyburn without Micklegate Bar, for breaking into the house of Thomas Hirst, of Bradley, on the night of the 22nd of October, 1758, and stealing out of a chest a leather bag, containing one hundred pounds in gold coin, and another bag containing forty guineas in gold, and a linen purse, containing twenty shillings and fivepence in copper; and Henry Nelson, for perjury and forgery. They both behaved in a very decent and becoming manner; but the former absolutely denied to the very last his being guilty of the offence for which he suffered.

BENJAMIN HOULT.

Saturday, April 9th, A.D. 1759.—Benjamin Hoult was

executed at the Tyburn without Walmgate Bar, for horse-stealing. He met his fate with great composure, and died very penitent, protesting to the very last his innocence of the crime for which he suffered.

EUGENE ARAM.

Monday, August 6th, A.D. 1759.—Eugene Aram, school-master, aged 54, formerly of Knaresborough, and after that of Lynn, was executed at the Tyburn without Micklegate Bar, and after that hung in chains, for the wilful murder of Daniel Clark, shoemaker, on the 8th of February, 1744-5. Clark had been recently married, and, under colour of having received a fortune with his wife, he entered into a confede-racy with Aram and Houseman, a flax-dresser, to defraud several persons of plate and other goods, which Clark was to borrow from friends and acquaintances, to make a first appearance in the married state. This he did, and obtained things of great value, such as linen and woollen drapery goods, besides three silver tankards, four silver mugs, one silver milkpot, one ring set with an emerald, and two brilliant diamonds; another with three rose diamonds, a third with an amethyst, six plain rings, eight watches, two snuff-boxes, &c., all from different people. Having fraudu-lently obtained the goods, the place of distribution was fixed upon at Aram's house, and Clark was soon afterwards missing. His intimacy with Aram and Houseman excited a suspicion that they might be concerned in the fraud. Search was made, and some of the goods were found in House-man's house, and another portion was dug up in Aram's garden; but as no plate was found, it was believed that Clark had gone off with that. The affair remained in abey-ance until the month of June, 1758, when Aram was found at Lynn, in Norfolk, where he was usher of a school, and he was then arrested for the murder of Clark.

The wife of Aram, after his departure from her—for she did not go with him to Lynn,—had intimated her suspicion of Clark being murdered, and of her husband and Houseman being concerned in the murder. Aram, on being told this, said to Houseman that " he would shoot her, and put her out of the way." This and other testimony being given on the coroner's inquest, Houseman, who was there, showed various marks of guilt; and, upon a skeleton which had been found being produced, he took up one of the bones and said, "This is no more Dan. Clark's bone than it is mine." In truth, these were not the bones of Clark, but were designed to bring the real body to light, which Houseman, after some evasion in his first deposition, discovered to be in St. Robert's Cave, near Knaresborough, where it was found in the posture described. He was then admitted king's evidence against Aram, and brought in one Terry as an accomplice in the murder. Houseman gave his deposition as follows :—

"That Daniel Clark was murdered by Eugene Aram, late of Knaresborough, schoolmaster, and as he believes, on Friday, the 8th of February, 1744-5 ; for that Eugene Aram and Daniel Clark were together at Aram's house early that morning, and that he (Houseman) left the house, and went up the street a little before, and they called to him, desiring he would go a little way with them, and he accordingly went along with them to a place called St. Robert's Cave, near Grimbald-bridge, where Aram and Clark stopped, and there he saw Aram strike him several times over the breast and head, and saw him fall as if he was dead, upon which he came away and left them. But whether Aram used any weapon or not to kill Clark he could not tell, nor does he know what he did with the body afterwards, but believes that Aram left it at the mouth of the cave ; for that, seeing Aram do this, lest he might share the same fate, he made the best of his way from him, and got to the bridge-end, where, looking back, he saw Aram coming from the cave-side (which is in a private rock adjoining the river), and could discern a bundle in his hand, but did not know what it was. Upon this he hasted away to the town, without either joining Aram, or seeing him again until the next day, and from that time to this he never had any private discourse with him."

Subsequently, however, Houseman said that Clark's body was buried in St. Robert's Cave, and that he was sure it was then there ; but he desired that it might remain where it was till Aram should be taken.

Aram being thus accused by Houseman, was apprehended

in the school at Lynn, and after some evasions on the first examination, he signed the following statement :—

"That he was at his own house on the 7th of February, 1744-5, at night, when Richard Houseman and Daniel Clark came to him with some plate, and both of them went for more several times, and came back with several pieces of plate, of which Clark was endeavouring to defraud his neighbours ; that he could not but observe that Houseman was all that night very diligent to assist him to the utmost of his power ; and insisted that this was Houseman's business that night, and not the signing any note or instrument as is pretended by Houseman. That Henry Terry, then of Knaresborough, ale-keeper, was as much concerned in abetting the said frauds, as either Houseman or Clark ; but was not now at Aram's house, because, as it was market-day, his absence from his guests might have occasioned some suspicion. That Terry, notwithstanding, brought two silver tankards that night, upon Clark's account, which had been fraudulently obtained ; and that Clark, so far from having borrowed £20 of Houseman, to his knowledge never borrowed more than £9, which he had paid him again before that night. That all the leather Clark had, which amounted to a considerable value, he well knows was concealed under a flat in Houseman's house, with intent to be disposed of by little and little, in order to prevent suspicion of his being concerned in Clark's fraudulent practices. That Terry took the plate in a bag, as Clark and Houseman did the watches, rings, and several small things of value, and carried them into the flat, where they and he (Aram) went together to St. Robert's Cave, and beat most of the plate flat. It was then thought too late in the morning, being about four o'clock on the 8th of February, 1744-5, for Clark to go off so as to get to any distance : it was therefore agreed he should stay there till the night following ; and Clark accordingly stayed there all that day, as he believes, they having agreed to send him victuals, which were carried to him by Henry Terry, he being judged the most likely person to do it without suspicion, for as he was a shooter he might go there under the pretence of sporting. That the next night, in order to give Clark more time to get off, Henry Terry, Richard Houseman, and himself, went down to the cave very early, but he (Aram) did not go into the cave to see Clark at all ; that Richard Houseman and Henry Terry only went into the cave, he staying to watch at a little distance on the outside, lest anybody should surprise them ; that he believes they were beating some plate, for he heard them making a noise. They stayed there about an hour, and then came out of the cave, and told him that Clark was gone off. Observing a bag they had along with them, he took it in his hand, and saw that it contained plate. On asking why Daniel did not take the plate with him, Terry and Houseman replied that they had bought it of him as well as the watches, and had given him money for it, that being more convenient for him to go off with, as less cumbersome and dangerous. After which they all three went into Houseman's warehouse, and concealed the watches with the small plate there, but that Terry carried away with him the great plate ; that afterwards Terry told him he carried it to How-hill, and hid it there, and then went into Scotland and disposed of it; but as to Clark, he could not tell whether he was murdered or not : he knew nothing of him, only that they told him he was gone off."

After he had signed this he was conducted to York Castle, where he and Houseman remained till the Assizes.

From the examination of Aram there appeared good reason to suspect Terry to be an accomplice in the murder. A warrant was therefore granted, and he was apprehended and committed to the Castle. Bills of indictment were found against them ; but it appearing to the Court, upon affidavit, that the prosecutor could not be fully provided with his witnesses at that time, the trial was postponed till Lammas Assizes.

On the 3rd of August, 1759, Houseman and Aram were brought up to plead. Houseman was arraigned on his former indictment, acquitted, and admitted evidence against Aram, who was thereupon arraigned.

Houseman was then called upon, who deposed,—" That in the night between the 7th and 8th of February, 1744-5, about eleven o'clock, he went to Aram's house ; that after two hours and upwards spent in passing to and fro between their several houses, to dispose of various goods and to settle some notes concerning them, Aram proposed first to Clark and then Houseman to take a walk out of town ; that when they came to the field where St. Robert's Cave is, Aram and Clark went into it over the hedge, and when they came within six or eight yards of the cave he saw them quarrelling ; that he saw Aram strike Clark several times, upon which Clark fell, and he never saw him rise again ; that he saw no instrument that Aram had, and knew not that he had any ; that upon this, without any interposition or alarm, he left them and returned home ; that the next morning he went to Aram's house and asked what business he had with Clark last night, and what he had done with him ? Aram replied not to this question, but threatened him if he spoke of his being in Clark's company that night, vowing revenge against him, either by himself or some other person, if he mentioned anything relating to the affair."

Peter Moor (Clark's servant) deposed,—" That a little before his disappearing, Clark went to receive his wife's fortune ; that upon his return he went to Aram's house, where Moor then was. Upon Clark's coming in, Aram said, ' How do you do, Mr. Clark ! I am glad to see you at home again ; pray, what success ? ' To which Clark replied, ' I have received my wife's fortune, and have it in my pocket, though it was with difficulty I got it.' Upon which Aram said to Clark (Houseman being present), ' Let us go up-stairs.' Accordingly they went, upon which this witness returned home."

Mr. Beckwith deposed,—" That when Aram's garden was searched on suspicion of his being an accomplice in the frauds of Clark, there were found several kinds of goods bound together in a coarse wrapper ; and among the rest, in particular, a piece of cambric which he himself had sold Clark a very little time before."

Thomas Barnet deposed,—" That on the 8th of February, about one in the morning, he saw a person come out of Aram's house, who had a wide coat on, with the cape about his head, and seemed to shun him ; whereupon he went up to him and put by the cape of his great-coat, and perceiving it to be Richard Houseman, wished him a good night, *alias* a good morning."

John Barker, the constable who executed the warrant granted by Mr. Thornton, and endorsed by Sir John Turner, deposed,—"That, at Lynn, Sir John Turner and some others first went into the school where Aram was, the witness waiting at the door. Sir John asked him if he knew Knaresborough. He replied, ' No.' And being further asked if he had any acquaintance with one Daniel Clark, he denied that he ever knew such a man. The witness then entered the school and said, ' How do you do, Mr. Aram ?' He replied, ' How do you do, sir ? I don't know you.' ' What !' said the witness, ' don't you know me ? Don't you remember that Daniel Clark and you always had a spite against me when you lived at Knaresborough !' The witness then asked him if he did not know St. Robert's Cave. He answered ' Yes.' The witness replied, ' Ay, to your sorrow.' That upon their journey to York, Aram inquired after his old neighbours, and what they said of him. To which the witness replied that they were much enraged against him for the loss of their goods. That upon Aram asking if it was not possible to make up the matter, the witness answered, ' He believed he might save himself if he would restore back what they had lost.' Aram answered that 'it was impossible; but he might, perhaps, find an equivalent.' "

Aram was then asked by the Judge if he had anything to say to the witness before him. He replied that, to the best of his knowledge, it was not in the school, but in the room adjoining the school, where Sir John Turner and the witness were when he first saw them.

The skull was then produced in court, on the left side of which there was a fracture that, from the nature of it, could not have been made but by the stroke of some blunt instrument ; the piece was beaten inwards, and could not be replaced but from within. Mr. Locock, the surgeon who produced it, gave it as his opinion that no such breach could proceed from natural decay ; that it was not a recent fracture, caused by the instrument with which it was dug up, but seemed to be of many years' standing.

Aram, on being asked what motive could induce him to commit the murder, answered that he suspected Clark to have had a criminal connection with his wife. It appeared further that Aram possessed himself of Clark's fortune, which he got with his wife a little before—about £100. The evidence having been closed, Aram delivered into court, in writing, the following masterly defence :—

" My lord, I know not whether it is of right, or through some indulgence of your lordship, that I am allowed the liberty at this bar, and at this time, to attempt a defence, incapable and uninstructed as I am to speak. Since, while I see so many eyes upon me—so numerous and awful a concourse, fixed with attention, and filled with I know not what expectancy, I labour, not with guilt, my lord, but with perplexity. For, having never seen a court but this,—being wholly unacquainted with law, the customs of the bar, and all judiciary proceedings,—I fear I shall be so little capable of speaking with propriety, that it might reasonably be expected to exceed my hope should I be able to speak at all.

" I have heard, my lord, the indictment read, wherein I find myself charged with the highest of human crimes. You will grant me, then, your patience, if I, single and unskilful, destitute of friends, and unassisted by counsel, attempt something perhaps like argument in my defence. What I have to say will be but short, and that brevity may be the best part of it.

" First, my lord, the whole tenor of my life contradicts every particular of this indictment. Yet I had never said this, did not my present circumstances extort it from me, and seem to make it necessary. Permit me here, my lord, to call upon malignity itself, so long and cruelly busied in this prosecution, to charge upon me any immorality of which prejudice was not the author. No, my lord, I concerted no schemes of fraud, projected no violence, injured no man's person or property. My days were honestly laborious ; my nights intensely studious. And I humbly conceive my notice of this, especially at this time, will not be thought impertinent or unreasonable, but, at least, deserving some attention ; because, my lord, that any person, after a temperate use of life, a series of thinking and acting regularly, and without one single deviation from sobriety, should plunge into the very depth of profligacy, and precipitately and at once, is altogether improbable and unprecedented, and absolutely inconsistent with the course of things. Mankind is never corrupted at once ; villany is always progressive, and declines from right step by step, till every regard to probity is lost, and every sense of all moral obligations totally perishes.

" Again, my lord, a suspicion of this kind, which nothing but malevolence could entertain and ignorance propagate, is violently opposed by my very situation at that time with respect to health ; for, but a little space before, I had been confined to my bed, and suffered under a long and severe disorder, and was not able for half a year together so much as to walk. This distemper left me, indeed, yet slowly and in part ; but so emaciated, so enfeebled, that I was reduced to crutches, and was so far from being well about the time I am charged with this fact, that I have never to this day perfectly recovered. Could, then, a person in this condition take anything into his head so unlikely, so extravagant ? I, past the vigour of my age, feeble, valetudinary, with no inducement to engage, no ability to accomplish, no weapon wherewith to perpetrate such a fact ; without interest, without power, without motive, without means ?

" Besides, it must occur to every one, that an action of this atrocious nature is never heard of but when its springs are laid open. It appears it was to support some indolence, or supply some luxury ; to satisfy some avarice, or oblige some malice ; to prevent some real or imaginary want ; yet I lay not under the influence of any of these. Surely, my lord, I may consistently, both with truth and modesty, affirm thus much ; and none who have any veracity, and knew me, will ever question this.

" In the second place, the disappearance of · Clark is suggested as an argument of his being dead ; but the uncertainty of such an inference from that, and the fallibility of all conclusions of such sort, from such a circumstance, are too obvious and too notorious to require instances ; yet, superseding many, permit me to produce a very recent one, and that afforded by this Castle.

" In June, 1757, William Thompson, for all the vigilance of this place, in open daylight, and double-ironed, made his escape ; and, notwithstanding an immediate inquiry set on foot, the strictest search, and all advertisement, was never seen or heard of since. If, then, Thompson got off unseen, through all these difficulties, how very easy it was for Clark when none of them opposed him ! But what would be thought of a prosecution commenced against any one seen last with Thompson ? "

" Permit me next, my lord, to observe a little upon the bones which have been discovered. It is said, which is perhaps saying very far, that these are the skeleton of a man. It is possible, indeed, they may be ; but is there any certain known criterion which incontestably distinguishes the sex in human bones ? Let it be considered, my lord, whether the ascertaining of this point ought not to precede any attempt to identify them ?

" The place of their deposition, too, claims much more attention than is commonly bestowed upon it ; for of all places in the world, none could have mentioned any one wherein there was greater certainty of finding human bones than a hermitage, except he should point out a churchyard ; hermitages in times past being not only places of religious retirement, but of burial too. And it has scarce or ever been heard of, but that every cell now known contains, or contained, these relics of humanity, some mutilated, and some entire. I do not inform, but give me leave to remind your lordship, that here sat solitary sanctity, and here the hermit or the anchoress hoped that repose for their bones when dead they here enjoyed when living.

" All this while, my lord, I am sensible this is known to your lordship and many in this court better than I ; but it seems necessary to my case that others, who have not at all, perhaps, adverted to things of this nature, and may have concern in my trial, should be made acquainted with it. Suffer me then, my lord, to produce a few of many evidences that these cells were used as depositories of the dead, and to enumerate a few in which human bones have been found, as it happened in this in question, lest to some that accident might seem extraordinary, and consequently occasion prejudice.

" 1. The bones, as was supposed of the Saxon, St. Dubritius, were discovered buried in his cell at Guy's Cliff, near Warwick, as appears from the authority of Sir William Dugdale.

" 2. The bones, thought to be those of the anchoress,

Rosia, were but lately discovered in a cell at Royston, entire, fair, and undecayed, though they must have lain interred for several centuries, as is proved by Dr. Stukely.

" 3. But our own county—nay, almost this neighbourhood, supplies another instance ; for in January, 1747, was found by Mr. Stovin, accompanied by a reverend gentleman, the bones, in part, of some recluse, in the cell at Lindholm, near Hatfield. They were believed to be those of William of Lindholm, a hermit, who had long made this cave his habitation.

"4. In February, 1744, part of Woburn Abbey, being pulled down, a large portion of a corpse appeared, even with the flesh on, and which bore cutting with a knife, though it is certain this had lain above one hundred years, and how much longer is doubtful, for this abbey was founded in 1145, and was dissolved in 1538 or 1539.

" What would have been said, what believed, if this had been an accident to the bones in question ?

" Further, my lord, it is not yet out of living memory that, a little distance from Knaresborough, in a field, part of the manor of the worthy and patriotic baronet who does that borough the honour to represent it in parliament, were found in digging for gravel, not one human skeleton only, but five or six, deposited side by side, with each an urn placed on its head, as your lordship knows was usual in ancient interments.

" About the same time, and in another field, almost close to this borough, was discovered also in searching for gravel, another human skeleton ; but the piety of the same worthy gentleman ordered both pits to be filled up again, commendably unwilling to disturb the dead.

" Is the exhumation of these bones to be forgotten, then, or industriously concealed, that the discovery of those in question may appear the more singular and extraordinary ; whereas, in fact, there is nothing extraordinary in it ? My lord, almost every place conceals such remains. In fields, in hills, in highway sides, on wastes, on commons, lie frequent and unsuspected bones. And our present allotments for rest for the departed are but of some centuries.

" Another particular seems also to claim a little of your lordship's notice and that of the gentlemen of the jury ;

which is, that perhaps no example occurs of more than one skeleton being found in *one cell ;* and in the cell in question was found but *one ;* agreeable in this to the peculiarity of every other known cell in Britain. Not the discovery of one skeleton, then, but two, would have appeared suspicious and uncommon.

"But then, my lord, to attempt to identify these, when even to identify living men sometimes has proved so difficult, as in the case of Perkin Warbeck and Lambert Symnell at home, and Don Sebastian abroad, will be looked upon, perhaps, as an attempt to determine what is indeterminable. And I hope, too, it will not pass unconsidered here, where gentlemen believe with caution, think with reason, and decide with humanity, what interest the endeavour to do this is calculated to serve, in assigning proper personality to these bones whose particular appropriation can only appear to eternal Omniscience.

"Permit me, my lord, also very humbly to remonstrate that, as human bones appear to have been the inseparable adjuncts of every cell, even any person naming such a place at random as containing them, in this case shows him rather fortunate than conscious-prescient, and that these attendants on every hermitage accidentally concurred with this conjecture—a mere casual coincidence of *words* and *things.*

"But, it seems, another skeleton has been discovered by some labourer, which was fully as confidently averred to be Clark's as this. My lord, must some of the living if it promote some interest, be made answerable for all the bones that earth has concealed, or chance exposed? And might not a place where bones lie be mentioned by a person by chance, as well as found by a labourer by chance? Or is it more criminal accidentally to *name* where bones lie than accidentally to *find* where they lie?

"Here, too, is a human skull produced, which is fractured ; but was this the *cause,* or was it the consequence of death? Was it owing to violence, or the effect of natural decay? If it was violence, was that violence before or after death? My lord, in May, 1732, the remains of William, the Lord Archbishop of this province, were taken up by permission, in this cathedral, and the bones of the skull were found broken ; yet certainly he died by no violence offered to him alive that could occasion that fracture there.

Let it be considered, my lord, that upon the dissolution of religious houses, and the commencement of the Reformation, the ravages of those times both affected the living and the dead. In search after imaginary treasures, coffins were broken up, graves and vaults dug open, monuments ransacked, and shrines demolished. Your lordship knows that these violations proceeded so far as to occasion Parliamentary authority to restrain them ; and it did about the beginning of the reign of Elizabeth. I entreat your lordship, suffer not the violence, the depredations, and the iniquities of those times to be imputed to this.

"Moreover, what gentleman here is ignorant that Knaresborough had a castle which, though now in ruins, was once considerable both for its strength and its garrison. All know it was rigorously besieged by the arms of the Parliament ; at which siege, in sallies, conflicts, flights, pursuits, many fell in all the places around it, and where they fell were buried ; for every place, my lord, is a burial-place in time of war ; many, questionless, of these rest unknown, whose bones futurity shall discover.

"I hope, with all imaginable submission, that what has been said will not be thought impertinent to this indictment ; and that it will be far from the wisdom, the learning, and the integrity of this place to impute to the living what zeal in its fury may have done ; what nature may have taken off and piety interred ; or what war alone may have destroyed, alone deposited.

"As to the circumstances that have been raked up, I have nothing to observe, but that such circumstances have been frequently found fallible and frail. They may rise to the utmost degree of probability, yet are they but probability still. Why need I name to your lordship the two Harrisons, recorded by Dr. Howell, who both suffered upon circumstances, because of the disappearance of their lodger, who was in credit, had contracted debts, borrowed money, and went off unseen, and returned many years after their execution ? Why name the intricate affairs of Jacques de Moulin, under Charles II., related by a gentleman who was counsel for the Crown ? And why the unhappy Coleman, who suffered innocent, though convicted upon positive evidence, and whose children perished for want because the world uncharitably believed the father guilty? Why mention the perjury of Smith, incautiously admitted king's evidence, who, to screen himself, equally accused Faircloth and Loveday of the murder of Dun, the first of whom, in 1749, was executed at Winchester; and Loveday was about to suffer at Reading had not Smith been proved perjured to the satisfaction of the court, by the surgeon of the Gosport Hospital?

"Now, my lord, having endeavoured to show that the whole of this process is altogether repugnant to every part of my life; that it is inconsistent with my condition of health at that time; that no rational inference can be drawn that a person is dead who suddenly disappears; that hermitages were the constant repositories of the bones of the recluse; that the proofs of this are well authenticated; that the revolutions in religion, or the fortune of war, have mangled or buried the dead; the conclusion remains, perhaps, no less reasonably than impatiently wished for. I, at last, after a year's confinement, equal to either fortune, put myself upon the candour, the justice, the humanity of your lordship, and upon yours, my countrymen, gentlemen of the jury."

The jury, after some conference, pronounced a verdict of "guilty." Aram's sentence was a just one, and he submitted to it with that stoicism he so much affected. The morning after he was condemned he confessed the justice of it to two clergymen (who had a licence from the judge to attend him), by declaring that he murdered Clark. Being asked by one of them "what his motive was for doing that abominable action?" he answered that, "he suspected Clark of having an unlawful commerce with his wife; that he was persuaded at the time he committed the murder he did right; but since he has thought it wrong." After this, "Pray," says Aram, "what became of Clark's body, if Houseman went home, as he said upon my trial, immediately on seeing him fall?" One of the clergymen replied, "I'll tell you what became of it; you and Houseman dragged it into the cave, and stripped and buried it there, brought away his clothes, and burnt them at your own house." To which he assented.

He was then asked whether Houseman did not earnestly press him to murder his wife, for fear she should discover the business they had been about. He hastily said, " He did, and pressed me several times to do it."

This was the substance of what passed with Aram the morning after he was condemned ; and as he had promised to make a more ample confession on the day he was executed, it was generally believed everything previous to the murder would have been disclosed, but he prevented any discovery by a horrid attempt upon his own life. When called from bed to have his irons taken off, he would not rise, alleging that he was very weak : on examination, his arm appeared bloody. Proper assistance being called, it was found that he had attempted to take away his own life by cutting his arm in two places with a razor, which he had concealed in the condemned cell some time before. By proper applications he was brought to himself, and though weak was conducted to Tyburn, where, being asked if he had anything to say, he answered " No." He was then executed ; and his body conveyed to Knaresbrough Forest and hung in chains, pursuant to his sentence.

On his table in his cell was found the following paper, containing his reasons for the attempt on his life :—

" What am I better than my fathers ? To die is natural and necessary. Perfectly sensible of this, I fear no more to die than I did to be born ; but the manner of it is something which should, in my opinion, be decent and manly. I think I have regarded both these points. Certainly nobody has a better right to dispose of a man's life than himself ; and he, not others, should determine how. As for any indignities offered to my body, or silly reflections on my faith and morals, they are (as they always were) things indifferent to me. I think, though contrary to the common way of thinking, I wrong no man by this, and hope it is not offensive to that eternal Being that formed me and the world ; and as by this I injure no man, no man can be reasonably offended : I solicitously recommend myself to the eternal and almighty Being, the God of nature, if I have done amiss. But, perhaps, I have not ; and I hope this thing will never be imputed to me. Though I am now stained by malevolence and suffer by prejudice, I hope to rise fair and unblemished.

My life was not polluted, my morals were irreproachable, and my opinions orthodox.

"I slept soundly till three o'clock, awaked, and then wrote these lines :—

> Come, pleasing rest, eternal slumber, fall,
> Seal mine, that once must seal the eyes of all ;
> Calm and composed, my soul her journey takes,
> No guilt that troubles, and no heart that aches ;
> Adieu ! thou sun, all bright like her arise ;
> Adieu ! fair friends, and all that's good and wise."

These lines, found along with the foregoing, were supposed to be written by Aram, just before he cut himself with the razor. He was 54 years of age.

WILLIAM AND JOHN COCKBURN.

Saturday, August 18th, A.D. 1759.—These two brothers, William and John Cockburn, were executed at the Tyburn without Micklegate Bar, for breaking into the dwelling-house and shop of Joseph Powley, of Orton, in the county of Westmoreland, and stealing from thence a great quantity of mercery and linen goods. They were very penitent, and confessed the crime for which they suffered.

ANN RICHMOND.

Saturday, March 6th, A.D. 1761.—Ann Richmond, a fine young girl, was executed at the Tyburn without Micklegate Bar, for setting fire to a stack and barn belonging to her mistress.

ROBERT KING.

Saturday, August 1st, A.D. 1761.—This unfortunate man, Robert King, was executed at the Tyburn without Micklegate Bar, for stealing two young cows or heifers. They were found in his possession, and though it appeared probable that he had bought them, the jury found him guilty. He was respectably connected, and much interest was used to save his life, but of no avail. He resided at Todwick, near Rotherham. Before he was executed he showed great marks of penitence, and acknowledged himself guilty of the crime for which he suffered.

George Harger.

Thursday, March 18th, A.D. 1762.—George Harger was executed at the Tyburn without Micklegate Bar, for the wilful murder of John Moore, of Kirby Malzeard. After the execution his body was given to the surgeons, to be dissected and anatomized.

William Bell.

Monday, March 14th, A.D. 1763.—William Bell suffered the severe penalty of the law, for the wilful murder of his fellow servant, William Wright, at Allerthorpe, near Pocklington. He denied to the last ever having struck William Wright, either with a stick, or in any other manner, so as to injure him. He was executed at the Tyburn without Micklegate Bar.

John Hall.

Saturday, July 30th, A.D. 1763.—John Hall, *alias* Bloom, was executed at the Tyburn without Micklegate Bar, for stealing a yellow bay mare, the property of Mr. John Harrison, near Leeds.

Charles Singleton Dorrington.

Saturday, March 31st, A.D. 1764.—The above culprit was charged, on the oath of John Lee, with having stopped a post-chaise, which he (Lee) was driving between Ferry Bridge and Doncaster, on Thursday, the 27th of October, 1763; and robbing a lady and gentleman who were in the chaise (whose names do not appear) of a purse of money. He was a fine-looking young man, and of good connections, but would not declare his real name, or whence he came. About eight o'clock on the morning of the execution, his irons were knocked off, and he was locked up alone in his cell; but at nine o'clock, when the gaoler wanted to go to him, he found the door barricaded on the inside, which Dorrington had done by means of a bench that happened to be almost the exact length betwixt the door and the opposite wall. This he wedged up with an old chair, which he broke for that purpose, and it was about two hours before they were able to force the door open. On being asked his reason for so doing, he said life was sweet, and that he only did it to prolong time. He acknowledged the justness of his sentence, and was executed at the Tyburn without Micklegate Bar.

ABRAHAM CLAYTON.

Saturday, August 15th, A.D. 1763.—Abraham Clayton, aged 35, was executed at the Tyburn without Micklegate Bar, for the murder of his wife, Elizabeth, at Howden, in the East Riding. Drink and jealousy were the cause. His body was anatomized after execution.

JOSEPH HAIREE.

Saturday, March 31st, A.D. 1765.—Joseph Hairee was executed at the Tyburn without Micklegate Bar, for robbing and assaulting John Dixon, William Dorbury, and others, on the highway in the township of Bramley, in the county of York, and putting them severally in fear, taking from Dixon a watch, three shillings in silver, or thereabouts; from William Dorbury, five pence in copper; from John Feedham, one black silk handkerchief; and attempting to rob John Leech and Joseph Hammond. He confessed the crime for which he suffered, but persisted to the last in saying that it was the first robbery he ever committed, and that poverty drove him to it.

THOMAS TAYLOR, ABEL HOBSON, AND ISAAC TURNER.

Saturday, March 6th, A.D. 1766.—These three men were taken in a cart from the Castle, through Micklegate Bar, to the old gallows, and hung amidst a large concourse of people. Turner was a Sheffield man, and was committed from that place on the 21st day of August, 1765, charged with stealing out of the respective dwelling-houses of Caleb Roberts and Matthew Lambert, both of Sheffield, linen drapers, in the Market-place, divers goods and chattels; and Lydia Nicholson, was also committed to York, charged with being the receiver of the goods, but was acquitted. Hobson was charged with burglary and divers felonies, committed in the West Riding, along with Joshua Clayton. Taylor, otherwise John Scott, together with his wife and daughter, were charged with breaking into the shop of Richard Clough, linen-draper, of Slaidburn, and carrying off goods to the amount of £40 and upwards. Taylor received sentence of death, but the females, being compelled to act under his advice, were acquitted.

MATTHEW YOUNG AND RICHARD CLARK.

Saturday, April 18th, A.D. 1767.—These two men were hung at the Tyburn without Micklegate Bar. Matthew Young for robbing a Jew pedlar on the highway, and using violence in the North Riding; and Clark, for breaking into the house of Mark Hattersley, of Leeds, and stealing £23 in money, a watch (which led to his detection), a red waistcoat, and two handkerchiefs.

ANN SOWERBY.

Monday, August 10th, A.D. 1767.—Ann Sowerby, a native of Whitby, was executed at the Tyburn without Micklegate Bar, for poisoning her husband, Timothy Sowerby. She was drawn to the place of execution on a hurdle, where she was strangled to death and burnt, pursuant to her sentence. Just before she was brought out of her cell for execution, she declared that John Douglas brought her some *nux vomica*, in order to poison her husband, which she burnt, —that he gave his own wife some of the same poison, who died soon after,—that some days after he brought her some arsenic, and assisted her in mixing it with curds, which she gave her husband for breakfast, who died a few hours after eating them. She acknowledged the justness of her sentence, and died penitent.

THOMAS AND RICHARD BOYS.

Saturday, October 17th, A.D. 1767.—Thomas Boys, aged 27, and Richard Boys, aged 24, were executed at the Tyburn without Micklegate Bar, for the highway robbery of Mr. Abraham Earnshaw, of Ovenden, holding a knife to his throat, and putting him in fear of his life. They took eight guineas and two shillings in silver from him. These two brothers married two sisters, who, with their father, attended the execution, after which they conveyed away the bodies to Halifax for interment.

LEONARD HOWSON.

Saturday, March 19th, A.D. 1768.—Leonard Howson, a native of Doncaster, was executed at the Tyburn without Micklegate Bar, for larceny at the Doncaster post-office, a case which made considerable noise in the world. It appeared that the culprit was charged by John Thompson, of Ludgate-hill, London, with having offered to him and his partner, Mr. Routh, a bill for acceptance, drawn upon them by William Thompson, of Thirsk, on November 17th, 1766, for £98. 10s. 9d., payable to E. Story, to order, at a month after date, which was accepted accordingly; telling them (Messrs. Thompson and Routh) that his name was William Jackson. He discounted the bill at Messrs. Carr & Co.'s, mercers on Ludgate-hill. Mary Exley, servant to Mrs. Newbold, mistress of the post-office, Doncaster, (unknown to her mistress) three different times in the evening, after the family had retired to rest, admitted Howson into the office, he pretending to look for a particular letter which he wanted to see. He also stole a bill of £20, which he paid to Joshua Tindall, of Bishopsgate-street, London. At the trial it was clearly proved that both bills were stolen from the post-office at Doncaster. The trial occupied a considerable length of time. He was found guilty and hung accordingly.

JOSEPH HALL AND THOMAS LEE.

Monday, July 25th, A.D. 1768.—Joseph Hall, aged 27, underwent the severe sentence of the law for coining at Hull; and Thomas Lee, aged 25, for the wilful murder of Richard Petty, of Grassington. After execution Lee was hung in chains at Grassington-gate, near the place where the murder was committed. They were both executed at the Tyburn without Micklegate Bar.

JOSEPH STELL.

Saturday, August 6th, A.D. 1768.—Joseph Stell was executed at the Tyburn without Micklegate Bar for coining. He was drawn on a sledge to the place of execution, which took place at six o'clock in the evening. He died penitent, confessing his guilt.

VALENTINE BAILEY.

Monday, April 3rd, A.D. 1769.—Valentine Bailey was executed at the Tyburn without Micklegate Bar, for shooting at and murdering Mr. John Smith, of Scarborough, officer of excise, while in the due execution of his duty. On the jury returning him guilty, he knocked down a woman who stood near him, with whom he had been concerned in smuggling goods, and who was the principal evidence against him. He died penitent, acknowledging the justice of his sentence, and his body was sent to the hospital for dissection.

DAVID HARTLEY AND JAMES OLDFIELD.

Saturday, April 28th, A.D. 1770.—David Hartley and James Oldfield were convicted, on the oath of James Crabtree and others, of Halifax, for impairing, diminishing, and lightening guineas. They were detected at Halifax, and died penitent, acknowledging the justice of the sentence passed upon them.

MICHAEL NAYLOR.

Saturday, August 23rd, 1770.—This man was found guilty of the murder of William Lund, at Grimstone, near Tadcaster, and was executed at the Tyburn without Micklegate Bar.

LUKE ATKINSON AND JOHN WRIGHT.

Monday, March 18th, A.D. 1771.—These two men were executed at the Tyburn without Micklegate Bar. Atkinson was charged, along with Dorothy his wife, with the murder of

Mr. William Smith, of Skelton, in Cleveland, corn-miller. Atkinson received sentence of death, but his wife was acquitted. Wright was a soldier in the 37th Foot. He with two others murdered James English. The evidence not being sufficiently clear, and having other charges against him, he was acquitted of the murder, but found guilty of breaking into the house of John Green, of Leeds. They both were executed at the above place.

THOMAS LAWRENCE AND JOHN LAZENBY.

Saturday, March 21st, A.D. 1772.—Thomas Lawrence, a highwayman, for robbing William Knaggs, of Whitby, taking thirty shillings or thereabouts from him; also further charged with being a deserter. John Lazenby, a native of Sheriff Hutton, was also charged at the same time with the wilful murder of William Moore, oatmeal-seller, of Sheriff Hutton. They were both executed at the Tyburn without Micklegate Bar.

WILLIAM FISHER, JOHN EARLY, AND JOHN HORNER.

Monday, March 15th, A.D. 1773. — The above three culprits were executed at the Tyburn without Micklegate Bar : John Horner, of Ripon, for coining ; William Fisher, of Whitby, for breaking into the house of Thomas Walker, of Whitby, and stealing cash to the amount of £5 ; and John Early, of Huddersfield, for the murder of Thomas Ospling, at Doncaster.

The old Tyburn on Knavesmire underwent considerable alterations and improvements this year, and the above were the first executions that took place upon it.

GEORGE BELT.

Saturday, April 2nd, A.D. 1774. — George Belt, of Howden, was executed at the Tyburn without Micklegate Bar, for breaking into and robbing the dwelling-house of Mr. Althorpe, near Howden. Before the time of execution he confessed the crime for which he suffered.

John Scott.

Monday, July 25th, A.D. 1774.—John Scott was executed at the Tyburn without Micklegate Bar, for the wilful murder of Hannah Stocks, of Northowram, in the West Riding. He was hanged, and his body was afterwards sent to the county hospital for dissection.

Robert Thomas.

Saturday, August 6th, A.D. 1774.—Robert Thomas, *alias* Thomis, for being an accomplice in the murder and robbery of Mr. Deighton, supervisor of excise, at Halifax, was executed at the Tyburn without Micklegate Bar, and his body afterwards conveyed under a strong guard to be hung in chains on Beacon Hill, near Halifax.

Captain John Bolton, William Bean, John Vickers, and Matthew Normington.

Saturday, March 30th, A.D. 1775.—The above culprits, except Bolton, were executed at the Tyburn without Micklegate Bar. Captain Bolton, an officer, was sentenced for execution, for the wilful and deliberate murder of his servant girl, Elizabeth Rambourn, on the 6th of September, at Bulmer. He strangled her with a fife and buried her body in his cellar. He, however, contrived to hang himself in the cell where he was confined in York Castle. He was buried at the three lane ends near the York Barracks, at ten o'clock at night, and a stake driven through his body in the presence of the turnkeys of the Castle.

William Bean, for a highway robbery in the constabulary of Clifford, in the West Riding, near a place called Bielby Wood Nook. He assaulted Richard Waddington at that place, and took from him five guineas, twelve half-guineas, and twenty shillings in silver, or thereabouts. His coffin was six feet six inches long, by two feet one inch wide and fifteen inches deep.

John Vickers, of Attercliffe, near Sheffield, for assaulting and robbing John Murfin, on Saturday night, the 11th of

February, between eleven and twelve o'clock, near the "Blue Ball," Attercliffe, of threepence half-penny in copper, a bad shilling, a breast of mutton, and half a pound of butter tied up in a handkerchief. He also stood further charged with assaulting and robbing John Staniforth, to whom he had been previously apprenticed at Darnall, (in company with three others unknown) on the same Saturday night, the 11th inst., near the Glass-house, at Attercliffe, of three shillings and sixpence, a sacking wallet containing horns for knife scales, a leg of mutton, six pounds of sugar, and some flax. John Booth, his accomplice, was acquitted. Vickers was born at Hemsworth Back Moor, in the parish of Norton, near Sheffield.

Matthew Normington, of Halifax, aged 29, for being concerned in the robbery and murder of Mr. William Deighton, at Halifax, supervisor of excise, along with Robert Thomas, gibbeted in August previous. He also was hung in chains on Beacon Hill, near Halifax.

GEORGE BULMER AND JOHN WILLIAMSON.

Saturday, July 29th, A.D. 1775.—George Bulmer, a native of York, and servant to Mr. Simpson of that place, who resided in Stonegate, was executed at the Tyburn without Micklegate Bar, for the murder of his wife, Dorothy Bulmer ; and John Williamson was executed at the same time and place for robbing the Whitby mail, at Thornton Gate, of £66. 10s.

JOHN SMITH, JOSEPH RIDDLE, AND FRANCIS JEFFERSON.

August 19th, A.D. 1775.—The above three culprits were severally hung on the old gallows without Micklegate Bar. Smith for stealing seven sheep off Sandal Common, five belonging to William Shaw, farmer, of Sandal Magna ; one to John Nash, of Sandal, cordwainer; and one to John Linley, labourer. Riddle for the murder of Richard Marsden, of South Cliff; and Jefferson for a burglary at South Cliff.

Eliza Bordington and Thomas Akerman.

Saturday, March 29th, A.D. 1776.—Eliza Bordington and Thomas Akerman, aged 37, were executed at the Tyburn without Micklegate Bar, she for poisoning her husband, and he, as her paramour, for being concerned therein. Both these persons were natives of Flamborough, and an improper intimacy being carried on betwixt them, they resolved to poison the husband of the former, in order to the easier gratification of their wicked passions. Bordington was an industrious man, and resided at Flamborough ; and at a prior period Akerman lodged with them. She was a showy, worthless woman, some years younger than her husband. She was hanged and burnt close to the gallows.

James Rice, *alias* Michael Rice.

July 28*th,* A.D. 1777.—James Rice was executed at the old gallows without Micklegate Bar, for the murder of Thomas Westell, mariner of Staithes, in the North Riding, by stabbing him with a knife, in the parish of Henderwell.

Thomas Green, *alias* England.

Saturday, July 30*th,* A.D. 1779.—Thomas Green was charged, on the oath of William Habershon, sergeant in the 14th Regiment of Foot, with stealing a bay mare, the property of Anthony Surtees, Esq., of Ackworth, in the West Riding. The jury found him guilty, and he was hanged at the usual place.

William Meyers, Esq.

March 20*th,* A.D. 1781.—This young gentleman was executed for the murder of John Spink, an assistant bailiff, on the 18th of October previous. He had not been long married, but it appeared that he had had his house entered by the sheriff's officer, who left Spink (his assistant) in possession of the place until he went to Kirk Hammerton to see Mr. Meyers, Sen., for money or bail for his son.

During his absence young Meyers came home, and flew into a violent passion, and swore he would shoot the man unless he at once left the premises, which he refused to do. Mrs. Meyers fetched her husband's pistols, which were loaded, and put them into his hands; he at the same instant pointed the pistol at the man and shot him in the neck, which caused his death in a few minutes. Meyers gave himself up, and lying in gaol until the Spring Assizes, was found guilty. After his condemnation he appeared to be resigned to his fate. On the morning of the 20th of March he was taken in a mourning coach past his own house, a hearse attending to bring back his body. On arriving at the gallows he was put into a cart, where he remained an hour and ten minutes, speaking to the sheriff and addressing the spectators, declaring that he had no intention to murder the deceased, saying he had no ill-will, but, on the contrary, had a regard for him as an old servant in the family. He severely accused his wife, and blamed her much for the hardship of his situation. He was much respected in the City of York, and generally went by the name of " Meek Meyers."

JOSEPH LINWOOD.

Saturday, April 7th, A.D. 1781.—Joseph Linwood, a native of Sheriff Hutton, in the North Riding, was executed at the Tyburn without Micklegate Bar, for the robbery of Margaret, wife of William Lee, of Huntington, of 19s. 6d., a lawn handkerchief, and a cloak, near Huntington. Linwood was a labourer, and 27 years of age.

FRANCIS FEARN, JOHN COCKCROFT, JOHN WOOD, AND THOMAS GREENWOOD.

Tuesday, July 23rd, A.D. 1782.—The above four culprits were executed at the Tyburn without Micklegate Bar for the following crimes :—

Fearn was a file-smith of Sheffield, and a native of Bradfield, near Sheffield. He was hung for the murder of Mr. Nathan Andrews, a respectable watchmaker, in High-

street, Sheffield. What led to the man's ruin was his desire
to possess a watch. He called on Andrews a number of
times, desiring him to accompany him (Fearn) to Bradfield,
where a watch club was commencing or had commenced,
and in which Frank took a great interest. Andrews promised to go with him when twenty members were ready;
and on his telling Andrews that the required number were
already paying into the club, they set out together early one
afternoon, Fearn waiting at the "White Bear" opposite
until he was ready, Andrews taking a number of watches
with him. On arriving at a place called Kirk Edge, a
lonely, secluded spot, Frank shot Andrews in the back, and
he then pulled out his knife, and after stabbing him in a
number of places, finished his work by beating out his
brains with a hedgestake. The body was discovered the
same evening by a young man, who gave the alarm, and it
was removed to the workhouse, and there identified by the
young man as being that of the man he had seen in company
with Frank Fearn near the place where the body was found,
as he (Wood) was going to a field to work. He spoke to
Fearn, whom he knew, and found the body on his return.
It was first thought to be the parson, who wore a similar
dress. Andrews had on white stockings, short black gaiters,
black breeches, waistcoat, and coat. The news soon spread,
and Fearn was arrested in bed, at Sheffield, in Hawley
Croft, the next night. This crime seemed to be of such a
desperate character that the judge who sentenced Fearn's
body to be dissected appears to have altered it. The following order was sent to the governor of the Castle, as
copied from the register now in York Castle:—

I do hereby order that the execution of Francis Fearn be respited
until Tuesday, the 23rd of July inst., and that his body (instead of
being anatomized) shall be afterwards hanged in chains on a gibbet, to
be erected on some conspicuous spot, on Loxley Common, in the parish
of Ecclesfield, in the county of York, at a convenient distance from the
highway.   J. EYRE.

Frank's body was brought from York in irons, and gibbeted accordingly. The post was taken down by Mr.
Payne, of Loxley, on whose land it stood, in the year 1807,
having remained there twenty-five years.

John Cockcroft was hung for coining one shilling; John

Wood for coining one shilling ; Thomas Greenwood, otherwise " Great Tom," for having in his possession tools for
coining ; viz., iron fly-press, wrench rollers, and other instru-
ments used in coining.   These three men were hung along
with Fearn.

FRANK FEARN.

(Song by old Joseph Mather.)

Mortals all, in town and city,
   Pay attention to this truth ;
Let your bowels yearn with pity
   Towards a poor deluded youth.

Though with Satan's vile injunctions
   I was forced to comply,
Now it causes sad reflections,
   Since I am condemn'd to die.

Andrews !   Oh, that name ! it pierces
   Through my very inmost soul ;
And my torment much increases
   In this gloomy, condemn'd hole.

At Kirk Edge I shot and stabb'd him,
   Cut his throat, and bruised his pate ;
Of his watch and money robb'd him,
   Causes my unhappy fate.

Christians, pray that true repentance
   May be given a wretch like me ;
I acknowledge my just sentence,
   There's no law can set me free.

Let me make one observation :
   Though to sin I've been enslaved,
Through my Saviour's mediation
   My poor soul may yet be saved.

Hark ! I'm called to execution !
   And must bid the world adieu ;
'Tis the hour of dissolution,
   And my moments are but few.

Let me endless bliss inherit,
   Wash me from my guilty stains ;
Oh, receive my precious spirit,
   Though my body's hung in chains.

CHARLES COLDWELL.

Wednesday, April 30th, A.D. 1783.—Charles Coldwell was executed at the Tyburn without Micklegate Bar, for forgery. He was committed December 6th, 1782, upon the oath of John Sykes, of Lepton, in the West Riding, tanning weaver, that at the town of Wakefield, on Monday, the 11th of November, some person or persons unknown picked his pocket-book, containing two bills, one of the value of £5. 17s. This bill Charles Coldwell paid to Thomas Simpson, servant to Mr. Thomas Shirbrook, of Leeds Bridge, linendraper, on the day following, and endorsed with the name of David Butler. The crime was clearly proved and the justice of the sentence acknowledged by the unhappy sufferer.

WILLIAM EMMERSON, WILLIAM FIELD, JOHN RILEY, MARK TATTENSTALL, AND THOMAS SPENCER.

William Emmerson, late of Etherby, in the county of Durham, for stealing two heifers and two steers, from the pasture of George Gibson, farmer, of Eyreholme, his property, on the 21st of June, 1780 ; William Field, of Erringden, in the West Riding, papermaker, stealing from the shop of John Sutcliffe, of Stansfield, divers goods, consisting of groceries, linens, stockings, &c., on the night of the 16th of January ; John Riley, a native of York, for committing a burglary near York ; Mark Tattenstall, late of the 33rd Regiment, and Thomas Spencer, an out-pensioner, for high treason, breaking the peace, along with a great number of riotous persons, at the town of Halifax, on the 10th of June. These two were hung on the 6th of August, on Beacon Hill, near Halifax ; and the other three at York, on the 23rd of August, 1783.

LYDIA DICKINSON.

Monday, March 22nd, A.D. 1784.—Lydia Dickinson, a young girl under twenty years of age, was found guilty of the murder of her female bastard child, by drowning it in a pond. She resided at Clifton-upon-Calder, in the West

Riding, and was executed at the Tyburn without Mickle-gate Bar, in the presence of a large concourse of people.

JOHN STEWART AND BENJAMIN WOOD.

Stewart, for breaking into the dwelling-house and shop of Frances Peach, of Richmond, and stealing cottons, silks, and other divers goods ; Wood, for stealing a small bay pony, the property of Michael Gaggs, of Knottingley ; also a saddle and bridle. He was also charged with robbing upon the highway, Mr. William Milner, of Notton, corn-miller, on Sunday night, the 28th of December, 1783, about eight o'clock, taking from him half a guinea and a silver watch. They were executed at the old gallows without Micklegate Bar, on the 29th of March, 1784.

WILLIAM ASQUITH, *alias* SPARLING, AND THOMAS KNAPTON.

Tuesday, August 3rd, A.D. 1784.—The above two crimi-nals were executed at the Tyburn without Micklegate Bar. Asquith, *alias* Sparling, who was a butcher at East Ardsley, for stealing a number of sheep, the property of different people, pasturing upon Rothwell Haigh, and other places, in the township ; Thomas Knapton, late of Potter Newton, in the borough of Leeds, yeoman, for the murder of Hannah Wood, by giving her poison, of which she died ; she had no knowledge of its being poison at the time she took it.

JOSEPH CLOUGH AND WILLIAM RILEY.

Wednesday, April 2nd, A.D. 1785.—Joseph Clough, aged 23, and William Riley, aged 23, were executed at the Tyburn without Micklegate Bar. Clough was a labourer, and was found guilty of stealing a coat and waistcoat, and eight half-crown-pieces, the property of John Hodgson, of Burmi-stone, labourer, from his dwelling-house. There was no one in at the time ; the wearing apparel was valued at 5s. Riley, aged 23, for robbing John Borr, of Hull, upon the highway, near Newland, in the East Riding. They were both penitent, and regretted the crimes for which they suffered.

ROBERT CROSBY, JOHN BECK, JOHN EDWARDS, CHARLES SPENCER, ROBERT SMITHSON, AND MATTHEW MASON.

Robert Crosby, John Beck (a soldier), and John Edwards were convicted for setting fire to a dwelling-house and wind corn-mill, the property of William Jackson, of Danthorpe, in the parish of Humbleton; Crosby was a native of Lelley, in Holderness ; Charles Spencer, for stealing a bay gelding, the property of the Rev. Christopher Alderson, of Tickhill; Smithson, for stealing twelve ewes and twelve lambs, from different people, in the township of Gilling and Melsonby, in the North Riding ; Mason, for sacrilege, breaking into and entering the parish church of Hampsthwaite, in the West Riding, and stealing seventeen shillings, some copper, and two silver cups (they were found broken to pieces in his possession).   On the night preceding the execution, Crosby and Edwards effected their escape, and were never heard of afterwards ; the others were hanged at the old gallows without Micklegate Bar, on the 6th of August, 1785.

ROBERT WATSON, JUN., AND JOSEPH HARTLEY.

Saturday, April 8th, A.D. 1786.—Robert Watson, jun., aged 22, and Joseph Hartley, aged 34, were executed at the Tyburn without Micklegate Bar, for highway robbery. Young Watson, for robbing between Rotherham and Barnsley, Mr. William Bailes, of Wentworth, yeoman, taking from him a purse, containing seven guineas and a half ; Hartley, for robbing Mr. William Chambers, of Scarborough, mason, on the highway, leading from Ayton to Scarborough, of two bank-notes and some silver.   Hartley left a wife pregnant, and one child.

JAMES PROCTOR.

James Proctor, *alias* William Smith, was hanged at Tyburn, near York, April 29th, A.D. 1786, for uttering a

A woodcut of York from the early nineteenth century.

'Micklebar Gate' in early days, and the arrival of a Royalist baggage train.

The great seal of Henry VIII. Henry's Dissolution of the Monasteries was one of the factors behind the rising known as the Pilgrimage of Grace.

The banner of the Pilgrimage. (By kind permission of Howard Peach)

The original site of the Knavesmire Tyburn. (By kind permission of Howard Peach)

Another side of justice in York: stocks in Holy Trinity churchyard, Micklegate, York. (By kind permission of Howard Peach)

A model of an early Victorian policeman outside Ripon Police Museum. (By kind permission of Howard Peach)

An imitation banknote etched by George Cruikshank in 1818, satirising the infliction of capital punishment for forgery.

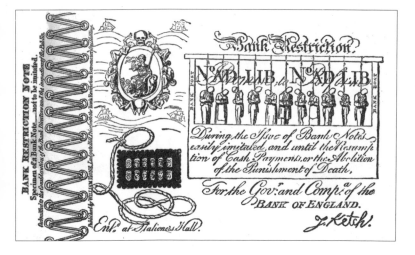

The famous Dick Turpin on his horse, Black Bess.

George Cruikshank

Turpin's grave in St George of the Beanhills churchyard, York. (By kind permission of Howard Peach)

A highway robbery in progress.

'Highwaymen at Work', from Major Arthur Griffiths' *Mysteries of Police and Crime*.

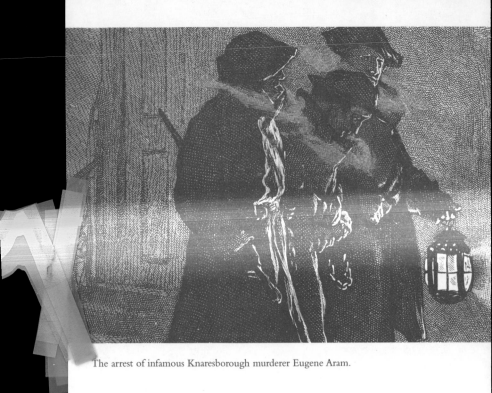

The arrest of infamous Knaresborough murderer Eugene Aram.

A contemporary portrait of
Aram. (By kind permission of
Howard Peach)

'The murder' – Eugene Aram commits his terrible crime. (By kind permission of
Howard Peach)

Mary Bateman, the 'Yorkshire Witch'. (By kind permission of Howard Peach)

Rawfolds Mill, site of one of the most serious Luddite attacks. (By kind permission of Howard Peach)

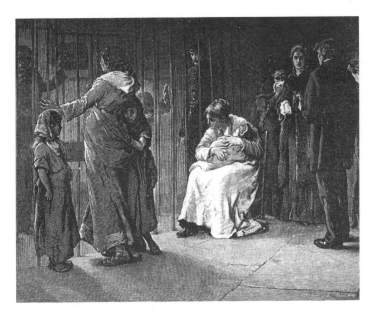

This image shows a felon 'committed for trial'.

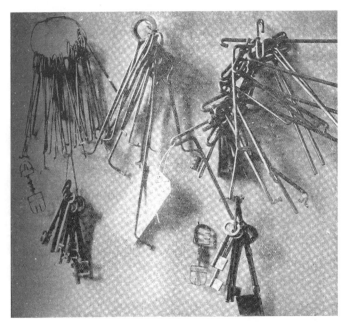

A large collection of 'skeleton keys'.

This stunning engraving by William Hogarth is known as 'the Idle Apprentice Executed at Tyburn'. It gives a vivid glimpse of what attending such an event would have been like; note also the skeletons on each side of the frame!

The dreaded Halifax Sharp Maiden. (By kind permission of Howard Peach)

Two turn-of-the-century engravings illustrating the process of the trial: 'waiting for the verdict', and, if you were very lucky, 'the acquittal'.

Micklegate Bar today. (By kind permission of Howard Peach)

forged bill of exchange, with intent to defraud J. Beckett, Esq., of Leeds. The forgery amounted to only fourteen guineas, and was instantly detected, so that he never received one farthing of the money. He was born at Dowholme, in Wyersdale, Lancashire, was thirty-five years of age, and left a wife and three children, and a father and mother, whose grief was beyond expression. He held a large farm in Wyersdale, and also a grocer's and draper's shop at that place; he was also a surveyor. His character was spotless, and he was in good credit with the first houses in Liverpool and Manchester. The interest made in his favour strongly corroborated this account, for no means were neglected or left untried to procure a pardon. J. Beckett, Esq., the prosecutor, applied to the judge for a petition, had it granted, signed by the judge himself and many others of distinction, and went to London himself with it; but alas! the fate of Dodd was held up as a barrier to a mitigation. Proctor was calm and resigned on the morning of his execution, said he was sensible of the violation of his country's laws, and hoped he should quit the world in peace. Being one day questioned why he offered the bad bill, when he had two good ones in his possession, he answered that he did not know it was a bad one. However this may be, his fate was surely to be pitied, as he confessed it was the first offence he had ever committed. The execution was delayed two hours beyond the usual time, as hopes were entertained of the arrival of a reprieve.

William Nicholson, John Charlesworth, James Braithwaite, William Sharp, and William Bamford.

Saturday, August 19th, A.D. 1786.—The above were all executed at the Tyburn without Micklegate Bar.

Nicholson, aged 27, labourer, for stealing two geldings, the property of Robert Athorpe, Esq., of Dinnington. Thomas Whitfield, Mr. Athorpe's man, was the principal witness against him.

John Charlesworth, of Liversedge, clothier, for breaking into the house of Susan Lister, of Little Gomersal, single woman, and stealing various articles of trifling value; also further charged with stopping William Hemmingway, of Mirfield, clothier, and robbing him of three guineas and a half and some silver and copper. He was 21 years of age.

Braithwaite, for breaking into the dwelling-house of Thomas Paxton, of Long Preston, innkeeper, and stealing various articles therefrom. He was a hawker and pedlar, and 30 years of age.

William Sharp, labourer, aged 26, and William Bamford, labourer, aged 28, for robbing Duncan M'Donald, of Sheffield, button-maker, by breaking into his house, and carrying away a number of horn combs, a silver threepenny-piece, and fourpence in copper. Sharp was a native of Conisbro', and Bamford, a native of Clifton.

DANIEL GOLDTHORPE, WILLIAM BRYAN, THOMAS WEST, JOHN THOMPSON, JOHN MORRITT, AND TIMOTHY O'BRIEN.

Saturday, April 7th, A.D. 1787.—The above six unfortunate offenders were all executed at the Tyburn without Micklegate Bar, in the presence of a large concourse of spectators.

Daniel Goldthorpe, of Holmfirth, clothier, for stealing from Thomas Beaumont, clothier, in the township of Almondbury, a piece of narrow woollen cloth, cutting it off the tenters. It is said that his wife attended the execution, and had a long altercation with Jack Ketch respecting his clothes, which she carried home to Holmfirth with her.

William Bryan, labourer, for stealing four shillings and sixpence, four farthings, and some wearing apparel, from John Ricardy, weaver, of Common Dale, in the North Riding.

Thomas West, of Woodhouse, near Leeds, for stealing two geldings, the property of Matthew Mawson, of Dunkeswick, in the West Riding; he was also further charged with stealing some geese.

John Thompson, of Skyehouse, near Thorne, labourer, was charged upon the oath of Samuel Mitchell, of Rotherham, butcher; and also of William Tyzack, of Rotherham,

constable, with stealing eight oxen, the property of Samuel
Scatcherd, of Pollington, farmer, from a field at Pontefract,
belonging to William Roberts, innkeeper, of that place.

John Morritt, a labourer, aged 34, for the murder of
John Argyle, *alias* Roundell, of Howden.

Timothy O'Brien, for stealing a dark bay mare, the
property of Robert Duck, of Lyth, in the North Riding.

ELIJAH AND JOSEPH PULLEYN, CATHARINE SAVAGE,
THOMAS GREENWOOD, DAVID LORD, JAMES ASHFORTH,
JOHN EASLEWOOD, AND JOSEPH KING.

Saturday, April 5th, A.D. 1788.—The above were all
executed at the old gallows without Micklegate Bar.

Ashforth and Easlewood, both of Dewsbury, worsted
weavers, for killing one fat ewe sheep, belonging to Thomas
Walker, of Hadfield, in the township of Thornhill, farmer,
and carrying away the carcase.

Catharine Savage, of Holme-on-Spalding Moor, in the
East Riding, for entering the house of Stephen Ridsdale,
of Welton, tailor and stay-maker, and stealing wearin
apparel of no great value. Her husband, Abraham Savage,
was concerned in the robbery, and received sentence of death,
which was afterwards reprieved to transportation.

Joseph King, of Knowlton, near Todmorden, clogger, for
uttering a forged note at Halifax, with intent to defraud
Samuel Roberts, of Halifax, hosier, of £8, the amount of
the note.

Thomas Greenwood, of Erringden, weaver, for breaking
into the warehouse of John and James Knowles, of Stodley-
in-Langfield, near Halifax, worsted manufacturer, and
carrying away divers parcels of worsted; along with David
Lord, also of Erringden, weaver.

Elijah and Joseph Pulleyn, for robbing and ill-treating
Elizabeth Carbutt, near Nun-Monkton, a few miles from
York.

WILLIAM BRAITHWAITE

Was a native of Staveley, in the county of Derby. He was

found guilty of sheep-stealing, and ordered for execution, July 20th, 1788, but died in gaol the night before his execution.

GEORGE LOCKEY

Was executed at the Tyburn without Micklegate Bar, York, on the 23rd day of March, 1789, for the wilful murder of Christopher Barker. Lockey was born at Easby, near Richmond, in the North Riding. He was a middle-aged man, about five feet nine inches high, stout, and ruddy complexioned. As frequent remarks were made upon the atrociousness of the crime, it must almost appear needless to further preface the account of it, but we will at once proceed to the particulars of this horrid deed, which were briefly these:—

Lockey and Barker had been intimate friends for many years; but, in consequence of a misdemeanour committed by Barker, he was brought to trial and transported for seven years. This sentence of course disunited their friendship, but on Barker's return, after having suffered the punishment inflicted by the laws of his country, they once more resumed their former attachment to each other. They now began criminal practices in a more daring manner than at any prior period, and even proceeded to the most violent outrages. One evening, as they were drinking at a public-house in Catterick, a farmer, who resided at Hornby, having ordered his horse, they were observed to leave the room and part of the liquor they had called for. However, on that night the man was robbed and murdered, about a mile from the town, and it was remarked that Lockey and Barker did not return. This led the company to suspect that these two men were concerned in the affair; but as no substantial proof could be brought against them, they were dismissed by the justices. To confirm this suspicion, however, it must be remarked that Lockey hinted to the court during his trial for the murder of Barker, that if Barker had got the better of him he would not have been the first man he had killed.

We now come to the particulars of the offence which occasioned the execution of Lockey, and cut him off in health and vigour. A short time previous to the murder, Lockey and Barker had a difference, when Barker threatened Lockey that he would inform. A few days only elapsed before Lockey called upon Barker to go a nutting. He complied with the request, but when they arrived at a place called the Rush Green (which is remarked for its solitary situation), Lockey took the opportunity to knock him down with a hammer, stabbed him in various parts of the body with a shoemaker's knife, and finished the barbarous deed by dashing out his brains with a sharp stone. The cries of the poor victim were heard by a farmer and his servants, who were in a field not far distant. The master, who had a bull grazing in an adjoining pasture, concluded that some person was attacked by the beast. He called his servants together, and ran to the place from whence the groans proceeded. Petrified with horror and astonishment, they beheld Lockey with his knees upon the deceased, and a bloody knife in his hand. He was asked what he had been doing. He replied, " I have been killing Barker."

Being thus detected in the very act, he was properly secured, and the coroner's jury sat on the body of Barker. They were seven days before they brought in their verdict. This delay was occasioned by the absence of a pedlar who, they were informed, had something material to relate. Diligent search was made, and having found him, they were acquainted with all he knew. The verdict given in was wilful murder by George Lockey. He was accordingly committed to York Castle, where he behaved himself in a becoming manner during his confinement.

Lockey was a shoemaker by trade, but being of a disorderly turn of mind, had pretty much relinquished his calling for that of cock-feeder. He left a wife, who was parted from him, and who lived in London, on account of his irregular habits. The only material plea he made on his trial was that of self-defence ; but as the hammer and knife with which he perpetrated the deed were proved to be his property, he was found guilty, and sentenced to be hung, and his body given to the surgeons. He exhibited great contrition prior to his execution; and confessed his guilt in having violated the laws of his country, but as a last refuge he relied on the merits of an all-forgiving Saviour, who pardoned the dying thief at the last moment, and implored the prayers of the numerous spectators who had assembled to witness the tragical end of this dangerous assassin.

ROBERT WILKINSON.

Saturday, April 11th, A.D. 1789.—Robert Wilkinson was executed at the Tyburn without Micklegate Bar, for a robbery committed on Mr. Fowler, on the highway near Dunnington, of one guinea, eight or nine shillings in silver, and a silver watch, and using him in a cruel manner. Wilkinson was born at Brampton, in Cumberland, of creditable parents. His father was a ship carpenter, and his son Robert engaged himself to Captain Wedderhead, in the ship called *Admiral Parker,* and sailed for Gibraltar, where he was taken prisoner, and remained as such in Spain for twenty-three weeks. He returned home in the year 1785, and then got acquainted with a set of bad women and thieves. He robbed, along with another man, a gentleman unknown, near Newcastle, of three guineas and several other things. Being arrested, together with a man named Blemitt, on the 14th of February, and committed to York Castle, Blemitt turned King's evidence, and Wilkinson received sentence of death. He wrote a letter to his wife the night before his execution, and the following is a part of it :—

MY DEAR, VIRTUOUS, AND LOVING WIFE,

'Tis a dreadful thing to be under sentence of death ! bound to a certain period of time. Night and day, hour and hour, moment and moment, the chiefest part of my thoughts employed about you and my children. Just after I had received my sentence, my aged father followed me to the Castle, dejected and sorrowful; almost terrifying me as much as my sentence, when he wrung his hands and burst into a flood of tears, crying, "O my son ! my most unfortunate son ! After all my care and diligence bestowed upon you, have I reared you up for the gallows tree ?"

The young man, for he had only been married a few years, met his fate with Christian fortitude, and died penitently confessing the error of his ways.

JOHN BARKER AND HANNAH WHITELEY.

Monday, August 3rd, A.D. 1789.—John Barker, aged 34,

and Hannah Whiteley, were executed at the Tyburn without Micklegate Bar, for the following crimes :—Barker was a native of Sheffield, and a baker by trade. He was found guilty of breaking into the dwelling-house of Francis Case, and stealing therefrom divers articles of wearing apparel of not much value. He was servant or journeyman to Case at the time of the robbery. His body was buried the same night at York.

Hannah Whiteley, wife of John Whiteley, of Hampsthwaite, for poisoning John Rhodes, a boy five years old, at the above place. It appears that she was related to the family, and put arsenic into a pie with intent to poison the whole of them.

JOHN STEVENS, THOMAS LASTLEY, GEORGE MOORE, EDWARD WILLIAMS, JOHN GILL, AND JAMES HARTLEY.

Saturday, April 17th, A.D. 1790.—The above six malefactors were executed at the Tyburn without Micklegate Bar, and their bodies interred the same evening. The crimes for which they suffered were as follow :—

Stevens and Lastley were button-makers at Sheffield. They, together with John Booth and Michael Bingham, also button-makers, were charged by John Wharton, small shopkeeper in the Bridgehouses, with robbing him on the highway, in the town of Sheffield, on the Lady's Bridge, on Saturday night, August 29th, 1789, and taking from him a basket containing a shoulder of mutton, one pound of tobacco, half a stone of soap, seven pounds of butter, and fourpence in money. Stevens and Lastley were committed to York on the 4th of September, and Booth and Bingham on the 28th of October. Stevens, Lastley, and Booth received sentence of death ; and Bingham, who it appeared was merely a looker on, was acquitted. Booth was reprieved, before the Judge left York, to transportation for life. This affair being looked upon in Sheffield as more of a " lark " than a robbery, caused considerable excitement on the news arriving announcing the result of the trial. Immediately a petition was got up, headed by the Master Cutler, and signed by the whole of the Cutlers' Company and principal inhabitants of Sheffield, and forwarded to London without delay, but owing to the then slow means of travelling, the reprieve arrived at York too late to save the men, although all was granted that was asked. Stevens and Lastley were executed on the 17th of April, and the reprieve did not arrive until the 19th. On the 30th Booth was on his way to Sheffield, having been turned out on that day with an unconditional pardon. Wharton, in addition to being a small shopkeeper, worked as a labourer for Mr. Hoole, at the top of Lady's Walk, near to where Mr. Berry's brewery now stands, who was an extensive butter manufacturer, and where also worked the prisoners. It appeared that all five had called at a public house, and had a little beer, and on Wharton leaving them to make his markets, the rest followed him, and committed the robbery. They took the basket containing the goods to a public house, the sign of the "Barrel," Pinstone-street, kept by a Mrs. Marshal, where Stevens lodged (he was a single man), and there had the mutton cooked the same night. The other things remained in the basket untouched, and they clubbed the money for the mutton to give to Wharton, whom they expected would come and sup with them. At that time blood-money was paid to parties on whose evidence a capital charge was proved, with a view to facilitate the ends of justice, and it was generally believed that these men were sacrificed to obtain it. On Booth's arrival in Sheffield, a great mob assembled in front of Wharton's house, which stood rising the hill, and became so infuriated that Wharton was in danger of being murdered ; and he, with much difficulty, made his escape and left the town, and afterwards set up in the same business in Manchester. The mob broke his windows, and nearly gutted the house. Lastley resided in Burgess-street, and left a wife and one young child.

A constable named Eyre, known at that time as "Buggy Eyre," got much blamed in this affair, as alluded to by Mather in his song, for Wharton afterwards said that he had no idea things would go so far ; that when he applied to Eyre, he told him the nature of the robbery, and all he desired was his basket and goods back. The newspapers of that time give no detailed account ; but according to old William Taylor (who was a tailor by trade, and at that time worked for Mr. Sanderson in Change-alley, resided in

Pinfold-street, and was a frequenter at the "Barrel"), one of the party at the supper, it appeared the four accompanied Wharton (being almost inseparable companions), in the town whilst he made his purchases ; after which they called at the "White Hart," now the Royal Hotel, and had some ale. Wharton, whose company they all appear to have sought after, said he was determined to go home and take the things, as his wife would probably be wanting them, with a promise to return. They, however, walked on with him to the Lady's Bridge, where there was a urinal, into which Wharton turned, and left his basket outside. They took it up, and said they were determined he should return with them to the "Barrel" in Pinstone-street, and were making off with it. A scuffle ensued, but they got the mastery over him, and made off, thinking he would follow them. On arriving at the " Barrel," they told the landlady what a spree they had with Wharton (she was at York, and spoke to that effect at the trial), when Stevens proposed and Lastley agreed that the mutton should be cooked, which was accordingly done, and the basket put carefully away, with its contents undisturbed, by the landlady. At the Lady's Bridge, in the scuffle, Bingham desired them to give him back his basket, which acquitted him on his trial ; and Booth hesitated as to the propriety of the mutton being cooked, which also told in his favour. Wharton being left at the bridge in a great rage, immediately set off in search of a constable, and meeting with Eyre, made affidavit of the robbery. Eyre went the same night to the "Barrel," and took possession of the basket and goods. The four men began to see the turn the things were taking, made their escape, and slept elsewhere. On the 2nd Stevens was arrested at the " Barrel," and Lastley the same day, in St. Paul's Churchyard.

THE EXECUTION OF STEVENS AND LASTLEY,

Who suffered at York, April 17, 1790.

(*Song by old* JOSEPH MATHER.)

O, Wharton, thou villain most base !
   Thy name must eternally rot ;
Poor Stevens and Lastley's sad case
   For ever thy conscience will blot.
Those victims thou wickedly sold,
   And into eternity hurled,
For lucre of soul-sinking gold,
   To set thee on foot in the world.

Thy house is a desolate place,
   Reduced to a shell by the crowd ;
Destruction pursues thee apace,
   Whilst innocent blood cries aloud.
Poor Booth in strong fetters thou'st left,
   Appointed for Botany Bay ;
He is of all comforts bereft,
   To die by a hair's-breadth each day.

Depend on't thou never canst thrive,
   Thy sin will ere long find thee out ;
If not while thy body's alive,
   It will, after death, without doubt.
When Stevens and Lastley appears,
   Requiring their blood at thy hands ;
Tormenting a million of years,
   Can't satisfy Justice' demands.

Those death-hunters, subtle and vile,
   That prompt thee to this wicked work
(In order to share of the spoil
   Thou got by the blood spilt at York),
Are equally guilty with thee ;
   And as a reward for your pains,
You ought to be hung on a tree,
   And then be suspended in chains.

Edward Williams, for robbing John Watson, on the highway, at a place called Win-Moor, in the parish of Barwick-in-Elmet, near Leeds, and putting him in fear and danger of his life. His wife, Lydia, was with him, and assisted in the robbery. She also received sentence of death, which was commuted to transportation for life. They took from him a canvas purse, containing three guineas and a half, and one shilling.

James Hartley, of Manchester, for breaking into the dwelling-house and shop of William Sanderson, of Preston, in the East Riding, on the 24th of August, 1789, and carrying away divers articles of women's wearing apparel.

John Gill, *alias* Best, of Framington, in the county of Durham, for stealing, on the 4th December, 1789, a dark grey galloway mare, the property of William Challoner, Esq., of York, value about £5.

George Moore, of Sheffield, a blade-forger, living in High-street, Park, known by the name of "Dockey Moore," for breaking into the shop of Mr. William Davis, of York, and stealing a number of articles of hardware goods. He had just enlisted into the 19th Foot, who were at that time recruiting in Sheffield, and whose head-quarters were at York. He was a fine-looking young man, had fought several pitched battles—a most desperate one on Crooke's Moor, with a man named Dewsnap. His father, old George Moore, a very stout man, worked for Mr. Senior, in Bank-street, Sheffield. He was apparently terribly cut up at the fate of his son, who had written to him, desiring to see his father before he died. A public subscription was made to enable old George to go to York. He got the cash and set out upon his sorrowful errand, and landed as far as Brightside, where he called to bait, having accomplished three miles of his journey. He there spent all the money, and returned to Sheffield, telling his friends that he had seriously considered the matter over, and could have done no good to his son, had he seen him.

These six unfortunate men were taken from the Castle at York in one cart, another following with coffins to bring back their bodies. Lastley delivered a long address to the crowd of spectators (which was very great), declaring his own and companion's innocence of any intention to rob, and that Wharton well knew it. They were executed April 17th, 1790, at Tyburn near York, and their bodies interred the same evening.

THE LAMENTATION OF SIX MALEFACTORS

Who were executed at Tyburn, near York, on Saturday, April 17th,
1790.*

Good Christians all, we pray attend
Unto these lines which here are penn'd ;
There's six of us, we do declare,
All ready for execution here.

I, James Hartley, do declare
Of sinning I have had my share ;
In paths of wickedness I've trod,
Offending the Almighty God.
But, now, alas ! I'm doom'd to die
For housebreaking, which makes me cry ;
Sweet Lord, show mercy and pardon me,
For I must suffer on Tyburn tree.

I, Edward Williams, must confess
The laws of England I did transgress,
By robbing John Watson on the highway
But, alas ! for it my life must pay.
Dear wife, I'm grieved to part with thee,
But yet I'm glad thou art set free
From a shameful death which I must die.
Have mercy, Lord, and hear my cry !

I, Thomas Lastley, with Stevens agreed
To join him in this simple deed ;
We took John Wharton's basket and meat,
But not with an intent to keep ;
Like Judas, he did us betray,
For money he swore our lives away.
Sweet Lord, for mercy we on Thee call,
From him we must have none at all.

I, John Giles, must tell the truth,
I've been a wild, extravagant youth ;
In drinking and gaming I've took delight,
Amongst loose women, which is not right ;
For horse-stealing, that heinous crime,
I must be cut off in my prime :
So all young men, be warned by me,
And shun loose, idle company.

I, George Moore, must tell you plain,
I lose my life for little gain ;
For shopbreaking, that shameful deed,
It makes my tender heart to bleed ;

* Taken from an old paper in the possession of the Editor.

A harlot's company I did keep,
To think of her that makes me weep ;
Through her I took to evil ways,
Which is the short'ning of my days.

———

JOHN BRIGG, ROBERT CRAMMAM, WILLIAM HOWSON, JAMES FERGUSON, AND HENRY BELL.

Saturday, August 14th, A.D. 1790.—The above male-factors were executed at the Tyburn without Micklegate Bar, for the following crimes :—

Brigg was a native of Southowram, a weaver by trade, for stealing, from a common in the township of Carlton in the West Riding, seven ewe sheep, seven lambs, two hogs, and one two-year wether, the property of William Driver, of Carlton, farmer.

Crammam, for stealing a chestnut galloway, the property of Ralph Lowe, of Penfold Howse, Wearsdale, in the county of Durham ; also for stealing a saddle and bridle from Charles Thompson, of Bowes, in the North Riding.

Howson, Ferguson, and Bell, for stealing a black mare, the property of T. Bell, of High Heworth, in the county of Durham ; also a black mare, the property of C. Sanderson, & Co., of Woodbourn, millers.

JAMES GOULD.

Saturday, April 9th, A.D. 1791.—James Gould was exe-cuted at the Tyburn without Micklegate Bar, for breaking into the house of John Irwin, sen., of Landmoth, in the North Riding, and stealing therefrom ten guineas in gold, one five-pound York note, and three pounds in silver, or thereabouts. The behaviour of this young man (he was only 19 years old) after his condemnation and at the place of execution, was resigned, but marked with a degree of firmness seldom witnessed on such occasions.

JOHN MINITOR, JOHN BENNET, AND ABRAHAM ROBERTSHAW.

Saturday, September 6th, A.D. 1791.—The above three

culprits were executed at the Tyburn without Mickle-gate Bar, for the following offences :—

Minitor was a native of Rotherham, near Sheffield, by trade a flax-dresser, charged upon the oath of Mr. John Whitehead, of Whiston, near Rotherham, farmer, with the suspicion that he did, on the night of the 17th of February last, wilfully and maliciously set fire to a certain barn belonging to the said Mr. John Whitehead, of Whiston, containing a quantity of lime and wood for husbandry pur-poses, and totally consumed the whole. The jury brought him in guilty, on which he received sentence of death.

Bennet was a native of Sheffield, where he resided in Waingate, at the time of his committing the crime which cost him his life. He, along with four others, named Frog-gatt, Johnson, Furness, and Ellis, were committed to York for divers outrages on the 27th of July last, and setting fire to the stacks at Broomhall, near Sheffield, the property of the Rev. James Wilkinson, justice of the peace, and vicar of Sheffield. The mob did much damage to the furniture, consumed a great number of books, and four stacks of hay.

Robertshaw was a native of, and resided at Stanningley, near Bradford, where he carried on the business of a butcher. His crime was forgery, by writing the name of John Ward as an endorsement on a bill originally drawn by Lodge & Co., Leeds, on Baron Dunsdale & Co., of London, for £5. 5s., which had been altered to £15. 15s., and paid by him (Robertshaw) as a good bill of that value, to Mr. Jacob Stubbs, of Whitwell, on the 21st of April last, in the parish of St. Dennis, York. After condemnation, he desired the governor to inform the public that he had no accomplice, that he had committed four other forgeries, but hoped that his death would atone for the injuries he had done to society.

They were all taken in a cart to the place of execution.

ELIZABETH ELLIOT.

Monday, March 26th, A.D. 1792.—Elizabeth Elliot, a woman who resided at Thornton Rust, in the North Riding, was executed at the Tyburn without Micklegate Bar, for the murder of Mary Walker, of the same place. She was found guilty on the clearest evidence, and received sentence of death, and her body to be anatomized. She was a most desperate and hardened woman, and persisted in denying her guilt under the gallows at the time the cart was moving from under her.

SPENCE BROUGHTON, JOHN LUCAS, THOMAS STEARMAN, THOMAS CRAWSHAW, AND JOSEPH BRIERLY.

Saturday, April 12th, A.D. 1792.—The above five unhappy victims were executed at the Tyburn without Micklegate Bar.

Joseph Brierly, a single man, about 30 years of age, was convicted of breaking into the dwelling-house and shop of Ann Booth, of Cleckheaton, in the West Riding, and stealing divers articles of not much value.

Thomas Crawshaw, of Snarth, near Selby, a single man, aged 42, by trade a corn-miller. He was found guilty of a burglary in the house of John Wilson, ale-house keeper, of Thorpe Willowby, in the West Riding.

John Lucas and Thomas Stearman, both of Leeds, the former a carpet-weaver, the latter a pattern-ring maker, for a burglary in the shop of Messrs. E. & J. Mandells, linen-drapers, of Malton. It appears they, with two others named Walker and Ambler, loitered about the town for some days, and went to the shop occasionally to purchase little matters, in order to lay their plans for the robbery. Even on this occasion there was a contemptible meanness discovered, which, however, out of kindness, was passed over, for Lucas was detected with a roll of ribbon in his pocket. They had by them a large and valuable assortment of goods, having removed them from Scarborough to Malton when the Spa season had closed. Walker turned King's evidence, and on his testimony it appeared they borrowed three horses of a person named Iveson, of Leeds, and came that night to York, where they slept. They left York next morning, dined at Spittlebeck, and got to Malton late in the evening. They put their horses into an empty stable, in a field by the roadside, and, about eleven at night, they broke open the shop, and took away goods to the value of several hundreds of pounds, and loaded their horses with them. They immediately set off on their return, but finding, when they got near Whitwell, that their horses would not be able to carry them and their goods, they buried nearly half of them in a dunghill by the roadside. They proceeded through York, and got to Walker's house at Methley, where they divided the goods. They were soon after pursued, and traced to Walker's house. Here the constables found his (Walker's) share of the various articles. They apprehended him and brought him to York, where he made a full confession of the robbery, in consequence of which the other two, Lucas and Stearman, were apprehended. Some of the goods were found in Lucas's possession; a part in the dunghill near Whitwell, and another part in a well near Leeds. Lucas was in the 37th year of his age, and left a wife and four children. Stearman was a single man, and about the same age as Lucas.

Spence Broughton, for robbing George Leasley, a boy, who carried the mail between Sheffield and Rotherham, on the night of the 19th of February, 1791, in company with John Oxley, taking from him the bags containing the letters, in one of which was enclosed a French bill of exchange, drawn by a Monsieur Virgelle, a merchant in France, on the house of Minnet & Fector, merchants in London, payable to Mr. Joseph Walker, of Masbro', near Rotherham, for £123 sterling, or thereabouts.

Few cases of this nature have excited more interest, not only in the neighbourhood where it took place, but throughout the whole kingdom, than the trial of these notorious mail robbers, a more full and particular account of which may be interesting.

The first account of them is, that on Monday, October 16th, 1791, a man, rather genteelly dressed, with a woman, called at Mr. Metham's, silversmith, Cheapside, London, bought a half-guinea ring, and required change for a Stamford bank bill of ten pounds. Not desirous of accommodating a stranger, and especially so trifling a customer, in a way that might subject him to inconvenience, Mr. Metham declined it, pleading want of cash. They then recollected that they wanted a cream-jug, and fixed upon one at a guinea and a half. Mr. Metham looked carefully at the note, and seeing nothing suspicious about it, gave the change, and they went away.

It presently transpired that the same party had bought a trifling article in the silk way next door, and changed a bill there also ; and some groceries of a Mr. Mosley, on the other side of the way, where they changed a third ; all of which, upon inquiry at the bankers', proved to have been stolen from the Cambridge mail, which was robbed in June last. Two days after, a boy, 18 or 19 years of age, who lived in the capacity of shopboy with Mr. Metham, in carrying a load on Blackfriars-road, was struck with the resemblance which a man passing on horseback bore to the person who paid the note to his master. He threw down his load, and ran as fast as he could after him over Blackfriars-bridge and along Fleet-street. At Snow-hill he would have entirely lost him but for some obstruction, which enabled the lad to turn the corner in time to see that he took the way leading to Smithfield : with fresh vigour he sustained the chase, till he saw him dismount and enter a public-house in Clerkenwell, opposite to which he planted himself, and remained a long time before he could get assistance ; at last, however, an officer was procured, whom the lad led on ; and upon a near view of the gentleman in the little room behind the bar (where he was seated at dinner with the landlord and landlady) the boy charged him with the fact, and he was led away.

When taken before Sir Sampson Wright, he said his name was Oxen, and that he had the bills of a Mr. Shaw, who desired him to get the bills converted into cash, which being done, he gave the cash and the articles he had brought to Mr. Shaw, at his house in Blackfriars-road.

The moment Shaw's residence was described, Townsend and Jealous, Bow-street officers, went out in search of him ; they had not arrived there three minutes before a rap was heard at the door. One of the thief-takers opening it, was asked by an uncommonly stout, tall, athletic man, if Mr. Shaw was at home ; he said yes, and desired him to walk in ; but instead of this he turned short round, took to his heels as fast as he could, and led them in pursuit all the way to the Obelisk, and nearly to the " Dog and Duck," in

St. George's-fields, before they could seize him or have him stopped.

They instantly searched him, and in his pockets found a handful of bank notes. With their prisoner and prize they hastened back to Bow-street, where the examination of Oxley had made but little progress ; and it had not transpired two minutes that one Broughton was concerned, and a principal in the business, when Townsend, with the bank-notes in his hand, exultingly entered, and said " We have got him." " What, Shaw !" said the justice. " No, a fellow worth a hundred Shaws !" and so it turned out, for according as things stood, it appeared that Shaw was a town agent, whose business it was to receive and put off the booty, whereas the other two did the robbing part of the business, which proved to have been carried out on a very extensive scale.

On Monday, October 25th, Spence Broughton, John Oxley, and Thomas Shaw were again brought up.

Thomas Shaw, when he found that the whole of this business must be brought to light, as some of the parties were in custody, first stipulated for his own safety, on which he took the opinion of counsel, and then impeached those whom he had seduced. His deposition was as follows :—

About a fortnight previous to the robbery of the Cambridge mail, on the 9th of June, Spence Broughton and John Oxley came to his house in Prospect-row, St. George's-in-the-fields, where they acquainted him with their design of robbing the Cambridge mail, near Bournebridge, and solicited his assistance. He declined, but as he was going to Cambridge on some business, he told them he would inquire about the mail, and give them such information as would the more easily enable them to execute their purpose. He accordingly set off from the " Queen's Head," Gray's-Inn-lane, in the fly ; and, what was a remarkable circumstance, was accompanied by Mr. John Palmer, of the Drury-lane Theatre, the eminent tragedian, who was summoned on a trial in that county. While at Cambridge, Shaw inquired at the post-office, and made it his business for several nights to learn how the mail was taken. After having made himself master of the whole system, he came to London, and disclosed his information to Oxley and

Broughton, who again pressed him to accompany them, but he declined, and they departed on the 8th of June to execute their purpose. On the 10th they returned, and sent for Shaw to the "Cannon" coffee-house, in Portland-road, where they told him they had completed the robbery, and Broughton gave him a handkerchief with all the notes in it, which he the same evening buried in the garden behind his house, in Prospect-row, St. George's-fields.

A few weeks after the robbery, Shaw took the notes out of his garden, and carried them to an empty house of his, No. 9, Middle-row, Holborn. There, in presence of Oxley and Broughton, the bundle was opened and examined. A few bills were taken out by each person for the purpose of negotiating, and within two or three days they passed to the amount of £150. Sir Benjamin Hammet, who was present, and who interested himself very much during the examination, questioned Shaw about the quantity and nature of the notes. Shaw said there were about £400 in value of the Bank of England notes, half of which were endorsed "P. post—Wood and Dowling." As it was not thought safe to negotiate these notes with that endorsement, Oxley extracted the writing with spirits of salt, and Shaw dried the notes at the fire. Shaw here observed that, having been concerned in a lottery insurance office, he knew that it must be spirits of salt that extracted the writing, as numbers which he had insured had often been erased, and placed in such a manner as led him to inquire how it could be done, and he had been informed it was by spirits of salt, but he positively denied ever having used them himself. When questioned by Sir Benjamin to what amount there were bills taken from the Cambridge mail, he declined giving any opinion; but as he acknowledged there were £400 in Bank of England notes, twelve or fourteen Stamford Bank notes of £10 each at least, one bill for £750, another for £350, and other bills which had either been passed or burnt; so that the whole must have amounted to between five and ten thousand pounds, or upwards; for by Shaw's own declaration, a thousand or two had been negotiated, and a large bundle, to no one knows what amount, destroyed when it was first known that Oxley was in custody. This much was disclosed by the deposition of Shaw.

George Thompson, the master of a coffee-house, said that he some time ago cashed a Stamford Bank bill for Oxley, which he paid to his brewers, Messrs. Gifford & Co., but they returned it, saying that it had been stolen from the Cambridge mail. Oxley was much surprised at this, and said he knew from whom he had received it, and would return it. During the whole of the examination, Oxley was not only ready but extremely anxious to disclose everything he knew, and, for the sake of brevity, we will begin with that which should properly be first.

Five or six days previous to the robbery of the Rotherham mail, he said Shaw came to him at his house, No. 1, Frances-street, Tottenham-court-road, and, after asking him if he was not well acquainted with the country between Rotherham and Sheffield, which was answered in the affirmative, he proposed that he and Broughton should go thither and rob the mail. Oxley partly agreed, and it was resolved that the next morning all the parties should meet at ten o'clock, at Shaw's house in Prospect-row, finally to settle the plan. Next morning Oxley went into the parlour, and found Thomas Shaw, Spence Broughton, and John Close, Shaw's partner in the lottery office, Mrs. Shaw, and a woman who lived with Close in London, although he had a wife and family residing in Change-alley, Sheffield, his place of residence. The men went out, and walked backward and forward between Prospect-row and the "Dog and Duck," where they arranged their plans, which were to be executed by Broughton and Oxley; but as these two were very poor, Shaw lent them ten guineas, which Broughton, as purse-bearer, received. They set off in the Nottingham coach from the "Swan with Two Necks," in Lad-lane. They proceeded next day, on foot, towards Chesterfield, in hope that the coach would overtake them, but as it was full it would not take them up. After partly walking and partly riding, they reached Sheffield, where they went to bed. On the following night, they walked out on the Rotherham road, and met the mail coming towards Sheffield; but as they designed to rob it as it was returning, they lay in wait until that time should arrive. Broughton, who Oxley said kept a number of smock frocks and other disguises at his lodgings, threw off his coat, and took out of his pocket a

smock frock and a little old hat, both of which he put on.
He lifted the gate which led into the field off the hinges
with his shoulders, saying that he would lead the boy and
cart into the field. He then gave his coat to Oxley, and
told him to wait in the field, which he pointed out, until he
came to him. Oxley lay there some time, and soon heard
the cart coming. He also heard the conversation between
Broughton and the boy, and presently the former came
running to him, saying he had got it, and desiring him to
follow, adding that he had secured the boy. Broughton
and Oxley proceeded on foot towards Mansfield, but before
they had got two miles on their road, they opened the
letters, when Broughton said there was only one that would
be safe to pass, which he put into his pocket, and threw the
bag into a brook. When they came to Mansfield, Broughton
pretended to be lame or sick, and said he could not then
proceed on his journey to London, but advised Oxley to go
and to pass the note which they had taken from the mail,
and which was on a merchant in Austin Friars, for £123.
Oxley accordingly came to London, and sent one Lisk, a
porter at the Temple, with the bill, who obtained the cash
for it, and received eighteenpence for his trouble. Oxley
further deposed :—About the 20th of May last, Shaw
proposed that they should go on horseback, and plan the
robbery of the Aylesbury mail, which they did, and
Broughton and Oxley executed it on the 28th, in precisely
the same manner as the Rotherham mail robbery, with this
difference, that they found no bills in it except some cut
bank notes, which were of no use. By this scheme, Shaw,
who had provided the money, complained that he lost £14.
Oxley added :—To reimburse Mr. Shaw, the robbery of the
Cambridge mail was projected. It was entirely of Shaw's
planning, who went down to Cambridge for the purpose of
learning the best mode of effecting it. Shaw found the
money, and they together accomplished it.

The particulars of the robbery of the Cambridge mail
Oxley related to be the same as what Shaw had stated, with
this difference—that Broughton was the person who actually
committed the robbery. He put on a smock frock, as usual;
and after he had taken the bag, he joined Oxley, who was
at a little distance. They concealed the large bag among

some stones on the roadside, and carried the smaller ones with the letters into an adjoining wood, where they opened them; and after taking out all the bills, which they put into a handkerchief, buried the letters underground, and proceeded on foot to Biggleswade; from thence they came up to London, on the outside of the Nottingham and Leeds coach. Lisk, the porter at the Temple, proved having received the bill stolen out of the Rotherham mail, and getting it cashed for Oxley. A mail coachman proved having brought Oxley a part of the way from Rotherham. And the Cambridge mail-boy gave it as his opinion that, although it was a very dark night when he was robbed, yet, from the size of the two men, it was (as he believed) Broughton, and not Oxley, who stopped and robbed him.

On Thursday, November 1st, the three men were again brought before Sir Sampson Wright to be re-examined, respecting the robberies of the Rotherham, Cambridge, and Aylesbury mails. The solicitor from the Post-office attended as usual, but nothing new transpired, except that the boy George Leasley, of Rotherham, who drove the mail from Sheffield to Rotherham at the time it was robbed, attended to identify either of the prisoners, but he was unable to do so. They were fully committed to the following prisons: Broughton to Newgate; Shaw to Tothill-fields; and Oxley to Clerkenwell.

OXLEY'S ESCAPE.

The escape of this man from his confinement appeared at the first very extraordinary, and wore the feature of suspicion. It is possible that a combination of circumstances might have placed him in Clerkenwell prison; that he might have had light irons; might have been unguarded; that the window might have been open; that a ladder might have been left against the wall; that he might have ascended to the roof of the building; but still the greatest difficulty remained. Having reached the leads of the house, how was he to get down again if the affair was not preconcerted, and that he had no accomplices? How then walk the street at seven o'clock in the evening, and no one perceive his darbies? The other circumstances were still more mysterious. One of the keepers following him sees him enter a house; gives a hint sufficient to alarm him; and procures a constable just in time to discover that the bird had flown. The confidence, or rather temerity of this man, in the subsequent part of the night, was truly astonishing. About eleven o'clock on the night of his escape, a coach stopped at a house in Norris-street, Haymarket, where a hazard-table was kept, and was once the resort of Oxley. The coachman knocked at the door and inquired after several persons who seldom make their appearance at so early an hour; and the man of the house being at length called to the coach door, received with infinite surprise the salutation of his former customer. Not wishing to become either his accomplice or accuser, the man warned him of the danger of his situation, and prevailed upon him to depart. His next visit was paid to a favourite station, the "One Tun," where he met with some friends who were fit to advise him, and since that time has never been heard of.

Broughton was removed to York by writ of *habeas corpus*, in order to be tried for the Rotherham mail robbery, which appeared to be the clearest case. At nine o'clock on the morning of March the 24th, he was brought into dock, and at half-past ten had received his sentence. It turned out on the trial that some part of Oxley's statement was untrue. Shaw, who was admitted evidence against him, and was the most material witness, said that Broughton's account of the journey was, that he and Oxley came from London to Derby in a coach, and walked thence to Chesterfield, and slept at the "Three Cranes" on the Friday previous to the robbery; that on Saturday morning they proceeded to Sheffield, and robbed the mail that night; Oxley stopped the boy and the horse; Broughton opened the gate into the field; Oxley tied the boy to the hedge. All this was corroborated by the boy himself. When Broughton arrived in London and learnt that Oxley had got the cash for the bill, and gone to the cocking at Leicester, Broughton said that Oxley was a damned rogue; that he would go to Leicester, and if he did not give him some of the cash he would take it.

TRIAL OF SPENCE BROUGHTON, FOR ROBBING THE ROTHERHAM MAIL.

(Before Mr. Justice Buller, at the Castle of York, March 24, 1792.)

The charge in the indictment was, that on the night of the 9th of February, 1791, the said Broughton, in company with one John Oxley, did stop the post-boy carrying the mail from Sheffield to Rotherham ; did take away the said mail or bags, containing letters, in one of which letters so feloniously taken away was enclosed a French bill of exchange, drawn by a Monsieur Virgelle, a merchant in France, on the house of Minnet & Fector, merchants in London, payable to Mr. Joseph Walker, of Rotherham, for £123 sterling or thereabouts.

The post-boy proved the taking the mails on the above-mentioned night by two men, but could not attempt to identify either of them, on account of the darkness of the night. He said that they led his horse some distance from the place where they stopped him ; one tied his hands and fastened him to the hedge, whilst the other cut away the bag containing the letters, with which they made off.

Thomas Shaw deposed as follows :—On the Saturday or Sunday after the 31st day of January, 1791, the prisoner sent a message, desiring to speak to him, and they met at his house in St. George's-fields. Broughton inquired if he had seen Oxley, and if he knew whether he had got cash for a bill they had taken out of the Rotherham mail. Shaw said he had, for on Oxley's return to London he had called on the witness and produced a foreign bill of exchange, which the witness found was due. Oxley said he had given a man ten guineas to endorse it. Oxley and Shaw went together to the Inner Temple gate, where Oxley saw a porter, and sent him with the bill to the house on which it was drawn. Shaw followed and watched the porter, that in case any person came out of the house with him, he might give the alarm to Oxley. He saw the porter come out of the house alone; watched him to a banking-house in Lombard-street, came from thence by himself, and carried the money to Oxley, who was waiting for it at the Inner Temple-gate. After this conversation Broughton said, " Oxley was a damned rogue, for he had left with his wife only ten pounds or guineas; that they had gone together from London to Derby in the coach, and walked thence to Chesterfield, and slept at the 'Three Cranes' on Friday previous to the robbery; that on Saturday they proceeded to Sheffield, and robbed the mail that night; Oxley stopped the boy and horse—Broughton opened the gate of a field—Oxley tied the boy to a hedge—Broughton took the bag—and they proceeded on foot to Mansfield; Broughton fell lame, could go no farther, and stayed there all that day—but Oxley then went by the coach to London." Broughton added, he heard Oxley was gone to the cockings at Leicester; he said he would follow him, and if he would not give him his share of the money, he would take it from him. The witness saw Broughton after he returned from Leicester, who informed him he had got the greatest part of the money. A foreign bill was now produced in court and shown to Shaw; after examining it, he said he knew it, and was certain it was the same Oxley gave to him. He never saw it since but at Sir Sampson Wright's. He lived in Prospect-row, St. George's-fields; was agent to a gentleman in Birmingham. After Oxley was taken, he received a letter from Mr. Anthony Parkin, solicitor to the Post-office, and he surrendered himself;—had been in custody ever since, in Tothill Fields Bridewell. He was charged with being an accomplice.

John Close lives at Sheffield; he remembers Oxley coming to Shaw's, in Prospect-row. They went with him into Bedford-court, Covent Garden, where he showed them a French bill. He saw Broughton the Saturday following, betwixt the Obelisk and Blackfriars Bridge. Broughton told him, "That he and Oxley robbed the mail; he stopped at Mansfield, and that Oxley went in the mail coach to town; that he had heard Oxley had got the money for the foreign bill, and was going to Leicester cocking; that he would follow and take the money from him." The witness understood some time afterwards that Broughton had been at Leicester and got his share of the money. On his cross-examination he said, he lives partly in Sheffield and partly in London; in the latter place, perhaps, three or four months in the year; that he then keeps a lottery-office; that he knows William Woodward; that he met him some time since in Fleet-street; that Woodward accosted him and said he understood he had accused Broughton, and that his evidence would hang him. The witness replied, that if his own conduct did not hang him, his evidence would not. On being asked if he did not tell Woodward he had accused Broughton for fear Oxley should accuse him and take his life, he denied he had ever said so, or that he had informed Woodward he had disclosed nothing that could affect Broughton. He was then asked if Jane Hill, or Ireland, had called on him? He replied she had. She asked him what he had to say against Broughton; he replied he had nothing to say to her.

Charles Lisk is a porter at the Inner Temple gate. He received a bill from Oxley, who then said his name was John Taylor. He carried it to a merchant in Austinfriars, who gave him a check on his banker, of whom he received £123 14s. and delivered it to Oxley, who waited for it at the Temple gate, where he said he had business. He saw an advertisement stating this transaction, and therefore came forward; saw Oxley at Sir Sampson Wright's, and knew him to be the man.

Two coachmen proved the carrying of Broughton different stages on the road towards Chesterfield. Mrs. Martindale, the wife of an innkeeper in Chesterfield, and a shopkeeper there who knew Broughton, and into whose shop he (Broughton) went to ask how he did, both proved Broughton's being at Chesterfield the day before the robbery. A person also proved his being at Mansfield at the time he owned to Shaw to have stopped there after the robbery, on account of his lameness. Mr. Beeston, a feeder of cocks, proved both Broughton and Oxley being at Leicester cocking at the time mentioned by Shaw and Close. Mr. James, the postmaster of Sheffield, proved the sending of the mail-bag from Sheffield to Rotherham on the above-mentioned night. Mr. Townsend, one of the Bow-street officers, proved that being at Shaw's house waiting for his coming home, a rap was heard at the door, and on going to it, Broughton was there, and asked if Shaw was at home; being answered in the affirmative, and desired to walk in, on his perceiving the officers of justice, he instantly fled: he proved his being taken, and at his house, on a search, a great number of the bills taken from the Cambridge mail were found, and produced in court, to the amount it was said of nearly £3,000. Against this very strongly connected chain of evidence, the prisoner had little or nothing to offer. His counsel asked Shaw how he came to be so intimately acquainted with all this transaction, and he answered that he was looked on as an accomplice, and applied to be admitted evidence to save himself. His only hope seemed to rest on the invalidation of the testimony of Mr. Close, in which he was, however, completely disappointed. Close's evidence was very collected and given in a clear and manly manner. The counsel for the prisoner, on Close's cross examination, endeavoured to extort from him an acknowledgment made to one Woodward, in a conversation had between them about Oxley and Broughton, as to his motives for swearing against Broughton; but he positively, and in the most pointed manner, denied it. He was asked also if he did not keep a lottery-office? He said he did. He was then asked if he did not keep a gaming-house? and he said most positively, No, that he never did. Woodward was, however, produced, but could not by any means substantiate the conversation alluded to. On Townsend being asked if he knew Woodward, he said, Yes, he lived in Rathbone-place, and kept an E. O. table, and gave a very indifferent impression of his character. On being asked by the Court if he knew Close? he said, Yes, but that he never knew any harm of him. Did he never know of his keeping a gaming-house? He answered, No, he never did, nor ever heard of his doing so.

The jury immediately brought in a verdict—Guilty.

The judge then addressed the prisoner. He stated that he had been convicted, on the clearest evidence that could possibly be produced, of a crime which must have been long premeditated, and which, in its consequence, was most baneful to society; of a crime of such a nature as to leave him without a shadow of hope that he could receive any mercy on this side the grave. That, in order to deter others from offending in the like manner, it was necessary that his punishment should not cease at the place of execution; that his body should be afterwards suspended betwixt heaven and earth, as unworthy of either, to be buffeted about by the winds and storms. He then recommended to him that he should make the best use of the little time allowed him in this world, and afterwards passed sentence of death on him in the usual manner.

The court was exceedingly crowded. The unfortunate prisoner distinguished himself by a very calm, firm, and manly demeanour, and though much affected while sentence was passing on him, he bowed to it with a degree of fortitude and resignation which evinced his sincere intention of dedicating the short remains of his span of life towards making his peace with, and obtaining forgiveness of, that all-just and all merciful Judge to whom alone he is now accountable.

Execution of Spence Broughton.

The behaviour of the five convicts, on Saturday fortnight, at York, in their last moments, was very devout and penitent; Broughton's in particular was marked with a degree of fortitude and resignation seldom observed in persons in his miserable situation. He told the clergyman who attended him after his trial, that he did not rob the mail, —that he believed he was at Nottingham when it was robbed,—but that he knew of the robbery. He added, that by giving information of his accomplices, he could have done them much harm, but would rather die than be guilty of such dishonourable conduct. He freely forgave those who had been instrumental to his death; and, so far from wishing that Shaw might die at the gallows with him, he expressed much sorrow when told that Shaw was in durance for forging the endorsement on the bill. When getting into the cart that was to convey him to the place of execution, he said :—" This is the happiest day I have experienced for some time." On his way to Tyburn he prayed very much. When the prayers were concluded at the place of execution, he (Broughton) without any tremor or change of countenance, took off his neckcloth and carefully fixed the noose of the rope under his ear; with the cap over his face, he again prayed, and with his last breath said that he was a murdered man. His body was taken from York early on Sunday morning, and hung on the gibbet at two o'clock on Monday morning.

George Drabble, who kept the sign of the "Arrow," a

road-side public-house (now pulled down) on the same side, and about 250 yards nearer Attercliffe than Carbrook Hall, gave the following account of the arrival and suspension of Broughton :—During the whole of Sunday, hundreds of people visited the spot to view the post, which was made in the Nursery, and fixed on Saturday, the day of Broughton's execution. At eight o'clock the common was like a fair ; a messenger having arrived announcing that the body was within a few miles, caused great numbers to linger late on the spot. Drabble, who had not been in bed since the first sod was dug for the post, during which time, night and day, his house was crammed with people, about one o'clock on Monday morning, hit upon the following stratagem to clear it. He cried outside through the back window, " A fight ! a fight !" which was the signal for a general rush. In less than three minutes, the house was cleared, save some half-dozen whose heavy potations had got them too fast asleep to see the fight. He (Drabble) jumped in through the window, and secured it and the door just in time to answer the question from some score of inquirers as to where was the fight ? He told them to fight amongst themselves, and would not be prevailed upon by threats or entreaties again to open it. He had not been in bed more than half an hour, when the cart containing Broughton, and a post-chaise with the officials, stopped at the door. Drabble was called up, and he immediately led them across the common some 200 yards, to the post, with a lantern and candle. In the cart with the body was a ladder, rope, and pulley. Upon hoisting the body up, it was found that the ring at the top of the irons was too thick for the hook in the post ; it was again let down into the cart, and held upon its legs—Drabble being one to assist—whilst the man at the top filed the hook, which did not take him more than a few minutes, and on the second try it went on, when all returned to the " Arrow," and a good breakfast was prepared for the four who brought the body. The gibbet-post (which was the last put up in Yorkshire), with the irons, the skull, a few other bones and rags, was standing as late as 1827 or '28, when it was taken down. Drabble, who afterwards kept the " Green Dragon," at Attercliffe, used to say that whatever crimes Broughton might have committed before he was hung, he certainly made a man of him (Drabble) afterwards, for he caused such a sale for his ale that he never afterwards looked behind him. When the gibbet had been up about a month, a respectable middle-aged female called at his house, and sat at the window a considerable time, appearing to be greatly distressed. This was supposed to be his wife, from the description given.

It was said that Broughton and Oxley had squandered away more than £10,000, which they had obtained by robbing the mails. How they became acquainted does not appear, but probably it would be at the cocking, at Leicester, at which place they were known as old frequenters and heavy betters. Oxley was born at Wentworth, and was, when a boy, employed in the stables at Wentworth House; and for some time carried the letter-bag, on horseback, to Rotherham and back. He was respectably connected with good families at Greasbro' and Rotherham. His knowledge of the neighbourhood was no doubt the reason of their fixing upon the robbery of the Rotherham mail, as he knew how it was carried. At that period cock-fighting was carried on to an amazing extent by all ranks, in which Oxley soon became notorious. He abandoned his employment, and turned his attention entirely to cocking; and for a time was somewhat successful. His escape out of jail, and never afterwards being seen, led to many surmises as to accomplices. It was reported that he was murdered on the night of his escape, and his body thrown into a deep sink, the receptacle at that time of all sorts of offal and filth; and that parties in high positions were suspected to have had a hand in it, to stop his mouth, lest certain disclosures of a very serious nature might come to light.

The account was partially set aside early in the following year, by one or two persons declaring they had seen Oxley in the neighbourhood of Rotherham. But these rumours remained unheeded until the following account appeared in the papers. In the *Newark Herald*, of Wednesday, January 30, 1793, is the following, copied from the Sheffield papers :—
"On Friday last was found dead, of hunger and cold, in a barn, on Loxley-moor, above Sheffield, a man who had been seen for a few weeks before wandering about in that neighbourhood, in the evenings, but had concealed himself in the

day-time. It appeared, upon examining him, that his legs were marked and cut about the ancles, as if he had been manacled with heavy prison irons ; from which circumstance, and from his avoiding with the greatest care the sight of any person, it is conjectured that he had broken out of prison ; and that, dreading the consequences of a discovery, had preferred perishing as above to mixing any more with mankind. Turnips, partly eaten, were found in his pockets, and about the place where he lay. He was slenderly made, had very black hair, and rather low in stature ; had on a blue coat, and other apparel decently good ; silver-plated buckles, and silver studs on his shirt-wrists, marked 'D. E.' A person residing at Darnall, near Sheffield, who was well acquainted with Oxley, declared that the man found in the barn at Loxley was no other than John Oxley, the confederate of Broughton, although he did not see the body, but from the description given in the papers, on the coroner's inquisition, so exactly corresponding with the dress he wore at Darnall, where he had seen him (Oxley) some weeks before. Oxley told him he had been across the common, to look at Broughton ; and had, about that time, applied to his friends in the neighbourhood of Rotherham for assistance to enable him to leave the country, but which appeal met with a prompt refusal. Close used occasionally to come to the 'Arrow,' and, on one occasion, the conversation turned upon the probability of the body found in the barn being that of Oxley,—'As sure,' said Close, putting his hand on Drabble's shoulder, 'as Broughton's bones are swinging yonder (pointing to the gibbet), so sure are those of Oxley in a solitary corner of Bradfield Church-yard.' He (Close) mentioned at the same time the name of a notorious gambler in London, a great companion of Oxley, whose initials corresponded with the studs found on the shirt wristbands."

The writer has frequently heard old people, who well remembered the circumstance, say that it was very generally believed at the time to be the body of Oxley.

Broughton was born at Sleaford, in Lincolnshire, his father being an extensive farmer at that place. Spence married a young woman, when about twenty years of age, who possessed a handsome fortune ; by whom he had three children, two boys and a girl, who were all living at the time of his death. He lived with Mrs. Broughton several years, in apparent happiness, at Martin, a village between Lincoln and Gainsbro', and was an extensive farmer and grazier at that place. He had also a large farm at Horblin, lived in good style, and was in apparently prosperous circumstances, until he formed a connection with a female, who occasionally lived with him as his wife. Seeing nothing but ruin before her, Mrs. Broughton resolved upon a separation, which was agreed to, but not before he had squandered away about £15,000. After this he became the avowed companion of gamblers and sharpers, attended cockings and races, and was concerned in an E. O. table. However, it is some extenuation of his crimes to say that no act of cruelty attended any of his robberies. George Leasley, the boy who carried the Rotherham mail, deposed that his horse was led into the field, and he bid to get off; that a handkerchief was tied over his eyes, and he to a hedge; that in about an hour's time he freed himself, and found his horse tied to a gate, but the Rotherham bag was gone.

WILLIAM ATKINSON, RICHARD WATSON, AND THOMAS JEWET.

Saturday, April 12th, A.D. 1793.—The above three culprits were executed at the Tyburn without Micklegate Bar.

William Atkinson, aged 70, a native of Whitby, for aiding, abetting, and counselling a number of riotous persons in pulling down and demolishing the dwelling-house of John Cooper, of Whitley. He declared he was but a looker on, and to the last stuck to saying that he had no hand in the affair.

Watson was a native of Halifax ; for breaking open and robbing the dwelling-house of John Ambler, of that place, and stealing therefrom one mahogany desk, seven or eight guineas in gold, and other articles to a considerable amount.

Jewet, of Osbaldwick, for stealing five heifers from Anthony Jackson, of Askham Bryan ; two from Frances Scott, of Copmanthorpe ; two from Thomas Fearby, of Askham Bryan ; and two from Messrs. William and Anthony Jackson, of Askham Bryan. Jewet had a son hanged at York for a rape, in 1807.

They all suffered at the old gallows on Knavesmire, at twelve o'clock on Saturday, the 12th day of April, 1793.

JOHN HOYLAND.

Saturday, August 9th, A.D. 1793.—John Hoyland, a native of Attercliffe, near Sheffield, was executed at the Tyburn without Micklegate Bar, for bestiality. He was residing at Attercliffe at the time when he committed the offence for which he suffered death. He was 77 years of age, and was convicted on the oaths of John Hunt and William Warburton, both of Sheffield, labourers, who swore upon oath, that he did, on July 15th last, have carnal intercourse with an ass. This poor old man declared his innocence to the last, and few who knew him doubted his statement. He was a simple, apparently harmless man ; had reared a large' family, scarcely removed from a state of idiotcy, and some of them dumb. When the father and mother used to quarrel, which was by no means of rare occurrence—the sons took the mother's side, and would wait for an opportunity to seize the father, when they threw him down and thrashed him so severely, that he frequently was weeks together with bruises upon him. This was one of those cases which had much to do with the altering of the law in giving blood-money ; few doubted but that was the sole cause of these men swearing this charge against him. When taken to the gallows, he told the spectators that he would not change places with the men who had sworn his life away.

WILLIAM WADDINGTON.

Saturday, April 12th, A.D. 1794.—William Waddington, a native of York, was executed at the Tyburn without Micklegate Bar, for counterfeiting the coin of the realm, and paying the same to divers people in York. He was 42 years of age, and had hitherto been very respectable. He left a wife and seven children to deplore his unfortunate and untimely end. The parting with his wife and children, who visited him on the morning of his execution, was most affecting. After they had gone, he said the terrors of death were now over.

ANN SCALBERT AND THOMAS KIRK.

The above two unfortunate individuals were executed at the Tyburn without Micklegate Bar, on Saturday, August 30th, 1794. The former was the wife of Moses Scalbert, of Bartley, in the West Riding. She was found guilty of murdering her husband's mother by poison. Kirk was a worthless idle fellow, spent his time in a vagrant kind of life, was a very muscular powerful man, and well known at Raskelf, in the North Riding, where he committed the crime which cost him his life. In July of that year, Mr. Smithson, of Greenfield house, in the parish of Raskelf, was out hay-making with the whole of his household, excepting his daughter Elizabeth, a young woman who was left in charge of the house, which stands some distance from any other, though close upon the high road leading from Easingwold to Thirsk. A little before twelve o'clock, Kirk called at the house and asked for some relief. She gave him some milk and water to drink; but on finding she was alone, he demanded some ale, which she fetched him; he then seized her and committed a rape on her person, and otherwise roughly used her. Mr. Smithson soon after returning from the field, found his daughter in a very shocking condition. He immediately mounted a horse which happened to be in the stable, and pursued him. He met Mary Dale and her sister, who pointed out the direction Kirk had taken; he soon came up with him, and never lost sight of him until he was captured. Mary Dale swore to him at his trial at York. He appeared totally insensible of his situation, and died in a state of obstinate impenitence.

CHARLES ELLIOTT.

Monday, March 30th, A.D. 1795.—Charles Elliott, sergeant in Colonel Cameron's Royal Regiment of Wake-field Foot, was executed at the Tyburn without Micklegate

Bar, for the murder of John Meyal, near Huddersfield, a poor, industrious, labouring man, and who left a wife and large family of small children totally destitute.

George Fawcett, William Brittain, William Brammam, William Jackson, and Thomas Mann.

Saturday, April 25th, A.D. 1795.—The above malefactors were placed as usual in a cart at the Castle, York, and from thence conveyed to the Tyburn without Micklegate Bar, where they were executed in the presence of a large concourse of people. The following are the crimes for which they suffered death.

George Fawcett, aged 77, a native of Marsham, where he resided, was convicted of stealing four sheep off Roundell Common ; his two sons, George and William, also received sentence of death, but were reprieved to transportation, for the same offence. At the place of execution, this old man persisted in declaring his innocence, and said that though he drove the sheep away at the desire of his sons, he did not at the time suspect them to have been stolen.

Brittain and Mann were both of them wool-combers at Bradford. They were charged with breaking into the dwelling-house of Mary Thornton, of Bolton, and taking away sundry articles. Being found guilty, they were sentenced to be hung. These men also persisted in their innocence at the gallows.

Brammam was from Milford, and was found guilty of breaking into the dwelling-house of William Shillito, of Hampool, and stealing a silver spoon. Jackson, aged 25, of Keyingham, was found guilty of stealing ten sheep.

Thomas Maclean, James Smith, *alias* Freeman Sutcliffe, and Thomas Burch.

April 25th, A.D. 1796.—The above were executed at the Tyburn without Micklegate Bar, near York.

Maclean, who was quite a lad, and a native of Swambee, for robbing a Jew pedlar named Innocenti Rossi, of the

City of York, on the 10th of December, 1794, at Beaka Riggs, near a place called Stone Haggs, in the North Riding ; taking from him two pounds, four shillings, and sixpence in money, and a silver watch.

James Smith, *alias* Sutcliffe, for assaulting and robbing Mr. Wignall on the highway at Keighley, putting him in bodily fear, and stealing from him sixty guineas, and several notes and bills.

Thomas Burch was a private in the Surrey Militia. He was convicted of a burglary at York.

At these assizes Broadbent, a notorious highwayman and housebreaker, was capitally convicted, and received sentence of death, but was reprieved to transportation. He was better known by the name of " New Brass," and had been long the terror of the county. Since the memorable days of Turpin, New Brass stood unequalled both as to the variety and number of his achievements, and the audacity of his exploits. There was something odd in hanging the lad Maclean, and letting this desperate man off.

JAMES BEAUMONT.

Monday, July 18*th*, A.D. 1796.—James Beaumont, of Sheffield, a filesmith, was executed at the Tyburn without Micklegate Bar, for the murder of Sarah Turton, in the Nursery, at the second house from the white rails, coming towards Sheffield (now standing). Beaumont was parted from his wife (who at the time lived in Barley-field, and kept a small shop), and was living with Sarah Turton as his wife. He killed her by blows and strangulation, on Monday night, the 9th of May. After he had killed the woman, he went to his wife's house, and called her up, intending, it was believed, to murder her also ; she, perceiving something wild in his manner, refused to let him in. He left several children. His wife lived many years afterwards in a very creditable manner. She visited her unfortunate husband in the condemned cell, who told her that had he taken her advice, he would not then have been in that terrible situation.

Owen Pendegrass.

Saturday, April 8th, A.D. 1797. — Owen Pendegrass, a private in the 88th regiment of foot, and a native of Ireland, was executed at the Tyburn without Micklegate Bar, for robbing on the highway Mr. Thomas Todd, butcher, upon Heworth Moor, near the city of York. He died penitent, confessing his guilt.

Robert Dyson.

Wednesday, August 29th, A.D. 1797.— Robert Dyson, aged 35 years, late of the post-office at Bawtry, was executed at the Tyburn without Micklegate Bar, for embezzling a three months' bill and destroying letters. He was born at Misson, near Bawtry, and put out a town's apprentice. Being of an active turn of mind, he attracted the notice of a Mr. Bower, of Bawtry (a justice of the peace), who gave him a liberal education, and appointed him to be his clerk, in which situation he conducted himself with more than ordinary ability. He was afterwards taken into the employ of Mr. Fisher as a deputy postmaster, and continued with that gentleman upwards of seven years. During this period he acquired a handsome fortune, having successfully speculated largely in various matters. To this bent of mind may be attributed his untimely exit, for being rather embarrassed about July last, and not willing to make his case known, it unfortunately happened that in course of business he discovered a letter to have been forwarded to their office by mistake. On looking at the direction he recollected the hand-writing ; he opened it, and finding a remittance enclosed for a house in London, amounting to £70, in bills, &c., he applied the same for the relief of his exigency, and destroyed the letter. A monetary relief produced indescribable anguish. He said that he was prompted to the deed with the flattering hope that, 'as the letter was sent wrong, he should be able to make up the sum before any discovery was made. Such are the particulars of this unfortunate man, who left a wife and one daughter to lament his unhappy lot. On Tuesday afternoon, a pathetic and well-adapted sermon was preached by the Rev. G. Brown. During the greater part of the service he appeared to be much dejected, but was rather in a more composed state when the discourse was delivered.

He passed his last evening, as well as several former ones, in acts of true devotion, and was a sincere penitent.

He was conveyed in a cart to the usual place of execution, without Micklegate Bar. On arriving there he was attended by the ordinary, with whom he passed about half an hour in prayer. His devotions being ended, the awful preparations commenced, and about twelve o'clock he was turned off amidst a large concourse of people, including a great number of his neighbours from Bawtry and Doncaster, where he was well known and respected. His body, after hanging an hour, was cut down and put into an oak coffin, provided by his wife, upon which was a breastplate, with the following inscription:—

"ROBERT DYSON,

DIED THE 30TH OF AUGUST, 1797,

AGED THIRTY-FIVE YEARS."

His remains were conveyed to Bawtry direct from the gallows in a hearse, and there buried in the churchyard.

His wife and daughter afterwards kept a glass and china shop at Bawtry, where she and her husband were greatly respected; and much sympathy was manifested by the surrounding neighbourhood for their unfortunate and unhappy situation.

PETER BUCK, ROBERT HOLLINGWORTH, AND
GEORGE LEDGER.

Saturday, April 7th, A.D. 1798.—The above three unfortunate men were executed at the Tyburn without Micklegate Bar, for highway robbery at York.

Buck was a tanner at Ripley. He was charged with robbing on the highway Mr. Richard Terry, of Ripon, gentleman, on the 30th of August, 1797, in the township of Farnham; taking from him a pocket-book containing notes and bills to the amount of £1,500, or thereabouts ; also a common harding purse, containing £180 in gold, or thereabouts.

Hollingworth and Ledger, the former a labourer, and the latter a shoemaker, both of Rotherham, near Sheffield, had long been the terror of the neighbourhood, particularly to persons attending market leaving after dark for the country. They had robbed at different times, in the neighbourhood of Rotherham, Mr. William Wing, of Kimberworth Park ; Mr. Spurr, of the Ewes ; Mr. Matcham, of Ravenfield ; Mr. Hinchcliffe, of Rotherham ; Mr. Wood, of the Haugh ; Mr. Whitehead, of Whiston ; Mr. Shaw, of Whitwell ; Mr. Wildsmith, of Ravenfield ; and Mr. Parker, of Brinsworth.

Hollingworth confessed to these different robberies, also to breaking into the shop of William Thompson, shoemaker, at Tinsley, and taking thereout a quantity of hide and calf leather. It was most singular that these two were never seen together in the day time, but were, as was generally thought, perfect strangers to each other. That two men — one a stout tall man, and the other a broad-set man, were well known as being the parties who committed the robberies, and it was also believed that they were Rotherham men. This game they carried on several years, without being in the slightest suspected ; for Ledger, the lesser, kept a shoemaker's shop at the bottom of the Shambles, and was always at work, although a great cock-fighter. The other, also, was at no time seen idling or slinking about, and was never known to be in Ledger's shop. Though these robberies were frequent, and carried out with such desperate determination, the authorities were totally at fault, and seemed to suspect any one but the right men. That which led to their capture was, the stopping of William Nicholson, a carrier, on Thorne-common, near the Red House, at the dead hour of the night. This man made a stout resistance, being a very powerful fellow and good game. He and his dog held them at bay a considerable time, and a most terrible and bloody fight took place, after which the robbers deemed it prudent to retire. In the scuffle, Hollingworth's hat fell off, as did also Nicholson's ; and each got the other's hat. Nicholson called them up at the Red House (now occupied by Mr. Matthew Ellis) and presented a woeful appearance, being covered with blood and dirt. He then discovered that he had changed hats with one of the robbers, and early the next morning it was handed over to the authorities, who soon discovered, from the hatter's name, from whom it was purchased. The hatter, on being applied to, recollected selling such a hat to Hollingworth. They immediately sent a person with it to Hollingworth's wife, and on the question being asked if she knew it, she at once said it was her husband's. Hollingworth was arrested at his work the same day, and thinking to save himself, impeached his companion. When the constables went to arrest Ledger, who was hard at work in his shop, he was talking to several people upon the all-engrossing subject of the robbery, which had spread like lightning first thing in the morning. Thomas Raper, of the Ickles, who was waiting for him finishing mending his shoes, one of the parties in the shop when the constables entered, said his colour came and went very quick; and Ledger declared he did not know such a man as Hollingworth; that he was in bed at the time of the robbery; and, by his firmness, seemed to create doubts in the minds of the authorities, at first, as to whether he was really the right man. However, both were committed to the assizes, and, but for a fresh piece of evidence, which seemed accidentally to arise, it was believed that Hollingworth's evidence would not have hung him. As has been already stated, they stopped Mr. Wm. Wing, some years before, on his way home from Rotherham market to Kimberworth, and robbed him of his money and watch. This watch was sold by Ledger, some time after, to a recruiting sergeant, who was about leaving the town. The sergeant happening to return to Rotherham at the time when the chief topic of conversation was the enumeration of the robberies, as confessed to by Hollingworth; and Mr. Wing's watch being frequently named, it struck the soldier, that on his leaving Rotherham several years ago, he purchased a watch from Ledger, which he then had upon him. On this being made known, Mr. Wing's watchmaker desired to see the watch, and said that if it was the one stolen it would have in it a wheel of a certain description, different somewhat to the rest of the works; and this being found to be as the watchmaker stated, corroborated Hollingworth's statement, and both received sentence of death. After condemnation, it was found necessary to keep them in separate cells, for Ledger became so furious, bordering almost on madness, declaring he would murder Hollingworth, and even on their way to the gallows would have struck him had not the executioner taken the precaution to pinion him before he left the Castle. Hollingworth was a native of Bramley, near Rotherham, at which place his widow resided many years after his execution, and taught a small school.

WILLIAM LARKIN.

Saturday, August 18th, A.D. 1798.—William Larkin, aged 23, was executed at the Tyburn without Micklegate Bar, for forgery. This unfortunate man, after his conviction, conducted himself with great propriety, and died truly penitent, acknowledging the justice of his sentence.

RICHARD CLEGG.

Monday, July 15th, A.D. 1799.—Richard Clegg was executed at the Tyburn without Micklegate Bar, for the wilful murder of John Morson. After execution his body was delivered to the surgeons of the County Hospital for dissection.

MARY THORP AND MICHAEL SIMPSON.

Monday, March 17th, A.D. 1800. — Mary Thorp and Michael Simpson were executed at the Tyburn without Micklegate Bar.

Mary Thorp for the wilful murder of her illegitimate child. She was a decent, respectable looking young woman, and had, during the whole of her confinement in the Castle, manifested the most sincere contrition for the dreadful crime of which she had been guilty, and after her trial acknowledged herself to be verily guilty.

Michael Simpson, for the murder of Thomas Hodgson, by administering to him a dose of deadly poison. After execution, their bodies were delivered to the surgeons for dissection, pursuant to their respective sentences. The above unfortunate man persisted to the last in asserting his innocence of the crime for which he was about to suffer, which fact was proved eighteen months afterwards by the confession of the wretch who did the deed.

JOHN MCWILLIAMS, SARAH BAYLEY, AND WILLIAM DALRYMPLE.

Saturday, April 12th, A.D. 1800.—John McWilliams, aged 28, for forgery at Sheffield ; Sarah Bayley, aged 25, for paying forged notes, and William Dalrymple, aged 35, for robbing Mr. Green's bank at Malton. The three culprits were executed at the Tyburn without Micklegate Bar, in the presence of a large number of spectators.

ELIZABETH JOHNSON.

Saturday, August 23rd, A.D. 1800.—Elizabeth Johnson was executed at the Tyburn without Micklegate Bar, for uttering a forged one pound bill, purporting to be drawn by the Governor and Company of the Bank of England. At the time when the awful sentence of death was passed upon her, this unfortunate woman appeared totally insensible to her dreadful situation, and continued so up to the time of her execution.

JAMES DOUGHTY, RICHARD HOLLIDAY, EDWARD TATTERSALL, GEORGE SEDGWICK, AND THOMAS HODGSON.

Saturday, May 2nd, A.D. 1801.—The above culprits were executed at the Tyburn without Micklegate Bar :—

James Doughty, aged 22, and Richard Holliday, aged 25, for sheep-stealing. Doughty was a native of Haxby, near York, and Holliday was a native of Acklam, near Malton. Edward Tattersall, George Sedgwick, and Thomas Hodgson, for uttering forged notes, purporting to be one pound Bank of England notes.

SAMUEL LUNDY.

Saturday, April 11th, A.D. 1801.—Samuel Lundy,

aged 37, was executed at the Tyburn without Micklegate
Bar, for cow stealing. He was a native of Newbald, near
Market Weighton.

EDWARD HUGHES.

Saturday, August 29th, A.D. 1801.—Edward Hughes, a
private soldier in the 18th Light Dragoons, was executed at
the Tyburn without Micklegate Bar, for a rape. Great
interest was made to save the life of this unhappy criminal,
and a respite for fourteen days from the time prisoners are
usually executed, was obtained. But the crime was considered to be so peculiarly atrocious, aggravated by the
circumstance of his military profession, that no further re-
mission could be obtained. He was a Roman Catholic,
aged 19, and was attended after his conviction by a priest
of that persuasion. He was committed to the Castle on
the 27th day of April, on the oath of Mary Brown, of
Tollerton, with having actually ravished her, and having
had carnal knowledge of her body against her consent, in a
field in the parish of Easingwold, on Monday, the 20th of
April. He was the last executed at the old drop.

JAMES ROBERTS, WILLIAM BARKER, AND WILLIAM
JACKSON.

Saturday, August 28th, A.D. 1802.—The above three unfortunate fellows were executed behind the Castle walls, on
the new drop, which was the first time of its being used.

Thomas Roberts, for stealing nineteen sheep.

William Barker, for stealing three horses, and

William Jackson, for a robbery in the house of Mr.
Wetherhead, at Malton.

The new drop was erected by Mr. Joseph Halfpenny, of
Blake Street, joiner, of this city, and those unfortunate men
suffered by the hands of John Curry, the executioner, who
had been appointed at the summer assizes to that office.
He had been a convicted felon.

JOHN TERRY AND JOSEPH HEALD.

Monday, March 14th, A.D. 1803.—John Terry and

Joseph Heald were executed at the new drop at the Castle, for the wilful murder of Elizabeth Smith, near Wakefield. Their bodies were afterwards delivered to the surgeons for dissection.

ROBERT BURGESS.

Saturday, April 2nd, A.D. 1803.—Robert Burgess was executed at the new drop behind the Castle, for horse-stealing. He was 35 years of age, and was a native of Ackworth, near Wakefield.

MARTHA CHAPEL.

Saturday, August 1st, A.D. 1803.—Martha Chapel, a fine-looking young woman, only nineteen years of age, was executed upon the new drop, behind the walls of the Castle, for the wilful murder of her child. She died penitent, acknowledging the justice of her sentence.

JOHN MANSFIELD.

Saturday, August 20th, A.D. 1803.—John Mansfield, chimney-sweeper, was executed at the new drop, without the walls of the Castle of York, for attempting a rape on the body of Isabella Ord, the wife of John Ord, of Craythorne, in the North Riding, and afterwards robbing her on the king's highway.

The atrocity of this malefactor's crime cannot be more fully given to the world, than by the following facts, which were corroborated on his trial by evidence of respectability. It appeared that the above named Isabella Ord went on the 5th of April last to one Rachel Thompson's, who lives about eight miles from Craythorne, for the purpose of assisting her to remove some furniture, and received two shillings for her labour; that she returned between five and six o'clock, and on her road home between Harlsey and Ingleby, she met Mansfield, who demanded her money, and repeated to her three different times, "Your money, you bitch." She replied, "I have got none; where must such a poor old woman like me get any money ? " He then said, " You old bitch, I'll kiss you," and then threw her down, and tewed her very much with her clothes up ; upon which she told him, "I have got two shillings, if you release me you shall have it." She then rose from the ground, took her two shillings out of her pocket, and dropped it between her gown and her petticoat upon the road, thinking to save it ; he then caught hold of her again, and threw her down upon the dirt collected on the side of the turnpike ; she then called out, but he clapped his hand across her mouth and nose, and swore if she made the least resistance, he would ram his brush down her throat, and frequently said he would let her see her guts out ; he then tore her clothes off her back, all except her shift ; he then stood with his hand in his pocket, and looked down the road ; she thought he was upon the point of taking out of his pocket a knife, or some other instrument, for the purpose of murdering her. A gentleman happened then to be coming upon the road, whom she believed he saw, for he immediately gathered up her clothes. She still continued laying on the ground, and durst not stir, during which time he put the clothes he had gathered up into his soot-bag, took up the two shillings then lying upon the road and put it into his right breeches pocket, leaped over the hedge adjoining the road, and laid a heavy curse upon her. As soon as he had got over the hedge, she got up and saw a gentleman coming, and made a signal for him to come faster ; when the gentleman came up, he took her to the nearest farm-house, and gave orders that immediate search should be made, and he would pay all expenses. This was done, and Mansfield was apprehended at Lockley.

He said he had been nine years on board a man-of-war, was at the battle of Copenhagen ; that when there, he fell down the hatchway of the ship he was in, and had thereby received a severe wound in his head, since which the least liquor deranged his intellects, and that he recollected nothing of the commission of the crime with which he stood charged.

His behaviour since his condemnation has been truly becoming, and he yesterday attended Divine Service in the chapel, when the Rev. G. Brown, the ordinary, delivered an impressive discourse (with which the culprit seemed much affected) from the following text : " Because he hath appointed a day in the which he will judge the world by that Man whom he hath ordained ; whereof he hath given assurance unto all men, in that he hath raised him from the dead."—Acts xvii., 31.

He was conducted to the drop at eleven o'clock this morning, and after some time spent in prayer, he was cut off from this world to meet the righteous Judge of all.

JOSEPH WALLER.

Saturday, April 14th, A.D. 1804.—Joseph Waller, a native of Holme-on-Spalding Moor, was executed at the new drop, behind the walls of the Castle, for the robbery of Mr. Potts, near Fulford, of two five-guinea notes. This unfortunate young man acknowledged his guilt previous to his execution, and died truly penitent.

JONATHAN ELLIS.

Saturday, August 9th, A.D. 1804.—Jonathan Ellis, of Aldwick-upon-Dearne, was executed upon the new drop behind the Castle walls, for a rape, which he committed upon Elizabeth Widdeson. He confessed his guilt, and met his fate with composure.

JOHN WILKINSON AND ANN HEYWOOD.

Monday, March 18th, A.D. 1805.—John Wilkinson and Ann Heywood atoned their guilt upon the new drop behind the walls of the Castle, for the horrid crime of murder.

John Wilkinson, aged 32, for the wilful murder of his lawful wife, and Ann Heywood, aged 23, for the unnatural murder of her illegitimate child.

BENJAMIN ALDROYD.

Monday, May 29th, A.D. 1805.—Benjamin Aldroyd was executed at the new drop, behind the walls of the Castle, for the wilful murder of his own father. He confessed his guilt to the ordinary, the Rev. George Brown, and died truly penitent.

GEORGE ORMOND.

Saturday, April 5th, A.D. 1806.—George Ormond, butler, aged 30, a native of Hull, was executed at the new drop, behind the walls of the Castle, for forgery on the bank of Raper, Clough, and Swann, of York. He acknowledged the offence for which he was about to suffer, and declared that it was the only crime he had ever perpetrated.

PETER ATKINSON.

Tuesday, May 6th, A.D. 1806.—Peter Atkinson, not quite sixteen years of age, was executed at the new drop, behind the walls of the Castle, for the attempted murder of Elizabeth Stockton, by wounding her on the head and face with the claw of a hammer, in a most dreadful manner, and leaving her as he supposed for dead. This was the second that was tried and condemned under Lord Ellenborough's Act.

THOMAS RICHARDSON.

Saturday, August 16th, 1806.—Thomas Richardson was executed at the new drop, behind the Castle walls, for robbing on the highway near Stokesley, Mr. Melburn. He confessed his crime, and died penitent.

THOMAS JEWETT.

Saturday, April 5th, A.D. 1807.—Thomas Jewett, aged 24, was executed at the new drop, behind the Castle, for violating the chastity of Elizabeth Stabler, a girl under ten years of age, his master's daughter. Up to the time of this unfortunate affair he was well respected, and bore a good character in the town and neighbourhood of Old Malton. He was by trade a blacksmith, and lived servant with

William Stabler, of Old Malton, blacksmith, in whose family he was an inmate. It appeared upon his trial that on Sunday, the 27th of July last, Mr. and Mrs. Stabler went to Castle Howard, leaving the care of the family to Jewett. The family consisted of five children, the eldest of which was the child on whom the abominable crime was committed, and who was at that time under ten years of age. The two boys went to the Sunday School, leaving only this girl Jewett, and an apprentice boy, and two children under four years of age, in the house. The apprentice was sent out of the way to fetch some water, and in his absence Jewett committed the foul crime for which he suffered an awful and untimely death.

SAMUEL PARAMAR AND JOHN ROBINSON.

Saturday, August 8th, A.D. 1807.—Samuel Paramar, aged 68, a native of Sheffield, was executed at the new drop behind the Castle, for committing a rape upon a young girl under ten years of age ; and at the same time and place, John Robinson, for the wilful murder of Elizabeth Wilkinson. They both evinced contrition for their crimes.

THOMAS WILBE, WILLIAM BARBER, JAMES WINTERBOTHAM, AND EDWARD STRAHAN.

Saturday, April 20th, A.D. 1808.—The above four un-happy culprits were executed at the new drop behind the Castle for the following crimes :—

Thomas Wilbe, aged 31, a native of Hull, for committing a rape upon a young girl under the age of ten years.

William Barber, aged 21, for committing a rape upon a young girl not more than ten years of age.

James Winterbotham and Edward Strahan, each aged 23, for highway robbery near Howden. At the place of execution they all acknowledged to the ordinary, the Rev. George Brown, their guilt and the justice of their sentences.

THOMAS ALLINGTON.

Saturday, March 28th, A.D. 1808.—Thomas Allington,

aged 27, was executed at the new drop, behind the walls of the Castle, for robbing Mr. Edward Latham on the Cave-road, near Gilberdyke. He was a fine young man, six feet high, and made a confession to the Rev. George Brown, before his execution.

JAMES BROWN.

Monday, March 20th, A.D. 1809.—James Brown, aged 38, of Cawood, was executed at the new drop behind the Castle for the wilful murder of Elizabeth Fletcher by administering to her with her food a strong dose of poison.

MARY BATEMAN.

Monday, March 20th, A.D. 1809.—Mary Bateman, aged 41, a native of Aisenby, in the parish of Topcliffe, near Thirsk, in the North Riding of Yorkshire, was executed at the new drop behind the Castle, for the wilful murder, by poison, of Rebecca Perigo, at Bramley, near Leeds. After the trial, which lasted eleven, hours, the jury conferred together for a few moments and found the prisoner guilty, after which the judge passed sentence of death in nearly the following words : — " Mary Bateman, you have been convicted of wilful murder by a jury who, after having examined your case with due caution, have been constrained by the force of evidence to pronounce you guilty, and it only remains for me to fulfil my painful duty by passing upon you the awful sentence of the law. After you have been so long in the situation in which you now stand, and harassed as your mind must be by long details of your crimes, and by listening to the suffering you have occasioned, I do not wish to add to your distress by saying more than my duty renders. necessary. Of your guilt, there cannot remain a particle of doubt in the breast of any one who has heard your case. You entered into a long and premeditated system of fraud, which you carried on for a length of time in a most astonishing manner, and by means one would have supposed could not, in this age and in this enlightened country, have been practised with success. To prevent a discovery of your complicated fraud, and the punishment which must have resulted therefrom, you deliberately contrived the death of the person you had so grossly injured, and that by means of poison, a mode of destruction against which there is no sure protection. But your guilty design was not fully accomplished, and after so extraordinary a lapse of time you are reserved as a signal example of the justice of that mysterious Providence which sooner or later overtakes guilt like yours. And at the very time when you were apprehended, there is the greatest reason to suppose that if your surviving victim had met you alone, as you wished him to do, you would have administered to him a more deadly dose, which would have completed the diabolical project you had long before contemplated and planned, but which at that time only partially succeeded, for upon your person at that moment was found a phial containing a most deadly poison. For crimes like yours, in this world, the gates of mercy are closed ; but the law, while it dooms you to death, has in its mercy afforded you time for repentance, and the assistance of pious and devout men, whose admonitions, and prayers, and counsels may assist to get you all the better prepared for another world, where even crimes, if sincerely repented of, may find mercy. The sentence of the law is, and the Court doth award it, that you be taken to the place from ,whence you came, and from thence on Monday next to the place of execution, there to be hanged by the neck until you are dead, and that your body be given to the surgeons to be dissected and anatomized, and may Almighty God have mercy upon your soul ! "

The prisoner having intimated that she was pregnant, the Clerk of Arraigns said, " Mary Bateman, what have you to say that immediate execution should not be awarded against you ? " On which the prisoner pleaded that she was twenty-two weeks gone with child. On this plea the judge ordered the Sheriff to impanel a jury of matrons. This order created a general consternation among the ladies, who hastened to quit the Court, to prevent the execution of so painful an office being imposed upon them. His lordship in consequence ordered the doors to be closed, and in about half-an-hour twelve married women being impanelled, they were sworn in court, charged to inquire whether the prisoner was with quick child. The jury of matrons then retired with the prisoner, and on their return into Court delivered their verdict, which was that Mary Bateman was not with quick child,—in fact, she was not with child at all. The execution of course was not respited, and she was remanded back to prison.

As soon as she returned to her cell, she took her infant child and gave it the breast, a circumstance which considerably affected the gaoler who attended her on this melancholy occasion. During the brief interval between her receiving sentence of death and her execution, the Rev. George Brown took great pains to prevail upon her to acknowledge and confess her crime. On his touching on the subject of the Quaker ladies, whose sudden death he mentioned, she seemed perfectly to understand his meaning, but wished to avoid all further pressing upon the subject by saying she was at that time confined in childbirth, but the impression left upon the mind of the Ordinary was, that she knew much more on this subject than she chose to communicate. Though the prisoner behaved with her usual decorum during the few hours that remained of her existence, and readily joined in the customary office of devotion, no traces of that deep compunction of mind which, for crimes like hers, must be felt where repentance is sincere, could be observed. She maintained her caution and mystery to the last. On the day preceding her execution, she wrote a letter to her husband, in which she inclosed her wedding-ring with a request that it might be given to her daughter. In this letter she lamented the disgrace she had brought upon her husband and family, but declared her entire ignorance of the crime for which she was about to suffer, though she acknowledged she had been guilty of many frauds. The letter also stated that she had made her peace with God. It will hardly be credited, though it is a certain fact, that this unhappy woman was so addicted to fraud, that even when in confinement on a charge which affected her life, she was incapable of refraining from her witchcraft. A young female prisoner had, in her presence, expressed a wish to see her sweetheart. Mary Bateman took the girl aside and said, if she could procure a sum of money to be made into a charm, and sewed into her own stays, the young man would be compelled to visit her. The simple girl complied, and Mary Bateman having prepared a potent spell, it was bound round the breast of this young woman. No sweetheart made his appearance, and the faith of her young dupe, unlike that of Perigo's, began to waver, and, in a fit of despair, she unbound the charm to take out her money, but it had vanished away. This circumstance being represented to the Governor of the Castle, part of the spoil was refunded, and Mary Bateman directed that the girl should have clothes of hers to balance the account; but the balance was paid by the friends of the prisoner. On Sunday night the Ordinary visited her again, but finding her obstinately bent on denying the crime for which she was about to suffer, he represented to her the danger and folly of her conduct. Exhortations and remonstrances were alike in vain. At five o'clock on Monday morning she was removed from her cell and from her infant child, which lay sleeping on the bed, unconscious of the fate of its unhappy mother. She stopped a moment and kissed it for the last time. If anything could excite the tender emotions of conscience, we might well imagine the present events would tend to do so; but nothing seemed to touch the hardness and depravity of her nature. When the solemn rite of communion was proposed, the necessity of confession was again introduced, but without effect, and she joined in this rite without unburdening her mind of its guilty secrets. The hour of execution arrived,—the sheriff and his attendants demanded her body for execution, and, after a few moments, they proceeded to the fatal platform. The number of persons assembled was much greater than usual on such occasions, and many from a great distance, and a large company from Leeds and the neighbourhood. The appearance of the prisoner upon the platform created a visible emotion among the spectators—not of brutal insult, as once disgraced the British character in the metropolis, but of awe and deep commiseration. The most respectful silence prevailed during the few moments spent in prayer, except when interrupted by a half-suppressed ejaculation for mercy on the wretched sufferer. The moment when the executioner was preparing to finish his awful scene, the Ordinary again addressed the culprit in a low tone of voice, inquiring if she had any communication to make? She replied, she had not ; she was innocent. The next moment terminated her existence as to this world, and sent her to another more awful tribunal. Her body, after hanging the usual time, was cut down and sent to the General Infirmary for dissection. In this awful manner terminated the earthly career of Mary Bateman. The curiosity excited by the singularity and atrocity of her crimes extended to the viewing of her lifeless remains. Though the hearse did not reach Leeds till midnight, it was met by a considerable number of people, and so great was the general curiosity to see her, that the sum of thirty pounds was raised for the benefit of the General Infirmary, by receiving from each of the visitors the sum of threepence.

JONATHAN GRAHAM.

Saturday, April 9th, A.D. 1809.—Jonathan Graham, a young man, was executed at the new drop behind the Castle, for the wilful murder of his own father, by shooting him. This unfortunate young fellow acknowledged the crime for which he was condemned to suffer, and left this world under feelings of penitence and contrition.

DAVID ANDERSON.

Saturday, August 20th, A.D. 1809.—The above-mentioned culprit was executed at the new drop behind the city gaol, for uttering bad notes. He was taken in the house of Robert Dentis flour-dealer, in Low Ousegate, in this city, by whom he was betrayed, and who was the principal evidence against him. He was tried, convicted, and sentence of death was passed upon him at the Summer Assizes. When he arrived upon the new drop, he kneeled down upon a rug, which he spread there for the purpose, and uttered a most fervent prayer. When he rose from his knees he looked around him, and met his fate with fortitude and resignation. This was the first time the new drop was used belonging to the city gaol. The executioner's name was William Curry, of the Castle.

Edward Francis Spence, Robert King, Robert Vessey, Robert Burton, and Frances Thompson.

Saturday, April 7th, A.D. 1810.—The culprits above mentioned suffered at the new drop behind the walls of the Castle.

Edward Francis Spence, aged 31 ; Robert King, aged 40 ; Robert Vessey, aged 46 ; Robert Burton, aged 38 ; and Frances Thompson, a widow, of Beverley, aged 31, for circulating forged notes and counterfeit coin, at Kingston-on-Hull.

Joshua Beaumont.

Saturday, July 14th, A.D. 1810.—Joshua Beaumont, aged 35, of Kirk Heaton, was executed at the new drop behind the walls of the Castle, for the wilful murder of Lucy Brooks.

William Chester.

Saturday, April 6th, A.D. 1812.—William Chester was executed at the new drop behind the walls of the Castle for housebreaking. His execution attracted thousands of spectators. He was a young and respectable man.

The latter end of April, this year, was remarkable for the removal of the old Tyburn without Micklegate Bar. It was first erected on the 7th day of March, 1379, so that it appears to have stood there a period of 433 years. The last man that was executed at the old gallows was in the month of August, 1801. It stood eleven years after it was disused.

George Mellor, Thomas Smith, and William Thorpe.

Friday, January 8th, A.D. 1813.—The above three culprits were executed at the new drop behind the Castle walls.

George Mellor, aged 22, cloth-dresser, of Longroyd Bridge ; Thomas Smith, aged 22, cloth-dresser, of Huddersfield ; and William Thorpe, aged 23, cloth-dresser, of Huddersfield. The jury were charged with the prisoners in the usual form, upon an indictment which alleged that the prisoner Mellor, on the 28th of April last, fired a pistol loaded with bullets, &c., at William Horsfall, by which firing he received a mortal wound on the left side of the belly, of which wound he languished till the 30th of April, and then died ; and that the prisoners Thorpe and Smith were present, aiding and abetting Mellor to commit the said crime, and that the three prisoners wilfully murdered the said William Horsfall. The jury found them all guilty, and sentence of death was passed upon them by Justice Le Blanc. Their bodies were afterwards delivered to the surgeons for dissection.

Fourteen Malefactors.

Saturday, January 16th, A.D. 1813.—The following fourteen malefactors were executed on the drop behind the Castle, for various burglaries, felonies, and tumultuously assembling in the night-time, to destroy shearing-frames, machinery, to collect fire-arms, and to demolish mills, particularly that of Mr. William Cartwright, at Rawfolds, in Leveredge, near Berstall.

John Swallow, aged 37, late of Briestwhistle, near Wakefield, coal-miner.

John Balley, aged 31, late of Thornhill, near Wakefield, clothier, &c.

Joseph Fisher, aged 33, late of Briestwhistle aforesaid, coal-miner.

The above three unhappy men were convicted (together with John Lamb, who was afterwards reprieved), of a burglary in the house of Samuel Moxon, of Upper Whilley, in the West Riding of the county of York. They went armed and in disguise to the said Samuel Moxon's house on the night of the 3rd of July last, and feloniously entered the place, and by threats of violence obtained several notes, some silver, a quantity of butter, and wearing apparel.

Job Hey, aged 40 ; John Hill, aged 36 ; and William

Hartley, aged 41, were convicted of a burglary in stealing
fire-arms in the night-time out of the house of Mr. George
Haigh, of Copley Gate, in Skircote, near Elland, in the
parish of Halifax, farmer. These men went to the said
George Haigh's house armed with pistols, and, having by
intimidation procured admittance, succeeded in obtaining
by violence and threats a gun and a pistol, &c. While
they were knocking at the door, Mr. Haigh got up, and
standing upon the stair inquired, "Who's there?" The
answer from without was—"Our master, General Ludd, has
sent for your fire-arms"—they had got the gun and pistol.
They said to his servant, "Tell your master that if he does
not sell his milk in the neighbourhood at two pence per
quart, they would visit him again on a similar purpose."
The principal witness against them was an accomplice in
the robbery. The pistol was found in the house of Job
Hey, also three pounds and a quarter of gunpowder.

James Hey, aged 25.

Joseph Crowther, aged 31 ; and

Matthew Boyle, aged 46, were convicted of robbery, in
the house of James Brook, of Fair Town, in the parish of
Huddersfield, on the 29th day of November last, and stealing
a one-pound note, a three-shilling piece, and putting the
persons therein in bodily fear.

These three men were mere robbers, and do not appear
to have any other object in view but the obtaining of plunder.
In the course of the same night they plundered several
other houses in the neighbourhood of Fair Town, in the
said West Riding, and at the close of their wicked expedition shared the profits, amounting to £15 each.

James Haigh, aged 28, late of Dalton, clothier.

Jonathan Dean, aged 30, late of Huddersfield, cloth-
dresser.

John Ogden, aged 28, late of the same place.

John Walker, aged 31, late of the same place ; and

Thomas Brook, aged 32, late of Lockwood, near Huddersfield. The five culprits, after a trial which lasted the whole
day, were convicted on a statute of the 9th of George III.,
which made it a capital felony to demolish, or to begin to
demolish, any mill of any description whatsoever. It appears
that these deluded men, in company with George Mellor

and William Thorp, who commanded on that occasion, and upwards of one hundred other persons, marched in military order and array, being armed with guns and pistols, axes, hammers, &c., such as are used for breaking stones on the highways, and attacked the mill of Mr. Cartwright, of Rawfolds (about six miles from Huddersfield), who used machinery obnoxious to the people employed in the dressing of cloth, and which they unhappily conceived to be destructive to their regular work. The attack was made on the night of the 11th of April last, and commenced with a discharge of guns and pistols. They were resisted with great spirit by Mr. Cartwright, and two of the assailants were mortally wounded and died soon after. Great numbers of these misguided men were afterwards apprehended, but only eight were brought to trial. The above five were convicted, three acquitted, and the rest discharged by proclamation, or on bail.

The whole of the above unhappy men were truly penitent when they ascended the scaffold, and all joined in singing that beautiful hymn in the Wesleyan Hymn Book—

" Behold the Saviour of mankind, &c."

At eleven o'clock in the morning the following convicts were executed :—

Joseph Crowther, aged 31, for burglary, leaving a wife and four children.

Nathan Hoyle, aged 46, for burglary, leaving a wife and seven children. Crowther and Hoyle were interred in the hoppet at the back of the Castle.

The bodies of the following five, all executed for burglary, connected with the Luddites, were taken home by their friends :—

John Hill, aged 36, leaving a wife and two children.

Jonathan Dean, aged 30, leaving a wife and seven children.

John Ogden, aged 28, leaving a wife and two children.

John Walker, aged 31, leaving a wife and five children ; and

Thomas Brook, aged 32, leaving a wife and three children. And at two o'clock on the same day :—

John Swallow, aged 37, leaving a wife and six children.

John Batley, aged 31, leaving a wife and one child.

Joseph Fisher, aged 33, leaving a wife and three children.

Toby Hey, aged 40, leaving a wife and seven children.

William Hartley, aged 41, leaving a wife and eight children.

James Hey, aged 25, leaving a wife but no children.

James Haigh, aged 28, leaving a wife and two children.

Their bodies were received for interment by their friends. James Hey was the son of a Methodist preacher. By this severe judicial visitation, fourteen wives were made widows, fifty-seven children became fatherless, and eight were turned upon the world helpless. Thus ended the executions of this most terrible day. Baron Thompson passed sentence of death upon them.

JOHN SENIOR, HENRY SUTCLIFFE, JOHN ROBINSON, JOHN JAMES, AND ROBERT TURNER.

Saturday, April 3rd, A.D. 1813.—The above were executed at the new drop behind the Castle.

John Senior for defrauding his creditors. He was a very stout man, about 6 feet 2 inches high, was born at Alverthorpe, in the parish of Wakefield, was 40 years of age, and left a widow and two children. He had several children by a former wife. This unfortunate man was the first who had suffered for a similar crime in the county.

Henry Sutcliffe, aged 29, was born near Halifax, was executed for forgery. He left a widow, to whom he had not been married a year. He was a person much respected.

John Robinson, aged 40, for robbing Mr. John Naylor, butcher, of Boroughbridge. He was a native of Newcastle-upon-Tyne, and had been twenty years in his Majesty's service as a doctor's mate in the navy. After quitting that service he travelled about as a quack doctor, and had lately taken a house in York, where he was apprehended the day after the robbery. He left a wife and three sons. He protested his innocence to the last, and said he was a murdered man.

John James, aged 32, for stabbing William Ridley, a bailiff.

Robert Turner, for the wilful murder of Margaret Appleby, of Yarm, by poisoning her at Middleham.

On Thursday morning a respite was received from Mr. Justice Le Blanc, for Rindleburg and Bottomley, during his Lordship's pleasure.

The case of Henry Sutcliffe was similar to that of Dr. Dodd, who was executed at Tyburn, June 27th, 1777.

JOSEPH BLACKBURN.

Saturday, April 8th, A.D. 1815.—Joseph Blackburn, attorney at Leeds, was executed at the new drop behind the Castle, for forging a stamp. He died confessing the crime for which he suffered.

GEORGE WHITE AND MARK BRAMAH.

Saturday, August 5th, A.D. 1815.—George White, aged 50, was executed at the new drop, for committing a rape upon a little girl under ten years of age, and Mark Bramah, aged 21, a native of Sheffield, was executed at the same time and place for a similar offence. White was a native of Snainton.

JAMES ORD.

Saturday, April 6th, A.D. 1816.—James Ord, of Marston, near Stockton-on-Tyne, was executed at the new drop for cutting and maiming Anthony Wilson. Ord was by trade a butcher.

MICHAEL PICKLES.

Monday, March 17th, A.D. 1817.—Michael Pickles was executed at the new drop, for the wilful murder and robbery of Mr. Joseph Greenwood, at Heptonstall.

DOCTOR DIERING.

Saturday, April 12th, A.D. 1817.—Doctor Diering was executed at the new drop behind the Castle, for a rape.

Benjamin Micklewaite and Benjamin Gartside.

Saturday, April 12th, A.D. 1817.—The above-mentioned culprits were executed at the new drop, for a burglary near Halifax.

William King.

Monday, July 7th, A.D. 1817.—William King was executed at the new drop, for the wilful murder of his reputed wife. He confessed his guilt, and died penitent.

Isaac Bradshaw.

Saturday, August 13th, A.D. 1817.—Isaac Bradshaw was executed at the new drop behind the walls of the Castle, for committing a rape upon a little girl under ten years of age.

Samuel Leatherhead.

Saturday, April 4th, A.D. 1818.—Samuel Leatherhead, for uttering and paying bad notes, was executed at the new drop behind the walls of the Castle.

Joseph Clayton, Samuel King, and Samuel Booth.

Saturday, May 15th, A.D. 1820.—Joseph Clayton was executed at the new drop behind the walls of the Castle, for uttering and circulating counterfeit notes.

Samuel King was executed at the same time and place, for highway robbery ; and

Samuel Booth, for shooting Thomas Parkin, gamekeeper to Mr. Wortley.

Joseph Pickersgill, Charles Puncheon, William Kettlewell, and Thomas Smith.

Saturday, August 12th, A.D. 1820.—Joseph Pickersgill, aged 27, for a highway robbery.

Charles Puncheon, aged 20, and William Kettlewell, aged 20, for house-breaking.

Thomas Smith, aged 28, for sheep-stealing. These unfortunate men were executed at the new drop on the date above mentioned.

The following lines were cut in the wall at the southside of the low grates, in the month of June, 1820, by Thomas Smith.

> " This prison is a house of care,
> A grave for man alive;
> A touchstone for to try a friend ;
> No place for man to thrive."

WILLIAM THOMPSON.

Monday, March 19th, A.D. 1821.—William Thompson, aged 40, was executed at the new drop behind the walls of the Castle, for the wilful murder of his wife, Elizabeth Thompson, at Henley, in the township of Appleton-le-Moors, in the parish of Lastingham, in the county of York.

MICHAEL SHAW.

Saturday, April 14th, A.D. 1821.—Michael Shaw, aged 56, was executed at the new drop behind the walls of the Castle, for robbing the dwelling-house of Joseph Booth, of Sowerby, near Halifax, on the nights of the 6th and 7th of October last, and stealing thereout a great quantity of linen and woollen drapery goods to the amount of £50.

Joseph Kershaw was also tried with him and found guilty, but has since been reprieved.

It appeared in evidence that a part of the stolen property was found, as described by Kershaw, within an inner wall ; and in a chamber chimney at Shaw's house, also a plan of Mr. Booth's house, which cost 40s. drawing.

When the constable went to Shaw's house to search for th eproperty, he found Shaw in bed. He arose and came down in his shirt ; and on knowing the constable's business, refused to let him search ; when a desperate battle ensued, in which Shaw defended himself with an iron crow, but was at length overcome and securely handcuffed. When in custody, Shaw was heard by the constable to say to Kershaw, that as he would get off, he was to go to Magson-House wood, and under a certain tree-root he would find the skeleton keys ; the constable and Kershaw went to the wood and found thirty-four picklock keys, and some of the property stolen from the prosecutor.

The Jury found both the prisoners guilty.

Shaw has left a wife and five children to lament his untimely fate, and since he received sentence, has behaved in a manner becoming his awful situation.

Yesterday an impressive sermon was delivered at the Castle, by the Rev. Mr. Flower, jun., the Ordinary, from St. Luke xiii. 5.

At eleven o'clock this unhappy man appeared on the platform, when, after spending a few moments in prayer, he was launched into eternity.

WILLIAM BROWN, *alias* MORLEY STUBBS.

William Brown, *alias* Morley Stubbs, aged 23, was found guilty of robbing John Armstrong, on the New Walk, near this city.

John Armstrong deposed. I reside in Walmgate, and work at Mr. Swale's factory, without Walmgate Bar. About nine o'clock on the evening of the 23rd November last, I was going to the Barrack Tavern ; I went on the New Walk. It was a fine night, rather moonlight. When I got within a few yards of the Blue Bridge, I saw two men coming over the bridge ; they came up to me. One of them was Brown. He (Brown) came and took me by the collar. I knew him well. He lived in the same street as I did ; nearly opposite. He asked me if I had got any money. I told him what money I had, I had worked hard for it and said, "Brown, thou art not going to rob me." The other man was standing just behind him. Brown struck me six or seven times with a short thick stick ; one blow on the side of the head brought me to the ground. He then got upon my breast with both his knees. They rifled my pockets, and took what money I had, which was 16s. in my breeches pocket, and a York note in my pocket-book, which was 'in the inside coat pocket. After robbing me, Brown still remained upon my breast, and the other man got a rail from the hedge and said, "D——n him, let us heave him over into the water." I begged of them to save my life, and said they might take my money. They put the rail betwixt my legs, and one of them took hold of one end of the rail, and the other man hold of the other end; and threw me over the corner of the bridge into the river Foss. I went overhead, and on rising to the surface of the water I caught hold of a post which was in the water, and called out "Murder!" repeatedly, as hard as I could. One of them came over the hedge, and tried two or three times to reach me with the rail, but I being so far in the water, he was not able to touch me. He then went to the top of the bridge and tried from thence to reach me with the rail, but was unable. I continued crying out "Murder!" The men left me, but I could not see which way they went. I kept hold of the post until some persons came and got me out. I was in a state of insensibility at the time, and could not tell who they were.

Christopher Jackson, George Dale, and William Clark were the persons who assisted in taking Armstrong from the water; the two former knew Brown and were certain he was the person they saw run from the bridge. The prisoner made no defence.

After the evidence had been summed up with great precision, the jury, after two or three minutes' consultation, found the prisoner guilty.

Mr. Raine, who presided as judge, immediately proceeded to pass the awful sentence of death upon the prisoner, which he did in the most solemn manner, nearly in the following words:—William Brown, you have been found guilty, by an intelligent and humane jury of your country, of an offence, which, in its least extent, is, by the law of this country, punishable with death. But the aggravated circumstances in your case in a double manner strongly urge this punishment to be inflicted; and were I not thus to speak and act, I should not be doing justice to the community at large, and likewise to my own feelings. I therefore in the most solemn manner inform you of the awful situation in which you now stand. I will not, I cannot, hold out a shadow of mercy ; for you not only robbed Armstrong of his little money (a great deal to him), but, with a most savage ferocity, maltreated him, and with another person, equally wicked and guilty as yourself, wished to add to the crime of robbing that of murder ; for you not only knocked the poor man down, but bruised him in that situation, and then, with ferocious cruelty, thrust him into the water, with the idea of taking away the existence of a fellow-creature, who had never done you the least harm, and thus thought of hiding the commission of a crime of so heinous a nature. I therefore beseech and strongly urge you, prisoner, to use the short time you have to remain on earth in a becoming and suitable manner ; attend to the instructions of your spiritual advisers ; apply to that Throne where mercy alone can be had ; confess this and all your other sins, and rest assured you may, even at the eleventh hour, obtain pardon from your offended God. I conjure you, with all the powers I am able, not to neglect this important concern, as there is no hope whatever that your life will be spared. Prepare, then, in the right manner, to stand before another and greater tribunal, at which you must shortly appear ; you may yet work out your salvation, but it must be with fear and trembling. It now only remains for me to add the awful sentence of the law, which is "that you be taken from hence to the place from whence you came, and from thence to the place of execution, there to be hanged by the neck till you are dead ; and may the Lord have mercy upon your soul."

Yesterday afternoon an appropriate sermon was delivered by the Rev. Mr. Flower, sen., from St. Luke xxiii. 42. Before Brown retired to his cell, he shook hands with all the prisoners, and said, "Farewell, I hope we shall meet in another world," and wept much.

About one o'clock this unfortunate young man appeared on the platform, and, after a few minutes spent in prayer, was launched into eternity in the presence of an unusual number of spectators.

It has been reported that Brown had nearly made his escape from prison, but this is not correct. He acknowledges taking the pocket-book, but denies throwing the man into the water. He has behaved himself with becoming resignation.

The above man is the second person that has suffered death at the City New Gaol. The first was David Anderson, who suffered on the 20th of August, 1809.

ANN BARBER.

Monday, August 30th, A.D. 1821.—Ann Barber, aged 45, was executed at the new drop, for the wilful murder of her husband by poison.

Ann Barber was married to James Barber in the year 1805, at Rothwell, near Wakefield, and from the evidence it appears she had formed an improper connection with a person of the name of Thompson, which in all probability has brought her to this untimely death. The trial was unusally long and interesting, the substance of which is as follows :—

John Hindle is a surgeon at Oulton, about a mile from Rothwell. Went to examine the body of the deceased on the 18th of March, the day on which the inquest was held. He opened it, and was enabled clearly to ascertain the cause of his death. The stomach was in a very putrid state ; the coats of it much corroded and inflamed. He attributed the immediate cause of Barber's death to mineral poison, which would produce all the effects he observed. Took mineral poison (white arsenic), from the coats of the stomach. He discovered it by tests ; a solution of the ammoniate of copper, which is of a purple colour, but when combined with arsenic becomes green. He tried it also with nitrate of silver, which is a very delicate test, and found the same result. He opened the body to the lungs. They were very black ; which he looked upon as a greater criterion of mineral poison having been received, than anything he can mention. When he first saw the body he was convinced the deceased had died by taking mineral poison. The body exhibited livid spots, and the skin of the stomach was very green, twice the breadth of a man's hand. The internal appearances confirmed this opinion. Thinks the deceased must have taken more than a drachm, from the account he received of the effects it produced.

G. B. Reinhardt is a chemist and druggist at Wakefield. Has seen the prisoner before. She has been at his shop several times. Remembers her being there on Friday the 16th of March, betwixt one and two o'clock. She wanted a pennyworth of mercury. He gave her it after some inquiry. She said she wanted it to poison mice. He gave her about six drachms. Arsenic is commonly called mercury. He is quite sure the prisoner is the woman to whom he sold it.

Jane Smirthwaite is mother to the prisoner, who was married to James Barber, for anything she knows, sixteen years ago, and lived with him up to his death. They had two children ; one of them is about sixteen, and the other ten. Remembers James Barber dying on a Saturday morning. Had seen him the day before several times. (The witness was here asked several questions, which she did not answer readily. Mr. Hardy reminded her, that though she was the prisoner's mother, she must give her evidence. She replied—" I am in years and very forgetful ; but must speak the truth as far as I can.")—She (the witness) called up Sarah Parker about five in the morning, because her daughter called her up and told her that James said he should not mend. Thinks the prisoner (her daughter) told her the night before that James would not get better. Thinks she had not been into Barber's house before she called up Sarah Parker. They went upstairs and found James very poorly. Sarah did not know whether he was dead or alive ; but he was alive when she got there. Sarah Parker came in, a little time after witness called her.

Thomas Spurr lives at Rhodes Green, three-quarters of a mile from the deceased. Saw him the night before he died, about half-past nine at night. Prisoner's brother was with him. Found deceased in the chamber. Prisoner was also there ; nobody else. The deceased was crying out, folding his arms across his bowels, " Oh ! dear me ; oh ! dear me." He was up, as if he had just got out of bed. He had on his coat and shirt. Conversed with him while the prisoner was by. She said to her husband, " Thou art going to run away, when they are coming to see thee." She took him by the arms and said, " Prithee get to bed again." He threw himself on the bed again, and still kept crying. Witness said to prisoner. " You've had a physician for the soul ; you want a physician for the body as well as the soul."

Deceased was then rolling about on the bed. He said it was her duty to take care of the body as well as the soul. She said, "There was no occasion; he would be dead before morning." Witness looked at deceased a few minutes, and then said to her brother, "Let us kneel down, John;" and he (the brother) went to prayer, and then the witness. Witness then shook hands with the deceased; and asked how he felt himself. He replied, "You have done me a deal of good." Witness soon after left him.

John Holmes lives at Potovens, near Wakefield. The prisoner took a house of him on the 21st of December. She wanted a small house and a stable. She said they were going to lead coals. The house had only one room. On the 26th she took possession of it; a young man was with her. He had a cart with "*Wm. Thompson*" on. They remained a week, living together in that house. They left because he wanted them to go away; he thought they were not man and wife.

Mark Parker is the husband of Sarah Parker, and a tenant of the deceased. Remembers the prisoner going from home. Before that, Thompson had come to live with her and her husband. He came at Martinmas. He had lived with a neighbouring farmer before then. Thompson went away with the prisoner on the morning of the 26th December. Had heard prisoner call her husband up before five o'clock, and say it was time for him to go to his work. Supposes he went; for witness never saw him that morning. A horse and cart came soon after. Witness got up, and went out; saw the prisoner and Thompson taking furniture out of Barber's house, and putting it into the cart. It was dark; but by the feel witness judged it was bed-stocks, a bed, and bed-linen. Witness went to Edward Barber's that morning, and told him. From what passed between them, witness watched where these people went to. They went to Potovens, near Wakefield. They had furniture and hay in the cart; "*Thompson, Rhodes Green*," was upon it.— He first saw the cart five weeks before Martinmas. It had not then Thompson's name upon it.

George Wadsworth, jun., is the son of the constable of Rothwell. Prisoner was in his charge on the 20th March, at William Farrow's. Brought her to York on the 22nd.

At Wm. Farrow's house on the evening of the 21st, she said she would tell him all the truth about it. She went to Wakefield on the 16th March, to Mr. Reinhardt's druggist's shop, and bought a pennyworth of mercury ; and when she got home in the evening, she put half of it in some warm ale and sugar, with intent to kill him. She said she was stalled (tired) of him. She said Thompson promised her marriage when anything ailed James.

George Wadsworth, sen., constable of Rothwell, was at the inquest. Prisoner was there. He took her into custody on the Tuesday morning following. She was taken by the witness to Wakefield and back that day. When taken to Reinhardt's at first she said she had never been there. A man reminded her he had seen her looking into the window ; she then said she might be on the steps, but was never in the shop. Witness gave her in charge to his son. Never used any promise or threat to induce her to confess. The postman came into the room and said, " You d——l at Lofthouse has let the cat out of the bag, and will hang you, mistress." She said, " Will he; will he ? but I'll take care he does not. It's all along of that devil I've done what I have done." Witness's son told witness what she had said to him.

John Smirthwaite is brother to the prisoner, and lived near her and her husband. Remembers there being a din in the neighbourhood ; witness sent for deceased, and asked if there was any difference between him and his wife. He said no ; but the neighbours made a disturbance, and called him a cuckold, and it unhinged his mind. He said he had thoughts of jumping into a pit as he came home. He said he would destroy himself some time or other.

After the evidence was gone through, his Lordship commented upon it for upwards of an hour. The jury then retired, and in about six minutes returned into court, and pronounced the prisoner—Guilty of Petit Treason and Murder. When called upon for her defence, she said, " I am innocent, sir, and leave it to God and my conscience."

The prisoner did not seem conscious of her situation during the trial ; but when the jury returned and gave their verdict, she became sensible of her dreadful situation, turned pale, trembled exceedingly, and fell upon the floor of the dock. She was raised by the gaoler; and his Lordship in the most impressive terms, passed sentence of death upon her, ordering her for execution this day, Monday. While his Lordship was passing sentence, she frequently interrupted him by protestations of her innocence.

This unhappy female was drawn to the place of execution on a sledge, and after spending a short time in prayer was launched into eternity.

Since sentence was passed upon her, she has behaved with becoming resignation. She has left two children, one sixteen, the other ten years of age.

There have been five women in the Castle for Petty Treason within the last seventy years, viz. Mary Ellah, hanged and burnt in 1757; Ann Sowerby, hanged and burnt in 1767; Eliza Bordingham, of Flambro', hanged and burnt in 1776; Ellen Bayston for poisoning her husband in 1785, sentenced to be kept in York Castle for life, being insane; and the above, Ann Barber.

GEORGE SMITH, JAMES BUTTERWORTH, JAMES BENNETT, WILLIAM BUCK, AND JAMES LAW.

Saturday, September 1st, A.D. 1821, the above five criminals were executed at the new drop behind the Castle.

George Smith for committing a rape upon a young lady of the name of Miss Robinson.

James Butterworth, for a burglary.

James Bennett and William Buck, for a highway robbery, and

James Law, for housebreaking.

JAMES MOSELEY AND WILLIAM ROBERTS.

Saturday, April 6th, A.D. 1822. —James Moseley, aged 31, was executed at the new drop behind the Castle, for the wilful murder of John Mackey. He was late of the parish of Sheffield, in the West Riding. And at the same time and place,

William Roberts, aged 27, was executed. He was charged upon the oath of John Barlow, of Hoyland, in the

West Riding, with having on the 5th day of November 1821, on the king's highway, in the parish of Rotherham, in the said Riding, feloniously stolen and carried away from the person of the said John Barlow, a red leather pocket-book, containing notes to the value of fifteen pounds and upwards.

WILLIAM JOHNSON.

Monday, March 24th, A.D. 1823.—William Johnson, aged 23, was executed at the new drop behind the Castle. He was charged upon the oath of William Stockdale, and others, with having feloniously robbed and murdered, upon the king's highway, in the parish of Leconfield, in the East Riding, on Friday the 27th day of December last, Richard Walker, late of Beverley, in the said Riding, servant.

Mr. Williams stated, very shortly, the outline of the facts. It appeared, that the deceased had been from three weeks to a month in the employ of Mr. Tygar, druggist, of Beverley ; that on the 27th of December, he was sent to take Mrs. Tygar in a gig to Driffield, in compliance with his master's orders. He left Driffield at two o'clock, in good health, on his return. He was seen at four o'clock, about five miles from Driffield on his way to Beverley, where, however, he did not arrive. It was not till some days after, his body was found in a ditch, in a field, in the parish of Leconfield, with his throat cut, and several contusions on his head and cheeks ; and it would be for them to consider whether he came to his death by his own hands.

He would now state the facts applicable to the prisoner at the bar. It would be proved, that on the road from Driffield, about four or five o'clock in the afternoon, the deceased was seen in company with the prisoner, four or five miles from the place where the body was found. Three days after what he was assuming to be a murder had been committed, the prisoner disposed of a watch which the deceased had in his possession some days before. The prisoner at the bar was taken up on the day the body was discovered, wearing a waistcoat of the same colour, and with the same kind of binding, which the deceased had on ; and a coat, lying on his bed, would be proved to be precisely of the same description as the one worn by the deceased; a hat, which the prisoner claimed, would be identified, he understood, to be the one worn by the deceased on the day he was murdered. There were some circumstances connected with the conduct of the prisoner, which he should not animadvert upon. The prisoner denied having been more than one mile and a half from Driffield, on the day in question. A button, apparently belonging to the dress of the prisoner, was found near the body; such a one was missing from his dress. The learned counsel stated the case with great forbearance as respected the prisoner.

Mr. Tygar was the first witness examined. He confirmed the statement of the learned counsel, as to the journey of the deceased to Driffield; his being missed, and the finding of the body with a severe contusion on the forehead, the brow being beat in, so that the interior of the head was visible; the right ear was torn off by the roots, the strings of the ear lying on the cheek; there was a small wound on the cheek, and the throat cut from ear to ear—the windpipe being completely severed. He described the clothes the prisoner had on.

Thomas Jefferson, the deceased's uncle, saw him on the 27th of December, and accompanied him about a mile from Driffield. He left him about three o'clock. Deceased had a watch.

Thomas Thomson, met the prisoner on the 27th of December, on the road from Driffield to Beverley, dressed in a smock frock, and a grey hat. It was about three o'clock in the afternoon. He inquired the road to Beverley.

Robert Pearson, saw the prisoner going from Driffield to Beverley, on the Friday in Christmas week. He asked, if that was the road to Beverley. He had no bundle. He saw him the next morning coming from Dawson's mill, which is situated about three or four hundred yards from the high road, with a bundle. He was dressed in a smock frock, and white hat.

Joseph Pike, met the deceased and prisoner on the 27th of December, about four miles and a half from Beverley. He was positive the prisoner was the man. The deceased had a red waistcoat on.

William Stockdale, deposed to finding the body, on the 6th of January, in a field in the parish of Leconfield, without coat, hat, or waistcoat, and with the wounds described by Mr. Tygar.

Thomas Potts, saw the prisoner in a field in Skirn lordship, in Driffield, about eight o'clock. He had on a white frock, and a black hat ; he had a bundle, and a grey hat with the bundle. Prisoner said he was running away from Hull Bank, because he did not like the country ; he had been used to the Wolds. He had a watch with a broken face.

William Taylor, constable at Driffield, took the prisoner into custody, at his mother's house, in Great Kelk, on the 7th of January. He was dressed in a white smock, and red waistcoat. A coat, with a hat and handkerchief, were lying on the bed, which he said were his. Prisoner said, he would take his oath he never had had a watch, either of his own or any one's else, since May last. Witness, on the 9th of January, got a watch from Mr. Lyon, watchmaker, of Bridlington.

The clothes and watch were produced.

Craven Lyon, a watchmaker at Bridlington, proved buying the watch from the prisoner, on the 30th of December, when he was dressed in a coat, waistcoat, and hat, like those on the table.

Daniel Foster, an apprentice to Mr. Tygar, identified the watch as having been in the possession of the deceased about ten days before he left Driffield on the 27th December ; and the coat and waistcoat, as being very like those he had on, on that day.

John Walker identified the watch as having once belonged to him ; he had exchanged it with his brother. He last saw it in his brother's possession in Martinmas-week last.

George Walker, another brother of the deceased, identified the coat as having belonged to his brother.

William Lockwood, a hatter in Beverley, identified the hat, as one he sold to the deceased on Christmas-eve ; and as having seen him on the 27th of December, dressed in a coat, &c., like those which were produced in court.

Pearson Fox, found a button, near the place where the

body was discovered. On examining the dress of the prisoner, it was seen, that a button was missing from his breeches. The one found was of the same description with those left on his breeches; but was a little smaller.

The prisoner, on being called on for his defence, said, he was innocent of the crime, as the child unborn, and the clothes found on him, he bought in London three weeks before Michaelmas. He called no witnesses.

The learned judge then summed up the evidence; and the jury immediately returned a verdict of guilty.

In passing sentence, the learned judge said—" Prisoner, you have been convicted, and, I must say, convicted on most unimpeachable evidence, of the highest crime that can be charged—the wilful and deliberate murder of your fellow creature. It would seem, from some circumstances of the case, that the eye of Providence had most clearly marked this murder for detection, so as to leave no possible doubt. Everything connected with it, together with the false account you gave of the manner in which you acquired the property found upon you, all tend completely to establish, without any doubt, that you are the person who committed this wilful and barbarous murder; and that you committed it for the sake of plunder. But this plunder has been the means of your conviction: the property you thus acquired, instead of serving your base purposes, has been the means of bringing you to justice. It is to be hoped, that as most of these circumstances, as appear from the depositions I have before me, were proved in your presence, and as you must have been conscious that there were no means of escape, it is, I say, to be hoped, that they may have brought you into a state of contrition and repentance. I beg of you to devote the very short time you yet have to live, in endeavouring to make your peace with the Almighty, for the horrible offence which you have committed. It only remains for me to pass upon you the awful sentence of the law, which must be carried into effect; for it is impossible for any person to stay the execution of the sentence in such a case as this."

Wm. Johnson, the unfortunate man who was executed this day, was committed to the Castle, on the 9th of January, last, was in size about five feet eight inches, stout made and has grown lustier since he was committed. His features were rather peculiar, a very round flat face, of sullen aspect, and seemed a complete lump of stupidity and ignorance. His behaviour has been singular during his confinement. At first he refused sustenance, then voraciously eat; and on one occasion, his companions in prison having taken some trifling liberty with him, he showed such power and strength as amazed every one. He appeared at the bar in his favourite dress, a smock frock which he could not be persuaded to put off and wear a coat, though much entreaty was used.

During his trial, he behaved with great indifference, and when the awful sentence was passed, left the bar with a smile, shook hands with the prisoners below, and told one he would leave him his braces. During the afternoon of Friday, he behaved rather better, and in the evening began to wish for a clergyman to pray for him. On Saturday morning he made full confession of his guilt, detailing the manner he committed the murder and how troubled he had been ever since; during the day he said he was much happier than he had been for years, and hoped his fate would be a warning to others: on Sunday he received the sacrament along with Belt (a prisoner in the Castle) and spent a long time in prayer. Both forenoon and afternoon he selected the prisoners he wished to spend the night with him, and this morning at eleven o'clock he appeared on the platform. After spending a little time in prayer he was launched into eternity, surrounded by an immense number of spectators; and after hanging the usual time his body was cut down and delivered to the surgeons for dissection.

JAMES RAMSDEN AND ROBERT GELL.

Saturday, April 12th, A.D. 1823, the above-mentioned culprits were executed at the new drop behind the Castle.

James Ramsden, aged 27, with stealing a number of gold watches, silver plate, and other articles from the shop of Philip Bright, in Doncaster, in the West Riding.

Robert Gell, aged 35, with being an accomplice in the above robberies, and with having committed other burglaries of a similar nature.

Morsire Camfield and Michael White.

Thursday, November 30th, A.D. 1824.—Morsire Camfield and Michael White were executed at the new drop behind the Castle, for robbing the Tollhouse near Wakefield.

Richard Holderness.

Saturday, April 23rd, A.D. 1825.—Richard Holderness, aged 22, was executed at the new drop behind the Castle. He was from Bishop Wilton, in the East Riding. He was convicted of shooting at Robert Manners, of Pocklington, with intent to kill and murder him.

The offence, for which this young man forfeits his life to the offended laws of his country, is almost equal in magnitude to murder; and renders it requisite, for the protection of the community, that it should be punished with the same degree of severity; for there is no doubt but murder was his intention, as he has since confessed that malice was the forerunner of the crime.

The particulars stated on the trial by the prosecutor are nearly as follows:—On Tuesday, the 19th of December last, Manners left Pocklington on his way to Hull, when he was joined near the former place by the prisoner, who accompanied him as far as Beverley, near which place the prisoner left him. He returned from Hull the next day, and arrived at Bishop-Burton about seven o'clock in the evening. Whilst he was baiting there, the prisoner came into the public-house. When he was about to pursue his journey, the landlady said—" You have got no passengers to-night." He said " No; there was a countryman of his in the house, but he did not know whether he would go with him or not." The prisoner never spoke. About a mile and a half from Bishop-Burton the prisoner came up to Manners, and observed it was a cold night. They walked some distance, and then got up and rode a short time, when the prisoner got down and walked a few minutes, then he got up a second time and placed himself near me in the waggon. When we got to the " Arrows " public-house, three miles from Market Weighton, I removed a sack to make room, and we both got in to ride again. I fell asleep, the horses stopped, which awoke me. I observed the prisoner laid as if asleep. When

I had got about 150 yards beyond the mile-stone near Market Weighton, I received a ball through my head, my mouth was instantly filled with blood, and I was nearly choked with smoke. When I was bleeding, and had my head hanging between my legs, the prisoner leaped down and said, " D—n those villains, they have nearly pulled my legs off." As soon as he had got down, I looked round ; I saw no person but the prisoner, who had his back to me and was walking away. I was afraid he was going to reload his pistol, so I set my horses off at full trot. Soon after I saw the prisoner running after me, and when walking down the hill he came up to me and said, " Manners, it's a bad job, it's fit to make my flesh creep upon my back." I said, " Well it might." When we got to Market Weighton, I went into the house where the York waggon generally stops, and the prisoner followed me. He said, " D—n the villains, they have nearly torn my hand off ;" and on showing his hand, it was all covered with blood. I told him that the blood which was upon his hand was mine. He said, " Oh ! Manners, how can you say so ? do you think I shot you ?" I replied, " I was sure of it." The pistol, with some balls and a bag, were found in a bush near the spot where Manners was shot at.

When placed at the bar to receive the awful sentence of the law, on being asked if he had anything to say why sentence of death should not be passed upon him, he fell upon his knees and said, " Oh, my Lord ! have mercy ; I hope you will have mercy ; all I desire is my life !"

Mr. Justice Holroyd then addressed him as follows :— Richard Holderness, you have been convicted of wilfully, maliciously, and feloniously shooting at Robert Manners, a carrier, who had taken you up in his waggon, and with whom you were travelling. The charge was that you did it with intent to murder him, and it was most perfectly clear upon the evidence that it was your full intent, and you did it under circumstances in which you thought you could not fail to carry into execution. Though by the merciful providence of the Almighty that has not taken place, the evidence against you was too clear to admit of the smallest scruple or doubt as to your guilt, notwithstanding the pretence that you used on your trial, that the pistol was fired, and the attack made, by two persons, whose intention it was to rob the waggon. Providentially the man's life has been spared, though no doubt if you had destroyed him there would still have been sufficient evidence to have convicted you through the providence of the Almighty; but as it was, without doubt, deliberately, when close by his side, you shot him through the head: the direction of the bullet—the finding of the pistol by the roadside after that pistol had been in your possession the day before loaded with a bullet—the taking out of the bullet for the purpose of showing your companion, who was a witness against you, how it was fired; and after firing reloading it with a bullet—all these circumstances are so clear, and coupled with the improbability of the story which you stated, are such as to exclude all hope of mercy being extended to you in this world. The safety of mankind absolutely requires that no judge should interfere between the full execution of the law so as to prevent it having its full effect. It only remains for me, after admonishing you to make the best use you can of the very short time that you have to live here, in making your peace with the Almighty, and in endeavouring to obtain from him that mercy which the safety of society prevents any hope of you receiving here, to pass the sentence of the court upon you, which is, that you be taken from hence to the place from whence you came, and from thence to the place of execution, and there to be hanged by the neck until you are dead, and may the Lord have mercy on your soul!

Yesterday a most excellent sermon was preached by the Rev. Mr. Flower, the Ordinary, from the following text:—
1 Peter ii. 21.—"For even hereunto were ye called; because Christ also suffered for us, leaving us an example, that ye should follow his steps."

At the appropriate time he was brought from the condemned cell to the drop, attended by the sheriff's officers; and after praying a short time with the Ordinary, he was launched into eternity—a sad example of depravity of the human heart. He was a single man, and only twenty-two years of age. Since his trial he confessed his crime, and appeared penitent. On being asked if he intended to rob the prosecutor, he said, "No;—but he shot him for an old quarrel which he had with him some time since.'

ISAAC CHARLESWORTH.

Saturday, August 13th, A.D. 1825.—Isaac Charlesworth, aged 22, was executed at the new drop for violently assaulting and robbing Joshua Cropper, of Halifax, taking from him £1. 14s. The assault was committed on the highway, in the parish of Sheffield.

PETER LITTLE AND JOSEPH LEE.

Saturday, April 22nd, A.D. 1826.—Peter Little, aged 26, was executed at the new drop behind the Castle, for feloniously assaulting William Sims, of Newton-lane-end, in the parish of Wakefield, twine spinner, and stealing from his person two Dewsbury Bank notes, twenty shillings in silver, and a half-sovereign.

Joseph Lee, *alias* Lees, aged 22, was executed at the same time and place, for stealing a grey gelding, the property of Richard Morton, of Horncastle, farmer.

LEONARD WILKINSON.

Monday, July 17th, A.D. 1826.— Leonard Wilkinson, aged 22, a native of Fingall, near Bedale, was executed at the new drop, for the wilful murder of Nicholas Carter, of Crakehall, in the parish of Bedale.

WILLIAM AND JOHN DYON.

Wednesday, April 2nd, A.D. 1828.—William Dyon, aged 45, late of Morton Carr, in the county of Lincoln, farmer, and John Dyon, aged 23, late of Filham Carr, in the said county of Lincoln, labourer, charged upon the oaths of William Wright, of Bawtry, in the county of York, surgeon, James Hodson, of Brancroft, in the said county of York, groom, Robert Farmery, of Brancroft aforesaid, servant in husbandry, and others, with the wilful murder of John Dyon, late of Brancroft aforesaid, farmer, on the 16th day of February last.

The prisoners, at half-past eight, entered the dock. They did not appear dejected by their awful situation. Although it was half an hour before his Lordship took his seat upon the bench, we did not observe them converse with each other.

The prisoners were placed at the bar, and the indictment read. They pleaded "Not Guilty," in a firm tone of voice.

Mr. Serjeant Jones stated the case to the jury. In alluding to the general nature of the inquiry, and the great interest which the awful circumstances of the case had excited, he earnestly implored the jury to dismiss from their minds, every rumour which they might previously have heard, and to give their verdict with feelings divested of every prior impression, and founded only on the facts which should be adduced in that court. The two prisoners at the bar were charged with the murder of John Dyon, a respectable farmer at Brancroft, near Doncaster, who was brother to the elder prisoner, and uncle to the younger, the two prisoners being father and son. The deceased had, by industry, acquired considerable freehold, leasehold, and other property, and has left a wife and three children. He was in the habit of attending Bawtry and Doncaster markets. On Saturday, the 16th of February, he set off for the market, at 11 o'clock in the forenoon, and remained the greater part of the day at Doncaster, whence he returned in the evening on the road homewards, but never reached his home. He was accompanied by Mr. Wagstaff, of Middlewood House, and Mr. Broughton, of Bawtry, solicitor, as far as the road leading to Brancroft, when the deceased and Mr. Wagstaff turned off the great North road, and Mr. Broughton proceeded to Bawtry. This was between eight and nine o'clock on Saturday evening—probably about half-past eight. The deceased and Mr. Wagstaff rode on till within a short distance of the gate of the deceased, where they wished each other "goodnight," and parted. It, however, was important to state, that Mr. Wagstaff struck into a smart canter, and was consequently soon far distant from the site of the murder. This was the last time, and the last place where the deceased was seen alive. Mrs. Dyon, the wife of the deceased, thinking him late, retired to rest, but he not having returned at two o'clock in the morning, she was so much alarmed that she ordered the servant to go and meet his master. On arriving at the first gate, he found the mare on which his master went to market, with the bridle entangled in the gate, but without a rider. On this discovery he returned in great alarm, and another servant was called to go with him in search of the unfortunate deceased. They passed the first gate together, and proceeded to the second gate which they found partly open, and having gone through it, they endeavoured to close it, but were not able, which caused them to look more minutely, when they found the dead body of their master laid partly in the gateway. The body was perfectly stiff and cold; being a severe night it was covered with hoar frost, which proved that it had laid on the ground some time. The deceased had £40 or £41, a watch, and other property in his pockets, none of which had been taken from him—hence it was clear that the motive of the murderers was not plunder. A cart was procured, and the deceased was taken home, and a surgeon immediately sent for, from Bawtry; who, on his arrival examined the body, and made the following report of the cause of his death. A ball had entered the left side, immediately upon the second rib, which it had fractured—it had then gone through the cavity of the chest; and, proceeding between the third and fourth rib of the right side, had lodged near the shoulder blade, which the evidence of the surgeon would prove must have caused instant death. These, gentlemen of the jury (said the learned counsel), are the circumstances of the case, as regard the condition and situation of the deceased. The next question is, by whom was the deed done?

Inquiries were made of a man of the name of White, who was the head farming man of the deceased, and had formerly been servant to the elder prisoner. He resided at Partridge Hall, and will prove that the prisoners went to his house on the 8th of February, and White being in bed got up, when they left two guns, the brother having previously made the inquiry if John Dyon was going to Doncaster market, and received a negative reply. On Saturday the 16th, however, the day of the murder, they came again to his house; the evidence would be produced that White had concealed the guns in an out-house, and that the time when they arrived at Patridge Hill, for the guns, was about seven at night. They said they had been at Bawtry with a cart. White, however, through fear of personal danger, did not state at first, all that he afterwards deposed to. There is another fact worthy notice, the elder prisoner had, when a young man, himself lived at Partridge Hill, with a Mr.

Conway. Independent of White's testimony, Mr. Turner, who married a daughter of the prisoner, will now prove that the prisoners were from home on the 8th, and did not return till late on the 9th. Mrs. Hornsby, who was staying at the house of the prisoners, will also prove that they were absent at that time.

On the 16th, the day of the murder, the two prisoners expressed an anxiety for an early dinner, and left immediately after it, and were seen no more till Sunday. Evidence would be produced to show that two men answering a description of the prisoners at the bar, were seen on the road towards Austerfield, on the night of the murder—they crossed the Ferry, and had two guns with them, though they had no guns when they left their own house. Witnesses would also be produced to speak to the identity of the prisoners, and positively swear to them.

The next evidence will be respecting the footmarks. On the morning of the 16th February, there was snow on the ground—the murderers had gone part of the way through fields, and the impression made by their feet was therefore strong and clear. The elder Dyon has a peculiar habit of turning out his feet—the footmarks corresponded with this peculiarity, and were traced from the road to the gate, and afterwards to the road where the prisoners were seen with the guns. On inquiring for the shoes, they were not to be found. Such is the evidence respecting the footsteps.

Upon such a subject, said the counsel, there must be much to doubt and much for discussion. The jury would however hear the evidence, and then decide how far they could connect the occurrences of Friday, the 8th, Saturday, the 9th, and Saturday, the 16th of February, with the charge against the prisoners. If they were not at home, where were they? On this question the father and son had in their examination, materially contradicted each other. Five persons had seen and traced them. It therefore was not requisite for him to add one word more. Nothing was wished for in this prosecution but that the dreadful affair might be fully and fairly investigated, and that the verdict should be governed alone by the evidence which would be produced.

About forty witnesses were then examined to support the statement of the learned counsel.

The part for the prosecution having closed, the prisoners were asked if they had anything to say in their defence, when William Dyon said—"Please you, my Lord, I have nothing to say. I have left all to my counsel." John Dyon said "No, I have nothing to say."

Mr. Baron Hullock then summed up the evidence which he recapitulated with great precision. The jury after retiring for five minutes, pronounced both the prisoners Guilty.

His Lordship, in passing sentence of death upon the prisoners, said—"Prisoners at the bar, you have been tried, and, after a patient investigation of all the circumstances of the case, convicted of murder. I am sorry to say that there is nothing to cause me to hold out the slightest hopes of mercy. Answer for your crime you shortly must with your lives, therefore you have no time to lose. I would exhort you, most earnestly, to seek peace with God, by prayer and repentance at the throne of grace, where alone mercy is to be found. In a very few hours you will be no more. It only remains for me to pass the awful sentence of the law upon you, and that is, that you be taken from hence to prison, and from thence on Wednesday next, to the place of execution, and there to be hanged by the neck till you are dead—that when you are dead, your bodies be dissected and anatomized ; and may the Lord have mercy upon your souls ! " The prisoners were then removed from the bar.

Mr. John Dyon harboured a presentment that he should at one time or other be murdered, and even expressed himself to that effect to Mr. Chadburn, of Rossington Bridge, on the Saturday previous to the sad event.

It is remarkable that William Dyon attended the funeral of his murdered brother and betrayed no visible emotion, neither at the sight of the body, nor when he was taken to the spot where the murder was committed. The son is rather taller than the father and has been recently married. A daughter of William Dyon also lately married into a most respectable family of the name of Turner, to whom this occurrence, however it may terminate, must be most heartbreaking.

The elder prisoner's wife, his youngest son, daughter, and

son-in-law, took their leave of him on Monday evening at nine o'clock, without any of the parties shedding a tear at the lamentable situation in which he was placed.

Everything has been done by the Ordinary to bring them to a proper sense of their guilt, but without effect, as they persisted in their innocence to the last.

Such was the interest excited, that at an early hour, an immense crowd had assembled to witness the awful ceremony.

At the appointed time they appeared on the platform, after spending a short time in prayer they were launched into eternity, surrounded by an immense concourse of spectators : and after hanging the usual time their bodies were given for dissection.

John Morrot, Matthew Harrison, John Coates, *alias* Wilkinson.

Saturday, April 26th, A.D. 1828. — The above unfortunates were executed at the new drop, for horse-stealing.

John Morrott, aged 26, a native of Lincolnshire.

Matthew Harrison, aged 40, of Beverley.

John Coates, *alias* Wilkinson, aged 30, of Wensleydale. They acknowledged their guilt and died penitent.

Martin Slack.

Monday, March 30th, A.D. 1829.—Martin Slack suffered death on the new drop behind the Castle of York, for the wilful murder of a female bastard child, at Sheffield.

The crime of murder has in all ages and in all civilized nations, been punished with death, for the Divine Law says, " He that taketh life, by man his life shall be taken."

Martin Slack, being arraigned at the bar, charged with the murder of his female bastard child, at Sheffield, pleaded " Not guilty."

Mr. Milner stated the case.—He said the prisoner was only 18 years of age, and was an apprentice to a brace-bit maker, at Sheffield. He became acquainted with a female at that place ; and the consequence was, the birth of a child in October last, which came to its death in the manner that would be stated by the witnesses.

Elizabeth Hague said, she lives in Sheffield, and knows the prisoner with whom she was acquainted. She was delivered of a child in October last. Slack was the father, and she filiated it on him before birth. He was sent to Wakefield House of Correction, but returned before the birth of the child. It was a girl. The child died on Sunday the 23rd of November. She saw Slack the day before ; and that morning he came soon after she got downstairs with the child. She was suckling the child when he came in, and as she was not quite dressed, she laid it down on a squab in the room, and went up to finish dressing. Her brother was asleep in a chair in the room with the prisoner. She had hardly got upstairs before she heard the child give a scream. She went downstairs, and the prisoner had the child in his arms. He had it with its head against his left shoulder. The mouth was against his left breast. He rose from the chair on which he was sitting and gave her the child. She was going to give it the breast, when she saw a blaze issuing from its mouth, and something like brimstone running down from it. She put the child's mouth to her cheek, which burnt it and left a mark. The stuff running from the child's mouth burnt her arm. The prisoner said he had given the child nothing, but said it was sick, and bid her give it some water. She told him he had given it poison. He denied it. She screamed for her father and mother, and he said if she screamed in that manner, he would go. Prisoner went out just as her father got to the bottom of the stairs, and did not return. Mary Wells came in, and witness gave her the child. A surgeon was sent for, but the child died in three-quarters of an hour. The sides of the child's mouth were burnt, and its fingers were also burnt with putting them against its mouth. The coat which was on the squab, on which the child was laid down, was also burnt.

George Hague, E. Hague's brother, Luke Hague her father, and Mary Wells, sister to the first witness, were examined; and confirmed her testimony. There was an inquest and the prisoner was committed.

They were cross-examined at great length by Mr. Cottingham.

William Woodward saw the prisoner go to Hague's house in the morning of the 23rd of November, and leave it at half-past seven. Joseph Wells, who married Hague's daughter, was called to prove that, on the Friday before the child died, he told Slack he was an unnatural father, on account of some expressions he made use of.

Mary Smith saw the child in Mary Wells' arms; there was stuff running out of its mouth.

John Pierce Lewis, surgeon, described the child when he was called in to be foaming at the mouth ; part of the face and the chin and neck were discoloured. He thought it was the effect of corrosive poison.

James Hardy, surgeon, said, corrosive poison was the cause of the child's death. Several other witnesses were examined: their evidence was not material.

Mr. Baron Hullock summed up the evidence at great length ; and concluded by putting two questions to the jury, 1st. Are you satisfied that the child's death was occasioned by poison? And if you are, then you must consider whether the prisoner was the person who administered it ? If you believe the witnesses, it is quite impossible, that it could have been any one but the prisoner, or one of those witnesses, who administered it. You must, however, be well satisfied, before you deliver your verdict according to your oath.

The jury consulted in their box about seven minutes, and then returned a verdict of guilty.

The Clerk of Arraigns asked the prisoner what he had to say why sentence of death should not be passed upon him, he replied—" Please you, my lord, I am not guilty of the crime, and as to the time given me to prepare to die, I am a murdered man."

Silence having been proclaimed, Mr. Baron Hullock after putting on the black cap, addressed him as follows :—

" Martin Slack, you have been convicted of wilful murder (Prisoner, " Yes, sir,") and it appears to me that that verdict, which consigns you to almost instant death,— (Prisoner, " Yes, sir,")—is a proper one, and I do not see that the jury could have found any other. The circumstances under which you have committed this crime render it, in its nature and character, one of the greatest enormity. Nothing remains for me now to do but earnestly to entreat of you to employ the short remnant of your life in imploring forgiveness, where alone it can be found. I can afford you no hope of mercy. You must die, according to the law ; a few hours must terminate your life ; I therefore entreat you to spend this short interval in the best manner ; to humble yourself, and by prayer and repentance to seek for pardon and forgiveness."

Slack, whose demeanour had hitherto been marked with propriety, now became violently excited, and interrupted his lordship, saying, "I have no occasion to go down on my knees and beg pardon, because I am innocent. I went to the girl's house. The child was crying. She went upstairs—but before she got to the top she returned and gave the child something out of a tea-cup. After that, she said—' Go off with you, Slack, for the child is poisoned.' I went away because I knew I was innocent. I went first to my mother's, I got my breakfast, part of it, however, and after that I went to Handsworth to see a fellow apprentice that was ill. Returning back, I met Mr. Waterfall, and he said I was charged with murder. I said I was willing to go with him. He said I must go immediately. They put me in custody, and there I remained. The evidence they have now taken against me, they have taken it completely falsely and in a different manner from what they gave it at Sheffield. I (raising his voice) have no reason to beg for mercy. The Lord is with me, and will save my soul, for he knows I am not guilty of the crime."

Mr. Baron Hullock.—I have only to repeat to you if you have any wrong impression, that you ought to seek forgiveness.

Prisoner.—I have no trouble upon my mind, because I know the girl is guilty of the crime for which I am now *arranged* at this bar.

Mr. Baron Hullock.—The sentence of the Court is that you be taken to the place from whence you came, and from thence, on Monday next, to the place of execution, there to be hanged by the neck till your body be dead, and that your body be afterwards dissected and anatomized.

Prisoner.—Well, my lord, that is just what they wanted. They have got their desire. They said I should be hanged. They said at Sheffield I should be hanged and dissected, but they have got it by false swearing.

In a moment the prisoner continued addressing his lordship—" I say you have not done your duty, to pass sentence of death upon me, for I am not guilty. I am a murdered man."

The prisoner was then taken out of Court, uttering imprecations against his sentence. When going out of the dock, he said, " I'll be d——d if I don't have my hat, if I never want it again. It's a d——d shame of the old ——.

In passing to his cell he continued to use the same kind of language as when leaving the dock, but when the clergyman went to him, he expressed regret that he had been so turbulent, and said he was subject to sudden ebullitions of passion. He was very calm when he went to bed, slept a good portion of the night, and during Saturday was very composed ; the second night he slept most of the time. When visited by the Ordinary he attended very devoutly to his instructions, but up to the morning of his execution, he denied giving the child the deadly dose.

He has a father and mother, five sisters, and one brother living. His mother and elder brother continued to visit him to the last.

At the appointed time this unfortunate young man was led to the place of execution, where after spending a short time in prayer he was launched into eternity, in view of a large concourse of spectators.

WILLIAM SHAW.

Monday, April 5th, A.D. 1830.—William Shaw, aged 25, was executed at the new drop behind the Castle, for the wilful murder of Rachel Crosley, in the parish of Kirkburton near Huddersfield.

William Shaw, aged 25, was, on Friday morning, April 2nd, placed at the bar, charged with the wilful murder of Rachel Crosley, in the parish of Kirkburton, near Huddersfield. On being arraigned, he pleaded, in a firm voice, " Not guilty."

Mr. Maude, in stating the case to the jury, said that this was a very serious inquiry, and would require their utmost attention. He should abstain from making any observations, and content himself by very briefly stating an outline of the evidence that would be adduced. The unfortunate young woman whose death was the subject of this investigation, was the daughter of very poor parents, who live at Thorncliffe Green, in the parish of Kirkburton ; her father was a working miner, and she was the youngest of fourteen children. The deceased, though she had nearly attained the age of 22, was of very short stature, and was generally called " Little Rachel." On Tuesday the 9th of March last, she was in perfect health and good spirits. She was at home that night, and at nine o'clock sat down to supper with her father and mother. She rose quickly from the supper-table, without partaking of anything to eat, went out, and never returned to her father's house alive. About ten o'clock, her family became alarmed at her absence, and search was made for her without success.

On the following morning, as some boys were lowered into a coal pit two hundred yards from the deceased's dwelling, to begin their work, they screamed out ; and on being drawn up, appeared greatly frightened, and said that there was a dead man at the bottom, without breeches. A man then went down, and at the bottom of the pit he found the body of the unfortunate woman ; another man was lowered, and the body was brought up. It was quite lifeless, and presented a most shocking appearance. The skull was fractured; some of the limbs were broken; the body dreadfully bruised and wounded ; her clothes were pinned round her thighs, in such a manner as to have prevented her walking far ; and her cap, gown, and other parts of her dress, were torn in a manner which could not have been done by her falling into the pit by accident. The prisoner had been the vowed lover of the deceased for several years. Four years ago she had a child, which was filiated on the prisoner, who paid a weekly allowance for its maintenance. At the time of her death, the unfortunate young woman was again pregnant to the prisoner, and was within a month of the time of her confinement. Her mother pressed him to marry her, and he promised he would.

About three weeks before the night on which the unfortunate occurrence took place, the prisoner was in the house of Mary Butcher, nearly opposite to the deceased's parents, when Mrs. Butcher and a young woman joked him about Rachel, and asked him what he was boon (going) to do. He replied that if they knew what he was boon to do, they would not rest either day or night. On the evening of the 8th of March, he was again at Butcher's, when a little boy told him that Rachel was boon for a warrant on the following day. He made no reply to this, but went away. On the night of Tuesday, the 9th of March, he was seen at a quarter-past nine, standing with the deceased behind her father's house ; at half-past nine he was also seen walking along with her up the croft, which was the last time she was seen alive. This was about 200 yards from the pit in which her body was found the following morning. On search being made for footmarks, those of a man and woman were traced along the croft, through two gaps at the corner of a field adjoining, and the one in which the pit was, and very near to the mouth of the pit. The prisoner's shoes were compared with the marks near the pit's mouth, and found to correspond, some of the nails being out. He surrendered himself to the constable the next morning. During the time the inquest was holding, some one said that the doctors were of opinion that the young woman had been murdered before she had been thrown into the pit ; on which the prisoner said, " Nay she wur not, for she wur alive when she went into the pit mouth." On being told what the verdict of the coroner's inquest was, the prisoner said, " I wish some one would come and pash my brains out."

Several witnesses were called, who proved the above facts. The prisoner made no defence, and the jury, after retiring three-quarters of an hour, pronounced the prisoner guilty.

Silence having been proclaimed, the learned judge put on the black cap. He addressed the prisoner nearly as follows :—

" William Shaw, the jury, after a long and patient inquiry, have pronounced you guilty of the dreadful murder of which you are charged. They have performed their duty, and it now remains for me to perform mine. You have been convicted of a most barbarous and brutal murder. There are instances in which, in the cases of persons who have suffered the last penalty of the law, there has been some reason for compassion for them, but your offence is such, no one can have pity upon you. That unfortunate young woman who was with child to you, and whom you had promised to become her husband, and ought to have been her protector, was enticed by you to the place where you destroyed her in the most dreadful, barbarous, and brutal manner. You have committed that crime which the law of God denounces. The law of your country gives you a short time, a few solitary hours, to seek forgiveness and mercy, and I entreat you to fall on your knees and pray to your Maker, that he may extend that forgiveness to you which you cannot possibly receive in this world. It now only remains for me to pass the sentence, not of mine but of the law, that you be taken to the place from whence you came, and from thence, on Monday next, to the place of execution, and there be hung by the neck till you are dead, and your body be given to the surgeons for dissection ; and may the Lord have mercy on your soul."

The prisoner was not in the least affected, and stood unmoved during the passing of the sentence. Every one else in the Court seemed deeply impressed. The Court was intensely crowded during the whole of the day.

JOSEPH SLATER.

Monday, August 2nd, A.D. 1830.—Joseph Slater was executed at the new drop, for the wilful murder of his own child, only three years old, by drowning it, near Guisbro.'

CHARLES TURNER AND JAMES TWIBELL.

October 5th, A.D. 1831.—Charles Turner, aged 19, and James Twibell, aged 19, were charged with robbing Jonathan Habberston, on the highway at Sheffield.

Mr. Elsley was for the prosecution ; and Mr. Cottingham for the defence.

The case was a very aggravated one. The prosecutor is the overlooker of a colliery near Sheffield, and was returning from Sheffield on the night of the 5th of October. When he arrived at a place called Manor Lane, he saw three men standing. He passed them, but they followed him, and one of them passed him. He almost immediately received a violent blow on the back of his head, and the blows were continued till he was felled to the ground. His pockets were then rifled, and the villains left him in a state of insensibility. He laid for about half an hour, when some one came past and took him home. A watch and some money was taken from him; and as the prisoners were found offering a watch for sale the next day, they were apprehended. Priestley, the third man turned King's evidence. The prosecutor; Henry Yaul, who assisted him home; Joseph Hunter, a surgeon, who found a large hedge-stake covered with blood near where the robbery was committed; Henry Walker, to whom the prisoners had offered a watch for sale; and James Wild, the constable who apprehended them, were examined, and deposed to the several facts.

When George Sidney Priestley was called, he denied all that he had sworn in his examination before the magistrates, and affirmed that what he had then said was forced from him by the constable's telling him that if he did not say what he said he would be transported.

Mr. Justice Parke ordered him into custody, saying he would have him indicted as an accomplice, and tried during the assizes.

Most of the witnesses who had been examined at Sheffield now pretended that "they did not know what they said;" and one said, when asked about signing his deposition, that "he could not write, but made his mark," and he "thought he took hold on the top of a pen."

The learned judge severely reprobated the tampering with the witnesses which had been adopted, and the jury returned a verdict of guilty.

His lordship put on the black cap, and addressed the prisoners in very solemn language. He said, " Charles Turner and James Twibell, the jury who have just found you guilty, have performed their duty to their country, and it now remains for me to perform mine. You have been justly convicted, and found guilty of the malicious assault committed upon this poor man; you have not been content with taking his money alone, but have beaten him in a most diabolical manner—beating him with a hedge-stake, and leaving him for dead.   Under the effects of those blows he still labours, and perhaps will continue to do so for the remainder of his life ; you therefore deserve the full weight of the law to fall on your heads.   It is not my sentence but the sentence of the law that I am about to pass on you ; I implore you both, therefore, the little time you have still left, to employ it, on your bended knees, in obtaining the pardon from God Almighty which you cannot hope for here ; and may God have mercy on your souls. The sentence of the law is, that you be conveyed from this place to the place from whence you came, and from thence to the place of execution, where you are to be hung by the neck till you are dead.

During the passing of the sentence, Turner wept bitterly, and at the conclusion exclaimed, " Oh, dear."   Twibell also sobbed and cried out " O Lord ! spare our lives."   They were then removed from the bar.

William Hodkin.

Saturday, October 18th, A.D. 1832.—William Hodkin was executed at the new drop behind the Castle, for committing a rape upon a little girl, under twelve years of age.

Mary Hunter, Ebenezer Wright, and Thomas Law.

Saturday, March 30th, A.D. 1833.—Mary Hunter was convicted for inciting and counselling a simple country girl, named Hannah Gray, to fire the stacks of her master, Mr. Marshall, of Lotherton.   The circumstances connected with this case show to what extent a spirit of revenge may be carried.   The unfortunate woman (who is mother of nine children) and her husband reside in the same village as Mr. Marshall, and were the keepers of the pinfold.   In August last a dispute arose about the pounding of some of Mr. Marshall's foals, for which Mrs. Hunter demanded fourpence. This sum was refused to be paid, and from words the parties got to blows, and ultimately the affair was settled by the

magistrate, much to Mrs. Hunter's dissatisfaction. Subsequently it appeared that Mrs. Hunter had declared she
would be revenged, if she was hung for it the next day, and
on Tuesday, the 22nd of January, Mr. Marshall had a stack
of wheat fired. Thomas Hunter was apprehended on suspicion, but afterwards discharged, and on the Sunday following three more stacks were fired and totally consumed.
The servant girl, Hannah Gray, then confessed that she
had fired the stacks on the Sunday, and that she did it in
consequence of Mrs. Hunter coming to her on the previous
Thursday, and asked her to set the stacks on fire, promising
her a new frock if she did it, and that if she did not she
would tear her liver out, and that if she told anybody she
would tear her to pieces. Such were the features of this
lamentable case, which has ended in a decent, respectable
looking female, at the age of 47, ending her days on a
scaffold, to atone for the breach of the law, has deprived her
husband of his partner in life, and brought the mother
of a numerous offspring to an untimely death, a melancholy instance of the danger of giving way to passion and
revenge.

Ebenezer Wright, one of the other criminals, was a
respectable-looking young man, about 26 years of age, full
six feet high, and stout made. He was convicted (along
with Samuel Norburn) of firing a stack of straw and a
stack of hay, the property of Mr. Oxley, of Rotherham,
solicitor, who had conducted a prosecution against him for
an assault. Wright, being determined to serve Oxley out
for this, fired his stack. The offence was committed in
August last, and for some time no clue to the perpetrator
was discovered. The offenders were, however, at last
detected by their own conduct. Norburn, having some suspicion that his companion was too familiar with his wife,
resolved, under the influence of jealousy, to confess the
transaction, to get his accomplice hanged, and by turning
King's evidence save himself. Wright was then apprehended, and he, finding that Norburn had been snitching,
also made a confession. The result was that both the
prisoners were tried and convicted on their own confession,
and received sentence of death. Norburn was subsequently
reprieved. Wright had lived some time at Rotherham, and

his mode of obtaining subsistence was, in many cases, anything but creditable.

Thomas Law, the other male culprit, was convicted (along with Robert Bingley) of a most aggravated highway robbery. The unfortunate individual who was the object of these men's brutality was a Mr. Thomas Atkinson, of Knottingly, near Ferry-bridge. He was returning from Pontefract market on the night of the 12th of January, and fortunately had taken the precaution to leave his money in care of the landlord of the inn where he put up. He had got to the cross roads on his road home, when two men, whom he knew to be Law and Bingley, came up to him, knocked him down, and rifled his pockets. Finding that they were known to Mr. Atkinson, they commenced a most horrid attack on him, beating him over the head with knob-sticks, and having inflicted about twenty wounds on his head, they left him laid on the road, apparently lifeless. He, however, survived the effects of the violence, and was so far recovered as to be able to give evidence against the prisoners, who were both convicted. Law behaved in the most disorderly manner during the trial, frequently interrupting the counsel and judge, and cross-examining the witnesses in the most impudent manner. His deportment fully showed that he was a reckless and desperate man, and after sentence of death was passed on him he exclaimed—"May the devil get the witnesses, they've sworn falsely against us."

At twelve o'clock the three unhappy culprits suffered the final sentence of the law. Wright and Law both ate a hearty breakfast, and the former remained perfectly callous ; the latter still protested his innocence.

Mary Hunter appeared penitent and resigned to her fate, but declared her innocence of the crime for which she was to suffer.

The Chaplain (the Rev. W. Flower, jun.) performed the sacred office of religion to the convicts, which were perfectly unheeded by Wright, and at twelve o'clock, the officer having previously pinioned their arms, they were taken to the scaffold.

Wright walked first ; Law followed. Hunter, who was much agitated, came last. As she got upon the scaffold she said—"Oh, I am innocent," and she kept uttering broken exclamations during prayers. The others said nothing, but Wright's countenance underwent a remarkable change whilst the chaplain was offering up the Lord's prayer, and he compressed his lips, as if in mental or bodily agony. As soon as prayers were ended the executioner put the halter round Law's neck. Whilst he was doing this Law said—"Gentlemen, before I drop I wish to say that I am innocent of the crime as any one of you. I never seed the man to my knowledge on that night. The Lord have mercy on my soul."

Wright did not utter a syllable, but he kicked his shoes off whilst the executioner was putting the rope round Law's neck.

Mary Hunter protested her innocence, said she hoped in a few minutes to be in Heaven, and called on the Lord Jesus to have mercy on her.

The last words she said were—"My dear brother will soon be here. I am dying for a innocent crime—I am in——" Before she got the last word out of her mouth the drop fell, and they were launched into eternity.

They all appeared to die with scarcely a struggle, and their bodies were cut down and delivered to their friends, after hanging the usual time. The number of spectators was very great. We should suppose that at least 4,000 or 5,000 were present. We understand that Wright was a resurrectionist, and he kept the body of his wife for two days under his bed, after which he sold it for a subject to save the expense of a funeral. He was certainly the most callous and hardened criminal we ever saw suffer.

They were executed upon the new drop behind the walls of the Castle of York. Mary Hunter was drawn up on the drop upon an hurdle.

CHARLES COOKE, THOMAS ROGERS, AND THOMAS MORRIS.

Saturday, April 26th, A.D. 1834.—The three culprits as above, were executed at the new drop, for the following crimes :—

Charles Cooke, aged 20, for highway robbery and attempted murder near Thirsk.

Thomas Rogers, aged 32, for an unnatural crime.

Thomas Morris, aged 23, for committing a rape upon Miss Mary Law.

URSULA LOFTHOUSE, JOSEPH HEELEY, AND
WILLIAM ALLOT.

Monday, April 6th, A.D. 1835.—Ursula Lofthouse, for the murder of her husband ; Joseph Heeley, for the murder of James Lee ; and William Allot, for the murder of Martha Hardwick, suffered death on the new drop behind the Castle of York.

The crime of murder has, in all ages, and in all civilized nations, been punished with death, for the Divine Law says, " He that taketh life, by man his life shall be taken."

The almost daily examples which the laws of the land oblige the power of justice to make, would, we might hope, deter persons from the commission of crime. But the cries of justice and the voice of reason are of no effect upon a conscience hardened in iniquity. Remonstrances, however reasonably urged, or movingly couched, have no more influence on the heart of such a one, than the gentle evening breeze has upon the oak when it whispers among its branches, or the rising surges upon the deaf rock when they dash and break against its sides.

Ursula Lofthouse, aged 26, was placed at the bar at York Castle, April 3rd, 1835, charged with the wilful murder of Robert Lofthouse, her husband, at Kirby Malzeard.

Mr. Cottingham and Mr. Dicken conducted the prosecution. Sir Gregory Lewin defended the prisoner.

Mr. Cottingham stated the case, and called nineteen witnesses, from whose evidence it appeared that the deceased went to Ripon market on the 6th of November, in good health, and on his return in the evening, he called at his brother's, who resides at Dalla Gill, and there partook of some bread and milk. He shortly afterwards left his brother's house and went home. On his arrival, he stated to his wife that he felt rather unwell; she said she would make him some tea, stating at the same time, that it would do him good. She prepared it accordingly, and they both partook of it. He had taken nothing to eat for dinner, and during the day had three gills of ale. His wife said, "I've made a cake on purpose for thee." The poor fellow without suspecting her diabolical object, immediately proceeded to take a meal of tea and cake, but before he had finished he said, "Bless me, I don't think I could swallow the piece of cake now in my mouth for all the world." Violent vomiting and purging ensued, attended with other distressing symptoms. She immediately went to his brother, and desired him to go to her husband, as he was taken dangerously ill. The brother went and found him as described by his wife; he grew gradually worse, and on the Friday morning a surgeon was called in, and found him dangerously ill. He attended him until the Saturday, when he died.

Thomas Thorpe.—I am constable at Kirby Malzeard, and know the deceased's house. I conveyed the prisoner to York in a gig. When we got about eighteen miles from Kirby, the prisoner began to talk about her husband. She said he had a disagreeable breath; that he would hardly allow her common necessaries to live; that she believed he had saved between £40 and £50; that he never told her what he did with his money; that she believed he carried it to Henry Lofthouse, and that he loved Ellen Lofthouse better than her, which made her very unhappy in her mind.

From the evidence of Lawrence Harland, it appeared the prisoner went to his brother's shop, to purchase two pennyworth of arsenic. He refused to let her have it, telling her it was rank poison, and sufficient to kill half the village. She said it was not for herself, it was for one Thomas Grange. Knowing Grange to be a respectable man, he let her have it.

Wm. West, an eminent chemist at Leeds, affirmed, that he analysed the stomach of the deceased, and found arsenicus cid or white arsenic. "I am inclined to the opinion that in the part of the body which came to me there was sufficient arsenic to cause death."

Other evidence was adduced, which left no doubt as to the guilt of the prisoner.

The prisoner, when called on for her defence said, " I have nothing to say, sir ; but I'm innocent."

The learned judge summed up the evidence.

The jury retired, and after an absence of twenty minutes, returned into court, and pronounced the prisoner guilty.

The judge, in a most affecting address, then sentenced the prisoner to be executed on Monday next. On hearing the sentence she wept profusely, and when removed from the bar was quite insensible.

———

Joseph Heeley, aged 29, charged with the wilful murder of James Lee, at Kirk-Burton.

Mr. Greenwood and Mr. Wortley conducted the prosecution. The prisoner had no counsel, but Mr. Baines undertook to watch the case for him.

Mr. Greenwood stated the case, and called seven witnesses, who proved that the prisoner, with several other persons, was drinking at three or four beer-shops on the 26th of November last ; a quarrel arose amongst them, and the prisoner was very violent, swearing he would stab three or four before morning, with a knife which he held in his hand.

Charles Moseley, who resided next door to the deceased, deposed that—On the evening in question I was lying down on the bed. Some one came to my door and burst it open. I went to the door, and saw Heeley (the prisoner) standing against Hardcastle's door, which adjoins mine. James Lee came out, and Heeley struck at him with his right hand. We followed Heeley till he got to the fold-yard end, the prisoner walking backward, and when he got there, he struck the deceased in the neck.

Kezia Hardcastle, the mother of the deceased, said her son was usually called James Hardcastle, but that he was born before she was married, and his name was Lee. She was at the door the time her son was stabbed, and he died the next morning.

Joseph Catterson, surgeon, deposed that he went to the house of the deceased, and found him nearly covered with blood. There was a transverse wound about two inches below the ear, and the carotid artery had been divided. The loss of blood proceeding from the wound was the cause of death.

Benjamin Fitton produced a knife which was found on the prisoner, and identified as one which he took from the pocket of a man named Hill.

The prisoner in his defence said, the witnesses had sworn falsely.

The learned judge having summed up the evidence, the jury, after consulting ten minutes, returned a verdict of guilty.

His Lordship then sentenced him to be executed on Monday next. The prisoner appeared to be quite unconcerned at his melancholy fate.

Wm. Allot, aged 35, was charged at York Castle, April 4th, 1835, with the wilful murder of Martha Hardwick, at Upper Heeley, near Sheffield.

Mr. Baines and Mr. Wortley appeared for the prosecution ; Sir Gregory Lewin defended the prisoner, who is a remarkably stout man, and in a firm voice pleaded not guilty.

Mr. Baines stated the case :—

Mrs. Hardwick, the deceased, was a widow, residing at Upper Heeley, two miles from Sheffield, and occupied a lone house ; the persons composing her family being herself, the prisoner, and a boy named Wolstenholme. She had a small milk-farm, which the prisoner managed, whilst she superintended the household affairs.

On the 9th of September last, the deceased was in perfect health, and between eight and half-past nine in the evening, received such injuries as caused her death two hours after. In the morning of that day, the prisoner and the boy went to Sheffield on some business at the town-hall, and afterwards went to a public house, where they continued drinking till three o'clock, when the boy left the prisoner, and returned home to attend to his work. The prisoner continued drinking till half-past seven, when he was seen going homewards the worse for liquor, and a few minutes before eight was observed crossing the garth within a few yards of home. The boy Wolstenholme left the house about eight o'clock, his mistress being then in good health. About half-past eight Mrs. Hardwick was heard to cry out, " Oh ! dear, he's killing me ! " Another shriek was heard, and the prisoner was heard using abusive language to the deceased, saying, " Thou's been robbing me every day."

At a quarter past nine, the prisoner went to a neighbour's house, and asked for a light, saying that his mistress was drunk—an assertion which was proved to be false. About half-past nine, Wolstenholme, the boy, returned home, and found the front door open, and no person in the front room, but a quantity of blood on the floor. On going into the inner room, he there found the prisoner dragging his mistress on to a bed, in a bleeding state, with her clothes torn, and her cap off. He was in his shirt-sleeves. The deceased's voice was very low, and she said, " Oh, help me." On the boy expressing surprise, the prisoner said he had seen two men run out of the house when he came in, who had done the deed, and he accounted for the blood on his clothes, by stating that he had dirtied them in lifting her on the bed.

A surgeon went the same night, but she was dead, and in a state too horrid to be described. Fifteen witnesses were examined, whose evidence confirmed the prisoner's guilt.

The judge having summed up, the jury retired, and returned with a verdict of guilty.

He was then sentenced to be executed on Monday (this day). After his sentence he requested that his body might be given to his father, but was told it could not be granted.

He concealed a large knife, with which it is supposed he intended to destroy himself.

To a clergyman who visited Ursula Lofthouse on Friday night, she acknowledged the justice of her sentence.

Joseph Heeley said that he was quite happy ; and William Allot became a true penitent.

At the usual time of execution, the culprits appeared on the platform of the drop. After a short time spent in prayer,

‚the bolt was withdrawn, and the awful ceremony concluded. The concourse of spectators was very great.

CHARLES BATTY.

Saturday, April 2nd, A.D. 1836.—Charles Batty, aged 28, was executed at the new drop, for an attempt to murder Elizabeth Brown, at Sheffield.

This unfortunate man was the last that John Curry executed upon the drop behind the walls of the Castle of York. He died soon after, having performed the onerous office of hangman since the year 1802.

THOMAS WILLIAMS.

Saturday, August 12th, A.D. 1837.—Thomas Williams, aged 29, for attempt at murder. A most savage and we fear successful attempt at murder was made on Friday afternoon the 14th day of March, in the workshop of Mr. Moore, basket-maker, Silver-street, Sheffield. The victim is Thomas Froggatt, and his murderer, Thomas Williams, both basket-makers. It appears that Williams has been for some time employed by Mr. Moore, who in consequence of his drunkenness and neglect of work gave him notice to leave, and set on Thomas Froggatt. Williams worked hard for some days after, but spent the remainder of the period of his employment with Mr. Moore, in drinking. About tea-time on Friday, he went into the workshop and began to look up his tools, some of which he could not find. Froggatt and another man from Worksop were working in the shop at the time. At a moment when the Worksop man's back was turned, Williams seized a bill which had been sharpener to cut willows, and struck Froggatt a violent blow on the right and posterior part of the head. The poor man fell bleeding on the floor, and the other man ran screaming out of the shop. The prisoner left the bill, and went by a back way to the " Windsor Castle," in Silver-street, where he was apprehended by Waterfall. Froggatt was raised from the ground, and medical aid immediately procured from Mr. Carr's, in Paradise-square. The wound inflicted is about

six inches long and one deep, forming a most fearful fracture
of the skull, and penetrating the brain, so that the hope of
Froggatt's recovery is very small. Before committing the
act, the prisoner had said to Mr. Moore's son that he would
do him a trick before the night, and his father also must
take care of himself. He afterwards expressed his regret if
he had failed to kill Froggatt, who he said, was taking the
bread out of his mouth, and if he was killed the trade would
benefit by it.

After his conviction he conducted himself becoming his
situation, and, acknowledging the crime for which he
was about to suffer, met his fate with fortitude and resignation.

THOMAS MUSGRAVE.

Saturday, April 6th, A.D. 1839.—Thomas Musgrave, aged
22, was executed at the new drop, for committing a rape
upon Hannah Appleyard, the wife of George Appleyard, at
Leeds. There was a large assembly of spectators.

JAMES BRADSLEY.

Saturday, April 11th, A.D. 1840.—James Bradsley, aged
28, was executed at the new drop, for the wilful murder
of John Bradsley, his own father, at Quick in the West
Riding. He was executed by Nathaniel Howard, of this
city, who, in consequence of the escape of Coates, was appointed executioner.

JOHN BURLINSON, CHARLES GILL, AND HENRY NUTTALL.

Saturday, August 7th, A.D. 1841. — John Burlinson,
Charles Gill, and Henry Nuttall, suffered death behind York
Castle, for the wilful murder of Joseph Cocker, at Knares-
borough.

Our criminal annals, black as they are with atrocity, have
not often recorded crimes of so deep a dye, and which exhibit
so much want of feeling, as the one for the commission of
which the above three miserable young men have this day

paid the forfeit of their lives. It appears, by the confessions of the parties, on being apprehended, that the murder of the unfortunate Cocker had been contemplated by them for some time previously; and indeed they went on the night preceding the execution of the fatal deed for the express purpose of committing it; but in consequence of Mr. Inchboard, tallow-chandler, coming in (with whom Nuttall had worked for some years), their bloody purpose was delayed being accomplished till the next night. By their own account of the horrid transaction they went into Cocker's (who kept a public-house in the neighbourhood in which they resided), and had a few pints of ale; and on a favourable opportunity occurring, by his back being turned, they struck him a severe blow with an adze, nearly severing one of his ears from his head; and which, notwithstanding the earnest but unavailing entreaties of the poor old man to spare his life, they continued to repeat till they finally left him for dead, after rifling his pockets of the money they contained. The following is an outline of the particulars as developed on the trial :—

John Burlinson, 24; Charles Gill, 19; and Henry Nuttall, 22, were charged with the murder of Joseph Cocker, at Knaresborough, the former as principal and the other two as accessories.

Mary Snow deposed,—I am the wife of Charles Snow, of Knaresborough. I live in the Market-place, there is a yard to our house; I knew Cocker; he lived going into the Market-place; he was a publican; he lived alone; he had no wife, no servant, and no child. He had a window that looked into our yard; it was high from the ground. I remember the evening of the 18th of June. At near twelve o'clock I heard a noise of groaning and beating : it appeared to come from Cocker's window. On hearing the noise I opened the door and went into the yard; I continued to hear groanings and beatings. It came out of Joseph Cocker's house. I went into our house again and got a bucket, and looked into the window. I stood upon the bucket, and kneeled upon a cover that covers the ash-place, that enabled me to see into the house. The window does not open. I saw three men standing, but I did not see Cocker. One of the men had a candle in his hand; there was another upon the window. I did not know the men at the time. They were in the kitchen, in the inside of the long settle. I heard them say, "Let us take him into the cellar." I opened our front door, and went to Cocker's front door. I shook the door with all my might, and I shouted, "Cocker, are they murdering you?" The door was fast. No one answered. I came round into our house again, and I came upstairs to awake my husband; he was in bed. I then heard a rush out of Cocker's house; I asked my husband to be quick. I came downstairs by myself, and looked out of our front door. It was dark; I heard some one whispering, but I saw nobody. I then went and looked into Cocker's back window, as before. I saw Cocker on his feet, and leaning against the fire-place. He was groaning and crying out. The floor where he was standing was covered with blood; I only saw one candle at that time. I went to urge my husband to be quick. We both came downstairs together, and went into the yard; I went before my husband. I looked into the window again, and I saw three men in the house again; two of them were standing, and one of them was knelt down. Cocker was laid across the floor. The man was knelt down by Cocker's head, near the long settle. The other two were standing near his feet, one of them had a candle in his hand. My husband followed me at the time. I did not see the men do anything but kneeling and standing. I went to the window before they left, and I left my husband looking. We went into our own house, and my husband got a pistol he had. He went to look into the window again, and we heard the men rush out; I was standing near him. We then went and awoke the police-officer. I knew Burlinson again as soon as I saw him in the jury-room.

After the examination of several other witnesses who corroborated the above statement, the learned judge summed up, the jury retired for a quarter of an hour, and on their return found all the prisoners guilty.

His Lordship then proceeded to pass sentence. His observations were brief, and he spoke in a low tone of voice, and seemed much affected. He observed that they had severally been convicted upon the clearest evidence of a foul and cruel murder upon the unfortunate deceased. For them there was no hope in this world, and he recommended them to seek to obtain that mercy which would prepare them for a future world. He then sentenced the prisoners to be hanged by the neck, and their bodies to be afterwards buried within the precincts of the jail. The prisoners on sentence being passed on them, were very much affected, and after sentence, were removed to the condemned cell bathed in tears.

The unfortunate young men after their condemnation, and up to the period of their execution, conducted themselves with the propriety becoming persons in their awful situation. They were regularly attended by the Ordinary, the Rev. W. Flower, and by that zealous and truly Evangelical Wesleyan minister, the Rev. J. Rattenbury, and others ; who administered to them those consolations which religion alone can afford, and to whose exhortations they paid the greatest possible attention ; at the same time expressing the utmost contrition for the crime of which they had been guilty. Nuttall, who seemed to be the most affected of the three, frequently expressed his anxious wish that the day of execution had arrived ; stating that if he had taken the advice of his friends, and paid attention to his religious duties, he would have escaped suffering so ignominious a death.

This morning (Saturday, August 7th), at the usual hour, the unfortunate young men came on the scaffold, behind the Castle, attended by the Ordinary, &c. ; when, after spending a few minutes in prayer, the caps were drawn over their eyes,—the ropes were adjusted,—the fatal bolt was withdrawn,—a shudder ensued,—and this world closed on them for ever. But though their lives were thus sacrificed to the violated laws of their country, and notwithstanding the enormity of their guilt, we sincerely hope that He who extended forgiveness to the expiring thief on the cross, and who, even in the bitterness of His agony, prayed for his own murderers, will have had compassion on these greatly erring young men. There was a large concourse of people to witness the awful spectacle, several of whom were acquainted with the unfortunate men, and had come from Knaresborough and its neighbourhood, to witness the closing scene of their wretched lives. Many of the spectators

were deeply affected at the melancholy occurrence, and
when we consider the youth of the sufferers, three young
men in the very blossom of their age, falling victims to their
vicious courses, it indeed affords ground for the most serious
reflections.

JONATHAN TAYLOR AND ROBERT NALL.

Saturday, April 9th, A.D. 1842.—Jonathan Taylor, aged
60, for the wilful murder of his wife Ellen Taylor, by
strangling her at Escrick, near York, on Tuesday, the 25th
day of October.—Also Robert Nall, aged 33, for the wilful
murder of his wife Mary Nall, at Sheffield. There was a
very large concourse of people to witness the awful tragedy.

JOSEPH DOBSON.

Saturday, January 20th, A.D. 1844.—Joseph Dobson,
was executed at the new drop, for the wilful murder of his
own father, by shooting him with a gun, at Mount Tabor,
near Huddersfield.

WILLIAM KENDREW.

Saturday, December 28th, A.D. 1844.—William Kendrew
aged 22, was executed at the new drop, for the wilful
murder of Mr. Inchbold, at Low Dunsforth, near Boro-
bridge. He acknowledged the crime for which he was about
to suffer and seemed penitent.

JOHN RODDA.

Saturday, August 8th, A.D. 1846.—John Rodda was
hanged on the new drop behind York Castle, for the wilful
murder of his daughter, at Skipton, in April last.

On Friday, June 17th, John Rodda was placed at the bar
charged with the murder of Mary Rodda, his daughter, at
Skipton, in April last, by administering to her a quantity of
vitriol. Mr. Hall and Mr. Wasney appeared for the prosecution ; the prisoner was defended by Mr. Bliss. The
prisoner pleaded " Not guilty."

Mr. Hall stated the case.—The prisoner stood indicted before them for the murder of his child—a charge so unusual and so repugnant to the ordinary feelings of human nature that he must caution them against being prejudiced against the prisoner, but to regard it as an additional circumstance of improbability of his being guilty of the crime imputed to him. The prisoner was a hawker of or dealer in mats, and a short time before the death of his child, was living at Skipton. He had a wife and some young children, the eldest of whom, Mary, was the person into whose death they were about to inquire. On Thursday, the 16th of April, the child, which was poorly, was taken by her mother to a medical man, who would be called as a witness, and the jury would learn from him his treatment of that child. It continued poorly, and on the evening of Sunday, April 19th, he should show them that about eight o'clock it was not so unwell, that it ate about a pint of porridge, and about half-past eight o'clock it was left nursing on its mother's lap. In half an hour afterwards—at nine o'clock—the child was found to be dying in consequence of having taken into its stomach some oil of vitriol. During that half-hour the crime must have been committed, if any crime was committed ; and the jury would have to ask themselves who were the persons about the child during that half-hour, and who committed the offence ? He believed that it would be shown the only persons about the child during that half-hour were the father and mother. This would give the jury a very natural wish that one of the two persons who might be charged with any offence that the other was present at, might be examined before them. There was, however, a wise and inflexible law which provided that in all cases where the husband and the wife were concerned, unless a charge was made of violence by the husband upon the wife or the wife upon the husband, neither the husband nor the wife could be heard as evidence either for or against one another. He begged that no inference might be raised for or against the prosecution or the prisoner, because the wife was not put into the box—they must regard the non-production of the wife as a witness as if she was actually dead. He (Mr. Hall) would endeavour, as far as he could, to fill up the history of the half-hour he had alluded to, by a statement which the prisoner made to the coroner. At that time, on being asked what he had to say, he replied that he had neither bottle, spoon, nor anything else about him but the two children ; that he put the deceased into the cradle when it began to vomit, and took it up again, when his wife came downstairs and asked what was the matter ; he re-plied the child had been throwing up ; that he went out and asked a doctor to go to his child ; that he got the stuff at a druggist's to rub on the wall, but being in a broken bottle he threw it away. The child died on the 19th of April, and he should show that on the 18th the prisoner went to a druggist's shop in Skipton, and bought a pennyworth of oil of vitriol, which he took away with him in a bottle. There was another fact throwing some light upon the matter, to which he would draw their atten-tion. Ten or twelve days before this unfortunate circum-stance happened, the prisoner, in a conversation with a witness he should call before them, stated that if the child were to die he would get 50s. for it from a dead club, and the sooner it was dead the better, it was so sickly. The learned counsel then called several witnesses who corroborated the above statements ; after which Mr. Bliss made a powerful speech in defence ; and his Lordship then proceeded to sum up the evidence, which he did in a most impartial manner. The jury then retired, and after an absence of an hour and a half they returned a verdict of guilty. His Lord-ship then passed sentence of death upon him.

After his conviction, the unfortunate young man became fully aware of the perilous situation in which he was placed ; and, as he could not entertain any reasonable hopes of obtaining mercy in this world, he sought for it where alone it might be found, at the hands of a crucified Re-deemer. Rodda was an Irishman, and, being, like a large majority of his fellow-countymen, of the Roman Catholic persuasion, he obtained the spiritual aid of the Rev. T. Billington, vicar-general and Catholic dean of this city, who was unremitting in his attendance on the miserable man, and administered to him all those consolations which re-ligion only can afford, at the same time strongly impressing on his mind the blessed truths of divine revelation, and pointing him to the Lamb of God who taketh away the sins of the world, and through whose mediation salvation might be obtained, and who could and would be found of all those who sought him with sincerity of heart. Rodda seemed grateful for the attentions paid to him by the rev. gentleman and others, and expressed his remorse, with tears, for the horrid crime of which he had been guilty. A few days previously to his execution, he made a full confession of his guilt, and stated that avarice was his only motive for sacrificing his innocent and unoffending child, whom it was his duty as a parent to have succoured and protected ; but whom he coolly, deliberately, and cruelly murdered for the sake of filthy lucre. But the day of execution at last arrived, and the greatly erring young man's earthly hopes and fears were soon to terminate. At an early hour on Saturday morning, August 8th, the workmen commenced erecting the drop in front of St. George's Field, and the solemn preparations for the awful ceremony were speedily completed. At the usual hour the wretched man, with blanched cheek and dejected look—his arms pinioned—appeared on the scaffold, attended by the regular officials ; after spending a few minutes in prayer, the executioner proceeded to perform the duties of his office, by drawing the cap over his eyes and adjusting the rope, when the fatal bolt was withdrawn—the drop fell—a convulsive struggle ensued—and the unhappy mortal ceased to exist.

There was a large concourse of spectators assembled in St. George's Field, and the intervening road, to witness the appalling spectacle, amongst whom were a great number of the lower orders of the Irish, who had congregated to witness the last moments of their fellow-countryman.

PATRICK REID.

Saturday, January 8th, A.D. 1848.—Patrick Reid, at the back of York Castle, for the Mirfield murders.

On Monday, December 20th, 1847, Patrick Reid and Michael McCabe were placed at the bar charged with the wilful murder of Caroline Ellis, at Mirfield, on the 12th of May. Both the prisoners pleaded " Not guilty."

Mr. Ingham then rose and said :—May it please your

lordship : gentlemen of the jury, you are now about to investigate the murder of Caroline Ellis. She was a young woman of about 20 years of age, and was the servant of Mr. James Wraith, who lived at a place called Water Royd Hall. Mr. Wraith was an old man, about 76 years of age ; Ann, his wife, was about 65 years of age : and these two, with the servant girl, Caroline Ellis, were the only inmates of the house. At half-past eleven o'clock on the 12th of May, Mr. Wraith went to Cripplegate, to request his nephew, Joshua Green, to go to his farm to pick up stones. About one o'clock a thunder-shower came on, and the nephew did not arrive till half-past. He knocked at the door and shouted, but received no answer ; he heard nothing but the ticking of the clock. From under the front door he saw blood, and then gave an alarm. Others came and got in through the kitchen window ; there they found Caroline Ellis upon her back, quite dead, though warm. Her throat was cut and her skull fractured. Mrs. Wraith was found in the passage dead, with her throat cut and skull fractured, and Mr. Wraith was in the parlour, dead, and in the same state as his wife and domestic. Mr. Wraith's pockets were turned inside out. In one a half-sovereign was found. His watch had been taken away, and money which he was seen with the day before, and the wedding-ring from Mrs. Wraith's finger. The drawers in this room had been broken. Reid lived about three miles from Wraith's. He was a hawker of hardware. On the day in question at half-past twelve he called at Lockwood's ; then he went towards Mr. Wraith's, and he was seen to go by a house belonging to people named Webster, at a quarter to one. All these places are close to Mr. Wraith's. The prisoner McCabe was likewise a hawker. At the former trial he was admitted evidence against Reid. When the surgeon examined Caroline Ellis she had only one garter on, and in McCabe's house a portion of a garter was found. Reid was taken into custody at his own home the day but one after, when in bed, at an early hour in the morning. His clothes were taken possession of ; they were the same that he had worn on the day of the murder, and were submitted to the examination of a chemist, and you will find that there were a great many spots of blood upon the coat, particularly before and behind.

The cap which he wore on the day in question was also found, and on this also were found spots of blood. When Reid was taken into custody he made a statement which I will read to you. He was told that he was suspected of the murder, and that he was seen near the house at the time the murder was committed. He replied " Well, I was at the house about the time you mention, with my basket hawking. I knocked at the door, no one answered, and I walked on." The witness who will speak to this conversation, then asked if he chose to state where he went after. He said, " Well, I went down the footpath by the side of Wraith's garden. Wraith's was the last house I called at; I went forward, struck down the footpath which brought me to the town-gate in Mirfield, and I went over the stile, and along the footpath which leads to Mirfield church." Gentlemen, I have now to call your attention to an important piece of evidence. The key of the kitchen-door was lost; there is a well a few yards from the back door, and on this well being pumped out on the 19th of May, a week after the murder— this key was found. In the same well was found an instrument called a soldering-iron, an exceedingly heavy blunt weapon, such, as I will show you was well calculated to inflict part of the injuries which I have described. Who put that weapon there, and when was it put there? I shall show you that it belonged to the father of the prisoner Reid; that it was borrowed some few months prior to the murder, by a person named Kilty; and that on the afternoon before the murder Reid went to the house of Kilty, and took it away. And now, gentlemen, having laid before you the facts of this very serious case, if you are satisfied that the evidence, taken altogether, makes out the guilt of the prisoners, it will be your duty, however painful, to remember what a solemn oath you took when you came into that box to discharge your duty to your country, as well as to the prisoners at the bar; and I pray that after a full and candid consideration of this case, you will a true verdict give according to the evidence, so help you God.

Witnesses were then examined who corroborated the learned counsel's statement, after which Mr. Seymour made an eloquent appeal to the jury for Reid, and Mr. Matthews followed on behalf of McCabe. The court then adjourned.

On Wednesday, Mr. Justice Patteson summed up with great minuteness, occupying upwards of three hours. The jury retired at half-past eleven, and returned at one, with a verdict of guilty against both prisoners. On the usual question being put, McCabe exclaimed, "Only one thing I can say; I am innocent of the crime laid to my charge." Patrick Reid remained silent. Mr. Justice Patteson then put on the black cap, and pronounced judgment. The circumstances under which the murder of Caroline Ellis was committed were of the most horrible description. He did not recollect ever to have heard or read of such an atrocious act having been committed in this country at any period, as that in the middle of the day a house should be entered, and three persons, the whole inhabitants of that house, an old man, his wife, and servant, cruelly murdered, beaten, their heads fractured, and afterwards their throats cut. (Here the prisoner McCabe fell in a state of insensibility in front of the dock. The officers of the gaol having placed him in a chair, he revived sufficiently to enable the court to proceed.) It seems to me that the object you had in view must have been plunder. Whether you went to that house determined to commit murder, or only to rob, it is quite impossible for me to tell. I cannot but fear that you must have gone there with the deliberate intention to kill the people in the house, because what was done was done so quickly, one after another evidently killed so rapidly, that I cannot think that the notion arose in your minds from meeting with resistance. The prisoners were then sentenced to death in the usual terms.

REID'S CONFESSION.

> "Condemned Cell, York Castle,
> 30th December, 1847.

"I, Patrick Reid, now lying under sentence of death for the murder of Caroline Ellis at Mirfield, hereby acknowledge the justice of my sentence, and I do hereby solemnly and sincerely declare that I alone am guilty of the murder of Caroline Ellis, James Wraith, and Ann Wraith, and that Michael McCabe, now also lying under sentence of death for the murder of the said Caroline Ellis, had nothing whatever to do with her murder, or the murders of James Wraith and Ann Wraith, any or either of them.

"I got up about nine o'clock on the morning of the murder, and thought I would not hawk that day. I afterwards changed my mind, and resolved to rob and murder the family of Mr. Wraith. I then went over to Mirfield ; I called at Lockwood's about half-past twelve, and proceeded down to Mr. Wraith's. I conversed with the servant girl, and took out the soldering iron, and struck her on the head ; she tried to open the door, but I prevented her ; I struck her again and she fell. I then did the same to Mr. and Mrs. Wraith. The soldering iron flew from the handle, and I got the kitchen poker. I heard a knock at the door, and I saw McCabe, who asked if we wanted anything in his line. I answered, 'No, sir.' I thought he would not have known me ; if he had, I should have murdered him too. I then ransacked the drawers, and taking out a razor, cut all their throats. I locked the kitchen door, and threw the key and iron into the well, and went home by the footpath.

"PATRICK REID."

THE EXECUTION.

After his conviction the unfortunate young man became fully aware of the perilous situation in which he was placed ; and, as he could not entertain any reasonable hopes of obtaining mercy in this world, he sought for it where alone it might be found, at the hands of a crucified Redeemer. Reid was an Irishman, and being, like a majority of his fellow-countrymen, of the Roman Catholic persuasion, he obtained the spiritual aid of the Rev. W. Fisher, who administered to him those consolations which religion only can afford, at the same time strongly impressing on his mind the blessed truths of divine revelation, and pointing him to the Lamb of God who taketh away the sins of the world, and through whose mediation salvation might be obtained, and who could and would be found of all those who sought Him with sincerity of heart. The day of execution at last arrived, and the greatly erring young man's earthly hopes and fears were soon to terminate. At an early hour on Saturday morning, January 8th, the workmen commenced erecting the drop in front of St. George's Field, and the solemn preparations for the awful ceremony were speedily completed. At the usual hour the wretched man, with blanched cheek and dejected look—his arms pinioned—appeared on the scaffold, attended by the regular officials ; after spending a few minutes in prayer, the executioner proceeded to perform the duties of his office, by drawing the cap over the prisoners eyes, and adjusting the rope, when the fatal bolt was withdrawn, the drop fell, a convulsive struggle ensued, and the unhappy mortal ceased to exist. There was a large concourse of spectators assembled in St. George's Field and the intervening road, to witness the appalling spectacle, amongst whom were great numbers of the lower orders of Irish, who had congregated to witness the last moments of their fellow-countryman.

The other prisoner, McCabe, who was tried and convicted along with Reid, received a respite from her Majesty.

THE MIRFIELD TRAGEDY.

The following lines were written on the barbarous and inhuman murders committed on the bodies of Mr. James Wraith, aged 77, Mrs. Mary Wraith, aged 70, and their servant Caroline Ellis, aged 20, on Wednesday, the 12th of May, 1847, at the village of Mirfield, near Dewsbury, in the West Riding of Yorkshire :—

You pious Christians, attention pay to what I now relate,
Concerning of this dreadful deed, for awful was the fate
Of those three unfortunate beings who fell by the murderer's hand :
A more horrid and brutal crime was never done in our land.

Chorus.

Let's hope their souls are happy now,
In Heaven among the blest ;
While their murderers do remain on earth,
Deprived of their rest.

In the pleasant village of Mirfield, near to Dewsbury town,
This aged couple lived for years, in the neighbourhood was well known,
Respected were by rich and poor, and all that dwelt close by,
Little thinking of the awful death that they were doomed to die

Their mangled bodies soon were found : after the deed was done,
A youth who was in their employ unto the house had gone ;
He found that every door was fast, no entrance could he gain,
He saw some blood beneath the door, and then gave the alarm.

An entrance then was quickly made, which caused great affright :
In the kitchen the murdered servant lay, a horrid ghastly sight ;
Proceeding further in their search, Mrs. Wraith they found,
Across her throat a dreadful gash, lying upon the ground.

With trembling limbs and horror struck to the parlour next they came,
They found the aged gentleman, his fate had been the same,
His hoary head was cruelly beat, his throat was cut likewise,
Those brutal deeds was done so quick it caused great surprise.

On Monday, the 19th of July, at the bar they placed Reid,
To take his trial for the murder, and to answer for the deed,
The crime that he was charged with, for the death of Mr. Wraith alone,
To prove if he was guilty, and how the crime was done.

McCabe, his supposed accomplice, in the witness box was placed,
He being admitted evidence, and to meet him face to face !
The evidence that he did give the jury could not believe,
For it is thought he is as guilty as the prisoner Patrick Reid.

The trial lasted full two days, and all were much surprised
To hear the verdict that was returned, for all thought he would die.
The Court, not being satisfied with the verdict that was given,
It was ordered then that both the men should be remanded back to
    prison.

Within York Castle's dreary walls they now are doomed to lie
Until the next Assizes, when again they must be tried
For the murder of Mrs. Wraith, likewise their servant maid,
And if they are guilty found, they may dread their awful fate.

Of all the murders that's been done in England near and far,
Greenacre, Good, or William Cooke, who murdered Mr. Pass,
There is none of them so horrid as the Mirfield tragedy ;
For they only took the life of one, but here they murdered three.

MICHAEL STOKES.

Saturday, May 13th, A.D. 1848.—Michael Stokes was executed on the new drop, in front of St. George's Field, for the murder of Mary Ann Garrad, at Leeds.

Michael Stokes was a private in the 57th regiment of foot, and at the time the murder took place, the regiment was quartered at the Leeds barracks. The deceased was a person of the name of Mary Ann Garrad, the wife of William Garrad, also a private in the 57th regiment. On the 20th of January, the deceased, her husband, and two or three other soldiers, were with the prisoner in one of the rooms at the barracks. While they were in that room, the husband of the deceased heard a musket go off, when his wife staggered and fell, and Garrad said something to the prisoner which the jury would hear. Two or three other persons, who were in the room, saw Stokes point the musket at the deceased, and fire it off. He did not raise it to the shoulder, nor in the attitude of "presenting," as the military phrase is. The deceased died in two or three hours, and on examination it was found that the ball had entered near the abdomen, passed through the body, and struck the wall behind her, the wall being broken to pieces. The surgeon stated that the death of Mrs. Garrad was caused in the manner above described, and one of the ball cartridges, previously in the prisoner's possession, was found to be missing. When Mrs. Garrad fell against the closet door, she exclaimed, "The Lord have mercy on me, what have you done?" Her husband then said, "You have shot my wife. I'll load my piece and shoot you." Stokes said, "Load it." The prisoner said he was not sorry for what he had done, but "could now die happy, for if she had lived he could not have died happy." On being asked the reason why he shot the deceased, he replied, "No one on earth shall know it but the priest."

After a lengthened investigation, Mr. Dearsley made an eloquent appeal to the jury on behalf of his client, who, he attempted to prove, was not in his right mind when he committed the fatal deed, or he would never have exposed himself to certain destruction. He proceeded to show the jury that if they acquitted the prisoner upon the ground of insanity, he would be confined in an asylum for life, which, therefore, was the safer course to adopt. If they sent him to the scaffold, the deed was irrevocable, it never could be undone. He solemnly conjured the jury to pause—allowing mercy to temper justice, to pronounce the man insane; and should they, after all, err and consign a madman to the scaffold, he solemnly prayed that his innocent blood might not fall upon their heads, nor those of their children.

The jury consulted together for a few minutes, and then returned a verdict of Guilty. The Clerk of Arraigns said, " You have been found guilty of the crime of murder, what have you to say why the sentence of death should not be passed upon you ?" The prisoner replied, " I hope, my Lord, you'll have mercy upon me."

His Lordship then put on the black cap, and sentenced the prisoner in the following terms :—" Michael Stokes, you have had the benefit of a full trial by an attentive jury, and have had everything that was possible suggested and urged upon me and the jury by your learned counsel. But the result of the trial has been to satisfy the jury, and unquestionably to satisfy me, that from some wicked and diabolical motive, into which I do not presume to dive, you deliberately, with the musket upon the day in question, deprived of life the unfortunate woman. What the motive was I cannot divine ; but I should indeed have trembled for the security of society if the defence attempted to be put forward had succeeded upon this occasion. It has been unfortunately but too common of late amongst the feelings of a large part of the community to think that they can discover in the very atrocity of crime itself a justification upon the ground that the party could not have been a responsible agent. I trust and hope, and I am sure there is no one who hears me but who does not trust and hope, that in the eyes of the Almighty there may be circumstances of palliation and mitigation which are hidden from human research. I trust and hope that may be the case, but these are questions with which human laws are incompetent to deal. We should be doing injustice if we were to attempt to act upon them. We must leave them in the hands of that Almighty Being who alone can understand their action." He then passed sentence of death in the usual manner.

On the day before the Assizes terminated, Mr. Dearsley moved for a copy of the indictment, in order that he might make application for a writ of error, to suspend the execution of the condemned man, so as to give time to have the matter argued before the fifteen judges, as to an alleged informality in the indictment. The point was argued by the prisoner's counsel on Saturday, April 29th. The learned judges took time to consider, and on Monday intimated to Mr. Dearsley that, in their opinion, the conviction was good and the cause of death stated with sufficient authority, the words " sent forth " being rejected as surplusage.

After his conviction, the unfortunate young man obtained the spiritual help of the Rev. W. Fisher and the Rev. J. Render, the two Roman Catholic priests resident in this city, he being of the Roman Catholic persuasion ; and, by their instrumentality, he was led to look for mercy at the foot of the cross, that being the only place where it could be found. He has paid great attention to their spiritual exhortations, and we trust that he will have made ample atonement for the heinous crime which he has committed. The day of execution at last arrived. At an early hour on Saturday morning, May 13th, the workmen commenced erecting the drop in front of St. George's Field, and the solemn preparations for the awful ceremony were speedily completed. At the usual hour the wretched man, with his arms pinioned, appeared on the scaffold, attended by the regular officials ; after spending a few minutes in prayer, the executioner proceeded to perform the duties of his office, by drawing the cap over the eyes of the culprit, and adjusting the rope, when the fatal bolt was withdrawn—the drop fell—a momentary but never-to-be-forgotten thrill of horror ran through the assembled multitude—a convulsive struggle ensued—and the unhappy man ceased to exist. There was a large concourse of people assembled to witness the last moments of the miserable man.

THOMAS MALKIN.

Saturday, January 6th, A.D. 1849.—Thomas Malkin was hanged on the new drop, in front of St. George's Field, for the murder of Esther Inman, at Hunslet, near Leeds.

It is again our painful duty to record one of those brutalizing spectacles, of which England, that land of Bibles and privileges, can boast so many, viz., the public strangling of a fellow creature. The extreme youth of the prisoner, he being only seventeen years of age, the irreproachable character he has hitherto possessed, and the interesting relation in which he stood to the unfortunate female, whose life he is charged with having taken, are all circumstances which militate greatly against the belief that he was in a sane state of mind when he committed the act. But however this may have been, his death upon the scaffold can only have the effect of rendering the public mind still more familiar with deeds of blood. The sacredness of human life can never be impressed upon the populace by exhibitions of judicial slaughter.

Esther Inman, the young woman who was murdered, lived at Hunslet with her step-father, a tailor there. The young man lived there also, and was working with Mr. Holdsworth, as a wood-turner. All the parties were highly respectable in their situation. The young man and young woman were both members of the Primitive Methodist Connection, attended the same school, the same chapel, and the same singing-seat in the chapel. This sort of meeting produced acquaintance, acquaintance strengthened into intimacy, and intimacy ripened into courtship. It is not unusual that that bright period of man's life should be chequered with clouds of sadness.

On the 8th of October, Esther Inman had been to Kirkstall, to see a sister of hers, and about ten o'clock that night she was sitting at home with her step-father, her elder sister, and two women named Smith, mother and daughter. While they were sitting they heard a whistle. Shortly afterwards, the younger of the Smiths left the house, saw Malkin, who desired her to tell Esther Inman to come out, as he wanted to see her. She went back and delivered her message. The deceased put on her boots and went out ; very shortly after her father heard a cry ; he rushed out, and found her laid prostrate in the garden ; he took her in his arms, and carried her into the house ; after a few ejaculations she instantly died. On further examination it appears she had two wounds on her breast. Malkin had been seen by two or three persons standing at the garden gate talking with Esther Inman, and after she cried out he was seen running out of the garden towards his own home, where he uttered some incoherent expressions respecting the fatal deed he had just done. An alarm was immediately given, but he was not taken until Monday night, when he was discovered in the Free Market, Leeds, in a very desolate condition. He was then committed to York Castle to take his trial for the murder.

The trial took place on Wednesday, December 20th, at York Castle, before Mr. Baron Platt and a respectable jury. Mr. Hall stated the case, and the foregoing particulars were corroborated by the various witnesses. Mr. Overend then made an excellent appeal on his behalf, after which his Lordship summed up in a clear and impartial manner, and the jury returned a verdict of Guilty, but recommended him to mercy on account of his youth. The learned judge then put on the black cap, and passed sentence in the following words :—" Thomas Malkin, you have been convicted by a jury of your country of the crime of murder. Yours is a case certainly exciting great commiseration, if a man committing so heinous a crime could be commiserated ; but that is impossible. Murder is of such diabolical malignity, that it is necessary to be punished when a party is convicted, and it is improper that mercy should be extended to those who have committed it. It is quite impossible for me to hold out any hopes of mercy to you. It seems to me that your case, although it has moved all who have heard it, is not one to which I can extend any hope. It is true you began life with respectability, but you forgot to curb your passion for resentment—you forgot to curb that malicious tendency of the human heart which, if not curbed, leads to every kind of malignant mischief." Sentence of death was then passed in the usual manner.

THE EXECUTION.

After the trial he manifested great indifference to what was passing around him, and seemed but little affected at the awful position in which he was placed. On Thursday he showed signs of contrition, and made a confession to Mr. Sutton of his having killed the young female, and that for a month or five weeks previously he had contemplated her death. He states that it was not jealousy which led him to commit the murder, but the thought came into his head, and he could not assign any particular reason for perpetrating the deed.

Since his condemnation the unfortunate young man has paid great attention to the spiritual exhortations of the chaplain, and seemed quite resigned to his awful situation.

At last the fatal hour arrived, and the wretched man was brought out upon the drop. He appeared to have undergone a considerable bodily change since his condemnation. At this moment the sensation produced was very great. Mingled emotions of horror, pity, and fear pervaded the vast multitude assembled in St. George's Field and the intervening road. After a few moments spent in prayer, the rope was adjusted—the fatal bolt was withdrawn—a few short convulsive struggles ensued—and Thomas Malkin was ushered into the world of spirits, there to render an account to his God for the deeds done in the body.

Thus has finished the unfortunate youth's career, of whom it may be truly said, " he has not lived out half his days." He has left a father and mother, and perhaps other relatives, to mourn his loss. He has left acquaintances ; and then there is the public at large, all of whom have some feeling in the matter. But what is that feeling ? With respect to his friends, it will be that of intense mental anguish ; with respect to others, in some cases it will be pity, in others a certain amount of gratification. So differently is the human mind affected by circumstances of this kind.

THE UNFORTUNATE CULPRIT'S LAMENT.

That night ! that night was calm and still ;
But was my inmost soul ?
Ah ! no, a fiend was lurking there
My youth could not control.

I knew not why, nor know I yet,
The promptance of my crime :
Unless 'twas jealousy, the bane
Of love, of faith sublime.

I lov'd my Esther with a love
Which could not brook the thought,
Much less the fact that she could slight
A heart with kindness fraught.

I lov'd her! yes, and hope for grace,
　For mercy from my God!
My curse upon that evil hour
　The murderer's steps I trod!

I lov'd her! yes, and could not bear
　To think she lov'd not me;
To think that some one else she lov'd,
　Whose own she wish'd to be!

My rueful life on earth is short;
　An ignominious death
Awaits my being—soon the cord
　Must stop my vital breath.

But can it kill my living soul?
　Ah, no! 'twill leave this clay,
And join with Esther's in the realms
　Of everlasting day;

When strife, nor envy, nor despair,
　But happiness and love
Fill every breast, and angels join
　Its consonance to prove.

Brothers and sisters, parents dear,
　Adieu! we meet no more
In this lower world—but shall again,
　I trust, on Heaven's blest shore.

GEORGE HOWE.

Saturday, March 31st, A.D. 1849.—George Howe was
hanged on the new drop, in front of St. George's Field, for
the wilful murder of his daughter, Eliza Amelia Howe, at
Yarm, on the 25th of January last.

On Saturday, March 10th, George Howe was placed at
the bar, charged with the murder of Eliza Amelia Howe, at
Yarm, by placing a quantity of oxalic acid in her food.

Amelia Wood, of Yarm, widow, deposed:—I live with my
uncle, Mr. Bray, at Yarm, and knew the prisoner. The
deceased was born about the end of October, and her mother
died on the 17th of November. After that, prisoner lodged
with the witness, and she nursed the baby. The prisoner

was working then as a labouring man. On the 24th of
January, the prisoner brought the carrier to take his boxes
away, which witness said she would not allow until he
had made arrangements about the children, and settled with
her. He had told her the day before that a person would
come from Middlesbro' and take the baby. Witness said it
was a very unlikely thing that the baby should be taken
away at night, and that she would make inquiries about it.
He went to a shop and bought a stone of flour, and then
said, " You must have a very bad opinion of me to think
that I shall go away and leave my children." Witness
replied, " George, you are so incorrigible a liar, that if you
speak the truth it is by accident." He then went to work.
That night witness was feeding the baby with milk and
bread. Her nephew called out to her to fetch the candle,
and she left the prisoner sitting at the side of the table.
When she returned she found him at the same place. He
took up the candle, and said, " You can spare the candle,
Mrs. Wood ;" and she said, " I shall be like, George."
Prisoner then went to bed, and she resumed feeding the
child by the firelight, and observed it put out a little bit of
bread. She then waited until she got the light from the
prisoner. When she began to feed it again, it made wry
faces. She looked into the can, and saw it looked very
watery ; and then stirred it up and took a spoonful, which
burned her stomach like very strong vinegar. Did not give
the child any more after she had tasted it, but took it upstairs, and Bray and Holmes tasted it. They got up, and
the food was taken to Mr. Dale, surgeon. Some time after,
Hardcastle, policeman, came and took the prisoner into
custody. The baby slept well that night, and was fed with
bread and water, sweetened with sugar. Next morning
witness observed the child's mouth was blistered and its
tongue was swollen. She got some magnesia from the
druggist's, and gave it a teaspoonful. The child continued
to get worse, and died on the Monday morning following,
after much suffering. In the first three or four weeks he
was a kind father to the baby, but after that he was off
drinking four or five days, and he began to say he wished
the child was dead, and who would have him with two
children. Witness replied that need not be any hindrance,

as she had no desire to part with it. One night he took and squeezed it to him until witness thought it would be suffocated. She would never allow him to have it after that.

Stephen Hardcastle, policeman, Yarm, said,—Holmes and Wintersgill went for him on the night in question, to take the prisoner into custody on a charge of attempting to poison his child. Witness searched his clothes, which were on the bed, and which were the same he has on now, except the breeches. Took him to the lock-up, but found nothing on him except a piece of paper, which he put his tongue to, and it had a very nasty taste, but different to tobacco. His boxes were searched, but nothing particular was found. Next morning searched again, and found a sack on a box near the bed-head, and folded in an old shawl was a bottle, containing something like crystals, and a small portion of liquid. A joiner was called in, and he drew witness's attento a board at the bed-head, on which was some powder. There was also a stain on the wall, as of some liquid having run down. On the Saturday he went again to Stockton, and took the prisoner with him.

Several other witnesses were examined, who fully established the facts, and after his lordship summed up the evidence, the jury found the prisoner Guilty, and the learned judge passed sentence of death upon him in a very feeling and impressive manner.

THE EXECUTION.

After his sentence the criminal appeared thoughtful and dejected, and was constantly visited by the Rev. T. Sutton, who has regularly attended him since his condemnation. He seems penitent and submissive to his fate, and relying on that Saviour who hath purchased the redemption of the vilest of sinners, he has in considerable placidity of mind anticipated the final day of his earthly existence.

At length the fatal day, on which the greatly erring man's earthly hopes and fears were to terminate, arrived, and this morning, at an early hour, the workmen erected the scaffold at the usual place in front of St. George's

Field, and as the time of execution grew nigh, an immense multitude of people began to assemble to witness the awful scene.

At twelve o'clock the unfortunate man walked on the drop with a firm step, but with blanched cheek and dejected look—his arms pinioned—attended by the regular officials ; he then knelt down, and appeared to pray most fervently for a few minutes, after which the executioner placed the cap over his head, and put the rope in its proper position. He then withdrew the fatal bolt—the drop fell—a momentary thrill of horror passed through the immense mass of people—there were a few short heavings of the shoulders—and the body of George Howe was a lifeless piece of clay—his spirit had fled into the boundless depths of an eternity whose mysteries have now been fully developed to his criminal soul, and whose blessings, we trust, he has received through the merits of a crucified Redeemer.

WILLIAM ROSS.

Saturday, August 17th, A.D. 1850.—William Ross was hanged on the new drop, in front of St. George's Field, for the wilful murder of Mary Ross, his wife, at Roughton.

The execution would have taken place on Saturday last, but in consequence of numerously-signed petitions having been sent to the Home Office, from York and other places, a respite for one week was received, in order that further inquiries might be made as to the truth of the prisoner's declaration of innocence. The result of this investigation was against him, and this day, whether he was innocent or guilty, his spirit has been ushered into the presence of that Judge from whom no secrets can be hid, there to give an account of the deeds done in the body.

The particulars of the case will still be in the recollection of our readers, but we cannot forbear giving a short account of the details connected with the melancholy transaction.

The prisoner was tried on Friday, July 19th, and pleaded not guilty. Mr. Bliss, Mr. Hardy, and Mr. Pickering were counsel for the prosecution ; Serjeant Wilkins and Mr. Dearsley for the defence.

Mr. Bliss stated the case. The learned counsel said that the prisoner was about 20 years of age, and the woman he was charged with having murdered was Mary Ross, his wife. The indictment charged the prisoner with having administered the poison in treacle, and he (the learned counsel) thought he should be able, partly by the statements which the prisoner had made, and partly by several minute and collateral circumstances, to establish the case. The place where this event occurred was Roughton, a small town on the confines of Yorkshire and Lancashire, and two or three miles from Ashton-under-Lyne. The deceased's maiden name was Bottomley, and she was married to the prisoner in 1849, at Ashton, where they then resided. In September, in the same year, they went to reside with his father-in-law, who, in January last, removed to Roughton, and occupied the house in which the murder occurred. In May last, a sister of the prisoner's paid him a visit, but she and Mrs. Ross not agreeing, the prisoner directed her to return to Ashton. She left on the 16th of May, and it would be proved that on the same day the prisoner purchased five ounces of arsenic at a druggist's shop at Ashton. He did not return to Roughton that night, and on making his appearance next day, a few words passed between him and his wife, and he was heard to say that she was " worth more dead than wick." It appears that on her death he would become entitled to £10. 6s. from two clubs of which she was a member. Up to this period the deceased had enjoyed her usual good health, but on Tuesday morning, May 28, she was taken ill, and was much purged and vomited. The prisoner left the house about ten or eleven o'clock, after having prepared her some potatoes and milk. That night Martha Buckley called to see her, and found her somewhat better. Next morning her sisters paid her a visit, when a desire was expressed that Dr. Scholefield should be sent for. Prisoner said he would go for him, and on his return, he said that the doctor was from home, but his lady had promised to send him as soon as he returned. This turned out to be a fabrication, as the prisoner had never called there at all. He went upstairs to her with a cup in his hand, and was heard to press her to take something, which she refused. Deceased rose on Thursday morning, apparently better, and having had some breakfast with her father and sister, they left to go to work, leaving the prisoner and his wife alone till between nine and ten o'clock, when he went out to the "George" public-house, where he spoke of the illness of his wife, and of the probability of her death. He was advised to procure medical relief, which he did. On his return home, he carried his wife from the bed she had hitherto occupied to one in an adjoining room. Martha Buckley was then at the house, and presently the doctor called, and asked to see her evacuations, but the prisoner replied he had thrown all away. The deceased lingered in great pain, and expired at about half-past two o'clock in the afternoon. Next day he made a statement insinuating that Martha Buckley had given the deceased some white powder, which had made her ill, and had been the cause of death. In consequence of this she was apprehended, but afterwards set at liberty. On the 18th of June, it occurred to the constable that he had not fully examined the prisoner's pockets. He commenced a search, and found a quantity of arsenic in his watch-pocket, on which he said he might as well tell all about it. Martha Buckley gave some of this poison to his wife in treacle, and the remainder he put into his watch-fob. He asserted that she and her husband knew all about it, and that the former had given him a shilling to say nothing about it, as she had made a mistake.

On Saturday morning his lordship summed up the evidence, and the jury, after a short consultation, returned a verdict of guilty. The judge, in a very feeling address, then passed sentence of death upon him, at the conclusion of which the unfortunate man exclaimed with strong emphasis, "Not guilty, my lord! I am not guilty of the crime."

Since his condemnation, Ross has had the spiritual assistance of the Rev. Thomas Sutton, the ordinary of the Castle, and we sincerely hope that he has profited by the exertions of that gentleman. He has made no confession, but protested his innocence of the crime for which his life has paid the forfeit. The workmen commenced erecting the scaffold at an early hour on Saturday, and at a few minutes to twelve o'clock, the mournful procession made its appearance. A short time was spent in devotional exercises, and the young man then took leave of those by whom he was surrounded. He was then placed in the hands of the executioner, and that functionary, after placing the cap over his eyes, and adjusting the rope, proceeded to the fatal bolt, which, in an instant was withdrawn, and he, who but a short time before was replete with life, was exhibited dangling in the air, as a warning to the multitude congregated together to witness the melancholy spectacle. After a few convulsive struggles, the sufferings of the unfortunate young man in this vale of tears were for ever at an end ; his spirit —released from its tenement of clay—had taken its flight, we trust, to a holier and happier region, where it shall remain until that day when the books shall be opened, the dead shall be raised, and the secrets of all hearts be made known.

After hanging the usual time, the body was cut down, and interred within the prison walls.

ALFRED WADDINGTON AND JAMES BARBER.

Saturday, January 15th, 1853.—Alfred Waddington and James Barber were executed at Sheffield for murder ; the former for that of his illegitimate child, and the latter for that of Mr. Alexander Robinson.

On August 19th, 1852, Sheffield was the scene of a horrifying murder. An illegitimate child has had its head cut off by its father, who also attempted to murder its mother and another young woman. The murderer's name is Alfred Waddington, a grinder, residing in Lord Street, Park, Sheffield. He is about twenty years of age, the associate of a notoriously bad character, and he has himself been tried for highway robbery. The child murdered was Elizabeth Slater, the daughter of Sarah Slater, of Brown Street, and was about a year and nine months old. On Monday the mother took out a summons against Waddington, for neglecting to maintain the child. He saw her in the street on Wednesday evening; she was left in care of a little girl called Barlow, while the mother went to attend the females' class at the Mechanics' Institute. At half-past eight Waddington appeared at the door of the class-room, and called out "Sarah Slater, you're wanted." She went to him, and he asked, "What have you done with the child? you must go with me; it has fallen off a wall and has broken its neck." She immediately ran out of the room with him. On arriving in Silvester Lane, he said she need not trouble, for he had murdered the child. He pulled out a clasp knife, and he said, "Here's some of its blood." The monster then fiercely attacked her, and attempted to cut her throat. She guarded her neck with her hands, which were shockingly lacerated. A little boy, who saw the struggle, called out "Murder." Waddington then went up to Eagle Street, and the woman was taken home. He was shortly afterwards met by a young woman, called Sarah Dobson, who resides in Duke Lane, Sheffield Moor, a companion of the young woman, Slater. Having heard rumours of the murder, and of the outrageous and diabolical attack upon Slater, the young woman asked him what he had done with her and his child. He at once, without answering, commenced a most fearful attack upon her with his knife, and wounded her in a very severe manner about the face. Her violent screams alarmed the neighbourhood and caused him to run away. At daylight in the morning, however, he gave himself up to a night-watchman, and on his being conveyed to the Town-hall, he described the exact place where the murdered child might be found.

He said he carried it into Cutters Wood; and there cut its head off. In the morning two policemen went to the spot mentioned by the prisoner, and there they found the body of the child. Its head was lying several feet from the body.

The prisoner was brought up before the magistrates at the Town-hall, on Thursday, at noon, when he was committed to York Castle to take his trial at the next assizes, for the inhuman deed.

The day of the trial Waddington was arraigned at the bar, when the facts recorded in the preceding pages were sworn to by the various witnesses, and the jury retired a short time and returned with a verdict of guilty.

The learned judge then put on the black cap, and proceeded to pass sentence of death on the prisoner in the usual manner, holding out no hopes of mercy in this world ; exhorting him to make his peace with his Maker.

On Friday, September 3rd, Sheffield was alarmed by another cruel murder, and inquiries strengthen suspicion that it has been a fearful tragedy, and that the unfortunate individual has been robbed, and met with a violent and bloody death. On Saturday an examination of the spot where the body was found was made by the police officers. A new silk hat was found, but was severely crushed by having been thrust among the bushes. There was also found secreted in the ditch a white silk handkerchief, marked with small black spots.

He had on a pair of tweed trousers, a black cloth waistcoat, a green and brown mixture coat, and a pair of good Wellington boots. The shirt was a coloured print cotton one, with a linen front. The body appeared to be that of a well-built middle-sized man, about thirty-three years of age, with light coloured hair and whiskers.

No money or valuables of any kind was found on the body. The wound is of that nature that it has more the appearance of being inflicted with a hatchet or scythe, than of being caused by a gun or pistol. The wound commences almost in line with the lips, and extends along the jaw, and then at an angle proceeding up the cheek. The appearance of the face thus gashed and mutilated was frightful. The jaw-bone is completely broken ; the legs are drawn up, or contracted ; the teeth are loose in the head, and several other cuts are on the cheek, so that it has the appearance of having been literally chopped. On his linen was found the name, T. Robinson. It is supposed he has been a hawker of drapery goods. The discovery of the body was made by two little boys gathering blackberries. The business of the deceased in such a spot is not exactly brought to light ; but there is a strong probability that he had been decoyed there by a female, and further, that she had had assistance in the affair.

THE TRIAL.

On Tuesday, Dec. 21st, James Barber was arraigned at the bar, charged with the murder of Alexander Robinson, at Sheffield. Mr. Pickering and Mr. Overend were for the prosecution, and Mr. Serjeant Wilkins and Mr. Hardy defended the prisoner.

Mr. Overend stated the case, and the witnesses were examined as follows,—

George Renton, a little boy, six years of age, grandson of a Mr. Renton, of Mayday Hill, was the first witness called. I was in Mr. Appleyard's field getting blackberries yesterday, about seven o'clock. We saw a man lying in the hedge bottom. His head was covered with brambles. I was frightened and ran down the hill for my grandfather. I told my grandfather's young man what I had seen, and he went up to the field. I followed. "John" told some Irishmen who were in the field cutting wheat. Three Irishmen came to the body. My grandfather came afterwards and pulled the body out.

Joseph Dixon (another boy), between nine and ten years of age, son of George Dixon, residing at Mr. Creswick's, East Hill Lodge, corroborated the last witness as to the time of night, added, as we were coming down the field, we saw a man in the hedge bottom.

James Somerset, a youth about seventeen, servant to Mr. Renton aforesaid, said, George Renton came to me about half-past seven o'clock and said—"Jem, there's a man shot himself in the field." The body and the man's head was covered with blood. The other boy remained in the field. I asked him where the body was, and he said in Appleyard's field, and he would take me. The body was lying in the ditch with its face downwards, and partly covered. He appeared to be lying on his knees, having one hand turned over upon his loins. I went down the field, and called to a man named Hemsworth, who was going towards Sheffield, and some Irishmen working in the adjoining field. Mr. Renton pulled him out of the ditch.

George Hind, farmer, Newfield Green.—On Thursday, Sept. 2nd, I sat on some steps smoking tobacco, just below

Mr. Renton's house, and saw two men coming up the road towards me, and I had to get up to let them pass into the fields. I said " I'll give you room to come over, gentlemen ; when the man without the bundle said, " What are you doing here ? It is proper you were at some employment." The taller man carried the bundle.

After a number of other witnesses were examined, the counsel then addressed the jury on behalf of the prisoner, and after the judge had summed up the case, the jury retired a short time, then returned with a verdict of guilty. The judge then proceeded to pass sentence of death on the prisoner.

HENRY DOBSON.

Saturday, April 9th, A.D. 1853.—Henry Dobson, aged 27, was hung at the drop behind the Castle, for the murder of Catherine Sheridan, aged 19, at Wakefield, on the 18th of February of the same year. He was convicted under the most clear and satisfactory evidence. He had committed the murder from a feeling of revenge and personal animosity, because the deceased would not submit to his rudeness and refused to keep company with him. The prisoner was of slender frame, below the middle stature, with small and regular features, light brown hair, fair complexion, and good-looking. On entering the dock he was slightly agitated, but pleaded not guilty in a firm though subdued tone of voice.

Mr. Blanshard and Mr. Shaw were for the prosecution, and Mr. Overend defended the prisoner.

Mr. Blanshard stated the case. He said the prisoner at the bar stood upon his trial for the wilful murder of Catherine Sheridan, who it appeared was a young woman not more than nineteen years of age. Previous to the murder, the deceased had lived a short time in Wakefield, and had formerly been the inmate of a workhouse. At a very early age, the deceased went into service ; and when she was not more than fourteen years of age, she became the victim of seduction, and was thrown upon the town as a common girl. Between four and five months before she was murdered, she became acquainted with the prisoner,

Henry Dobson, and cohabited with him till the 11th day of February last, but being afraid of his conduct, she left the prisoner and went to lodge at another home. The deceased had occasion to lay a complaint before the magistrates for ill-treatment on the part of the prisoner, and he was consequently taken into custody by an officer named Gibson ; to whom he remarked, when in charge, that if he got over the accusation brought against him, in a short time afterwards he should have to be taken into custody and tried at the assizes, observing, " I shall take her life for this." After this, she lived in continual alarm, dreading the vengeance of the prisoner. She went to lodge with a young woman named Ann Clough, who resided at Wakefield, and who was in the same unhappy position as herself, being a girl of ruined reputation. Ann Clough lived in a yard in New Street ; and between ten and eleven o'clock at night, on the 18th of February last, she and the deceased went in company together to a shop in New Street, where they purchased some bacon and bread, and then returned to the house. On arriving there they recollected that they had forgot to purchase some cheese. In consequence of this omission, Ann Clough went out again in order to procure the required article, leaving the deceased in the house by herself. She was absent little more than a quarter of an hour. On re-entering the house, she observed there was no light except the light of the fire ; and was alarmed on witnessing the girl, Catherine Sheridan, laid full length upon the floor. Her head was slightly underneath the table, and her feet rested upon a piece of carpet laid upon the floor. Ann Clough endeavoured to arouse the deceased, but immediately found that she was dead. An alarm was instantly made, and a man named Berkinshaw, and other persons living in the neighbourhood, quickly entered the house. A light was procured, and on examining the body of the deceased, it was found that the throat was cut from the back to the front of the neck ; the gash extending from ear to ear. Dr. Wood was called in, and he found the unhappy girl quite dead. A razor was found on the floor, which was stained with blood, and there was a small portion of hair adhering to the blade. It was proved from witnesses that the prisoner was seen in the yard in New Street at the time when Ann Clough was absent, just before the clock struck eleven ; also, that the prisoner, shortly after eleven o'clock, was seen coming out of the yard, at the very time the unfortunate young woman was murdered ; as she was alive and well shortly before eleven o'clock, and a lifeless corpse before a quarter of an hour past eleven. A married woman named Harriet Woffinden saw the prisoner in Kirkgate at a quarter past eleven. He was running, and Woffinden called to him, upon which he stopped and remarked to her, "Oh, Harriet, I've done the job ; I've cut Kitty's throat ! I have, I have, by God ! Give me in charge to the police !" The prisoner then ran away, but was followed by the police, and within two hours he was apprehended, when he avowed that he had done the deed—that he had murdered the deceased.

The learned Baron summed up very briefly, stating that if there had been any scuffle as was suggested by the learned counsel for the prisoner, and that in the heat of passion he had committed the awful deed, that would be an aggravated species of manslaughter. The jury would have to consider whether, however, this was the true explanation of the transaction, and if they found it was not, then they must give their verdict totally irrespective of the consequences which would follow. His Lordship then read the evidence, and concluded by observing that if they thought there had been any quarrel, then the crime might be reduced to that of manslaughter, but on the contrary, if they thought the prisoner had deliberately taken the life of the girl without any altercation, then they must find him guilty of murder.

The jury consulted together for a few minutes without leaving the box, and then returned a verdict of guilty.

On being asked if he had anything to say why sentence of death should not be passed upon him, the prisoner who retained his self-possession, and appeared unmoved by the verdict, shook his head and made no reply.

SENTENCE OF DEATH.

Mr. Baron Martin having assumed the black cap, passed sentence of death upon the culprit in the following terms.

Henry Dobson, you have been convicted upon very clear and most satisfactory evidence of the crime of wilful murder. Murder is caused by a variety of motives, but in your case it is impossible to tell what was the motive passing in your mind at the time you perpetrated this awful deed. It was not from any desire of personal gain, but probably from some mingled feeling either of love or jealousy ; or it might be from motives of revenge for some real or imaginary injury done to you. It is impossible to arrive at any other conclusion than that you made up your mind to murder this unfortunate young woman upon this night, and that you procured a razor with which you deliberately cut her throat. If it be that a period of a week, or I should rather say, a space of ten days elapsed, during which you nourished malice in your breast, your crime is very great. The law will give to you what you did not give to your victim—you will be allowed some time to make your peace with God for your guilt. I therefore entreat you to consider yourself from this moment, separated from the world, for I can assure you that there is not the least possible chance of your life being spared. I am not disposed to distress your mind by making any lengthened remarks upon the enormity of your crime, and therefore I shall merely declare the sentence of the law for the wilful murder of which you have been convicted. The sentence is, that you be taken hence to prison, and thence to a place of execution, there to be hung by the neck until your body be dead, that your body be then cut down and buried within the precincts of the prison, in pursuance of this conviction.

The prisoner remained perfectly unmoved during the delivery of the awful sentence, and left the dock with a firm step in charge of two of the turnkeys.

THE EXECUTION.

This day, immediately after the hour of twelve had struck, the culprit appeared on the drop attended by the chaplain, William Gray, Esq., the under-sheriff, and the other officials. Dobson walked without a faltering step, and engaged in prayer with the chaplain for a short time, when Howard proceeded with his duties, though somewhat tardily. The bolt was then drawn, and Dobson, after severe struggling, was launched into eternity.

The number of spectators did not exceed 5,000. The body, after hanging for an hour, was cut down, and, in accordance with the sentence, interred in the graveyard of the Castle.

A defunct "legal functionary."—The official career of Nathaniel Howard, who has been the executioner for this county since 1840, has been brought to a conclusion ; the painful exhibition of the execution of Dobson, showed that from old age and infirmity, he was totally incapable to perform the duties of his responsible situation.

He died on Friday, April 22nd, aged seventy-three years.

William Dove.

Saturday, August 9th, A.D. 1856.—William Dove, aged 28, was committed to the Castle on the 17th of March, for the wilful murder of Harriet Dove his wife, at the borough of Leeds, on the 1st of March last.

The prisoner was tried on Wednesday, July 16th, 17th, 18th, and 19th, and was indicted for the wilful murder of Harriet Dove, at Leeds, on the 1st of March last. He was also charged upon the coroner's inquisition with the murder of the said Harriet Dove.

Mr. Overend, Q.C., Mr. Hardy, and Mr. Bayley were counsel for the prosecution ; Mr. Bliss, Q.C., Sergeant Wilkins, Mr. Hall, and Mr. Middleton for the defence. The fees of the counsel for the prosecution amounted to 220 guineas ; and the fees of the counsel for the defence would be as large.

At ten o'clock, the governor of the Castle was directed to put up at the bar the prisoner William Dove. Dove stepped up quickly to the bar, when all eyes immediately became rivetted upon him. He appeared perfectly calm and collected, and assumed an attitude of composure and ease, placing his left hand to his side, whilst with his right he took hold of the bar at which he stood.

Mr. Overend opened the case for the prosecution. The prisoner, he said, had committed a cold-blooded, cruel murder, by the use of a subtle poison known by the name of strychnia ; that he used this poison on six occasions ; that he made five attempts on the life of his wife, which were unsuccessful ; and, finally, that he made a sixth attempt, which ended in the death of his wife. The prisoner, he said, was the son of a very respectable man, Mr. Christopher Dove, a leather-merchant, who lived in Leeds, and at Christmas, 1854, he left the prisoner an annuity of £90 a-year, upon which the prisoner lived at the time of his wife's death. He was brought up to farming ; but at the time of his wife's death he was without employment. Shortly before her death he had, however, been an applicant for the office of pay-clerk to the Board of Guardians for the township of Leeds, but he was unsuccessful. Mrs. Dove was the daughter of equally respectable parents. She was the daughter of Mr. Jenkins, leather-merchant, of Plymouth. Mrs. Dove's brother (Mr. Jenkins) married the prisoner's sister, consequently there was a double relationship betwixt them. In 1851, the prisoner first became acquainted with his wife, and paid his addresses to her. At the latter part of 1852 they were married. He then brought her to a small farm, which at that time he occupied at Bramham. They lived there from the end of 1852 to the beginning of 1855, when they removed to Woodhouse, near Normanton. There they lived from the beginning to the end of 1855 ; and at Christmas in that year removed to Cardigan Place, Kirkstall Road, about one mile and a half from the centre of Leeds. It was in this house Mrs. Dove died.

It appeared from the evidence brought forward at the trial, that shortly after their marriage there were several complaints of the prisoner's ill-usage of his wife. He was a man very much addicted to liquor, and very frequently got drunk. His wife had been educated in a very religious family, and so had the prisoner. Mrs. Dove tried to check his propensity for drink, and this was the cause of frequent quarrels. At various times Dove was kind to his wife ; at other times he was abusive, brutal, and violent. On some occasions when drunk, and sometimes when sober, he was very violent. At one time he threw a chair at his wife's head. He threatened to blow her brains out ; and in one instance Mrs. Dove was obliged to fly from his house between ten and eleven o'clock at night for fear of her husband's violence. At another time she waited till she thought he would have retired to bed, and then she returned to the house, got in at one of the windows, and crept under the bed of the servant-maid, where she lay all night in the greatest fear. Complaints were made to her mother of the cruel treatment she received from her brutal husband, and a separation was agreed upon in which Dove was to allow her £20 a year to live upon ; but unfortunately it was not carried into effect. About this time Dove became acquainted with a certain individual, ignorantly called a " wise man," a kind of astrologer, and one who professed to have some skill in drugs and chemicals. To such a person as this the prisoner applied ; and after he had done so, he told his wife that he had got to know when it was probable that she would die. He said that he had good reason to suppose that she would not survive the month of February ; and she died on the 1st of March. On one occasion he said to Mrs. Dove, in the presence of the servant-maid, " Never mind, I'll do your job for you one way or another." Some time after-wards, when sober, he repeated the same thing, viz., that " he would do her job for her, and she need not mind." He ordered the servant out of the room, and she went down-stairs, but hearing Mrs. Dove scream loudly, she ran up again, and found that the prisoner had his wife down, and had a carving-knife in his hand. Assistance was called in, and he desisted.

On the 3rd or 4th of January, Dove sent for a person of the name of Harrison to a public-house, the New Cross Inn, in Meadow Lane ; and Harrison read to him, in the *Times* of that date, the announcement that Dr. Taylor could not discover strychnia in the body of Cook. Im-mediately after this had been read to the prisoner, he said to Harrison, " Can you get me, or make me any strychnia ?" to which Harrison replied, " No, not for the world." The prisoner replied, " Well, I can get some if you will not." Towards the end of January, he went to the surgery of Mr. Morley, a medical practitioner at Leeds, where he first met with a youth of the name of Peacock, and had some conversation with him about the killing effects of strychnia ; also to another youth at the same place, of whom he procured the poison which destroyed the life of his wife.

On Monday, the 25th of February, Mrs. Dove got up, between eight and nine o'clock in the morning, quite well. She and the prisoner breakfasted together ; but very soon afterwards she was taken ill. Her legs became stiff; there were twitchings of the legs and arms ; her body was thrown back ; there was the arching of the back, and all the symptoms of poisoning by strychnia. This was repeated over and over again ; and on Saturday, the 1st of March, she died in the greatest possible pain and agony, about twenty minutes to eleven o'clock. The pain was intense ; her body was arched, her hands were clenched, and her agony was so excessive that her screams were heard for a considerable distance.

After the trial the jury retired at five minutes past ten o'clock p.m., the summing up having occupied nearly six hours.

The jury returned into Court at twenty minutes before eleven o'clock, after an absence of thirty-five minutes, and their names having been called over, the Clerk of Arraigns said,—Gentlemen, have you agreed on your verdict ?

The Foreman.—We have.

The Clerk of Arraigns.—Do you say the prisoner at the bar is Guilty, or Not Guilty ?

The Foreman.—Guilty, but we recommend him to mercy on the ground of a defective intellect.

The Clerk of Arraigns then said,—William Dove, you have been convicted of murder, have you anything to say why sentence of death should not be passed upon you according to law ?

The Prisoner.—The only thing—

These were the only words he was heard to utter.

Proclamation being made for silence whilst the sentence of death was being passed upon him—

SENTENCE OF DEATH.

Mr. Baron Bramwell then assumed the black cap, and proceeded to pass sentence upon the prisoner, which he did in a low tone of voice. His lordship spoke to the following effect. Prisoner at the bar, you have been found guilty of the crime laid to your charge, the crime of murder—and you have been found guilty upon evidence that cannot leave a doubt on the mind of any one who has heard your case. You have been found guilty of a murder, the most dreadful of all crimes, and it is in your case one of the worst description— the murder of your own wife, whom you had sworn to cherish and preserve—a woman who had committed her fate to your keeping—murder by the most dreadful of all modes of murder, poison—and it is a murder which, I fear, from the circumstances, is one of the most aggravated that can be committed. The jury, in my judgment, have done their duty to their country and their consciences. They have done their duty in repelling the kind of defence that has been made for you, that your mind was in such a condition as that you were not to be held responsible for the consequences of your act. I have no doubt you were responsible in point of law, and by the verdict the jury have given, they have shown a firm determination to do their duty, while at the same time they have yielded to their natural impulses in recommending you to mercy. That recommendation shall be forwarded to the proper quarter, and if that recommendation should be concurred in mercy will be extended to you. My duty, however, is to pass upon you, not my sentence, but that of the law, and it is also my duty to caution you not to expect that the recommendation of the jury will be concurred in, but to anticipate that the solemn sentence of the law I have to pronounce upon you will be carried into effect, and that you have but a short time to live, and I recommend you therefore to employ that time in preparation for that fate. I doubt not, from what I have heard, that you have a capacity—an ample capacity— as to the knowledge of religious truths, and I doubt not you may now profitably employ the time reserved to you in con- sidering them, and in receiving that advice and assistance that will be offered to you. Do not cherish any hopes, but prepare yourself for the worst. The recommendation of the jury, I repeat, will be forwarded to the proper quarter, but I caution you not to expect it will be entertained ; whether it will be or not, it is not for me to say. My duty is now to pronounce the solemn sentence of the law, and the sentence of the Court upon you is that for the crime of wilful murder, you be taken from hence to the prison where you shall be confined, and from thence to the place of execution, where you shall be hanged by the neck until you be dead, and that your body be taken down and buried within the precincts of the prison in which you have been confined after this your conviction, according to the law in that case made and provided ; and may the Lord have mercy on your soul.

Previous to his execution, the prisoner made a confession of his guilt, and of the justice of the sentence, in the presence of Mr. Noble, the governor of the Castle. He avowed freely that he administered the poison *strychnia* to his wife, and that he knew at the time that what he was administering was poison.

THE EXECUTION.

The celebrity which the murder and the criminal had attained throughout the country, and especially in the neighbourhood of Leeds, was sufficient to justify the expectation that an immense concourse of spectators would assemble to witness the last scene of the dreadful tragedy. These anticipations were realized, for the morning trains were unusually heavy, but no cheap excursions took place. About eleven o'clock about 1,000 persons had assembled in front of the scaffold, and from that hour till the time of execution, the approaches to the vicinity of the gallows were filled with hurrying crowds. At the time of the execution, we should estimate that not less than from 15,000 to 20,000 persons were present, a number exceeding anything we have ever seen.

About a quarter to twelve o'clock, the under-sheriff arrived at the Castle, and shortly afterwards the convict was removed from the room in which he was placed to the waiting witness room, where his arms were pinioned by the executioner. The Rev. J. Hartley then read a portion of the Church of England burial service, and offered extempore prayer. The clock struck the fatal hour. The party moved forward to the scaffold. The prisoner appeared perfectly calm and collected, and walked on the scaffold without faltering. He was attended by the officials, with whom he shook hands. The executioner then adjusted the rope round his neck, and placed the cap over his head. The bolt was drawn, and Dove was launched into eternity. He expired with scarcely a struggle. Previous to going upon the scaffold he stated to Mr. Barrett, his solicitor, that he had nothing to add to the previous statements he had made as to his guilt, and taking him by the hand he said, " Tell my poor mother that I die happy." These were the last words that he uttered, except joining in prayers, and taking leave of the persons whose names have been mentioned.

The crowd dispersed peaceably. The body after hanging until one o'clock, was taken down and buried at three in the afternoon within the precincts of the prison.

Thomas Askren, a debtor in the Castle, was the executioner.

JOHN HANNAH.

Saturday, December 27th, A.D. 1856.—John Hannah, aged 22, for the wilful murder of Jane Banham, at Armley, near Leeds, on the 11th of September last, by cutting her throat with a razor in the parlour of the Malt Mill Inn. The culprit had cohabited with her and had two children by her. He was tried on the 13th of December, and Mr. Justice Erle then proceeded to sum up. He (the judge) could not find anything like provocation by blows, and it was his opinion that what was called provocation by saying she would not live with the prisoner would not palliate the crime of murder—neither words nor disappointed affection would palliate the offence.

THE VERDICT.

The jury retired at ten minutes past three o'clock, and were absent a quarter of an hour. On their return into Court—

The Clerk of Arraigns, said,—Gentlemen, have you agreed on your verdict ?

The Foreman.—Yes.

The Clerk of Arraigns.—Do you say the prisoner at the bar is Guilty or Not Guilty ?

The Foreman.—Guilty.

The Clerk of Arraigns.—John Hannah, you have been convicted of murder. Have you anything to say why sentence of death should not be passed upon you according to law ?

The prisoner (faintly),—" I wish to say," but proceeded no further.

Proclamation was then made for silence, and the judge put on the black cap.

SENTENCE OF DEATH.

Mr. Justice Erle (addressing the prisoner), said—Prisoner at the bar, you have been convicted of murder upon evidence which is perfectly clear to satisfy the jury, and to satisfy my own mind; and it is now my duty to pass upon you the sentence of the law. The sentence is that you be taken to the prison from whence you came to the place of execution, and that you be there hanged by the neck till you be dead, and that your body be afterwards buried within the precincts of the prison in which you have been confined.

The prisoner was removed from the bar in a fainting condition by the officers of the Court.

THE EXECUTION.

The execution of the culprit took place at noon to-day. Crowds of people began to assemble in front of the scaffold in the course of the forenoon, and at the time of execution about 5,000 persons would be present, a number not half so large as that which assembled to see Dove's execution.

Shortly before twelve o'clock, William Gray, Esq., the under-sheriff, proceeded to the Castle, in order to see the sentence enforced according to law. On his arrival the executioner (Askren) was introduced to the culprit, who at this time was in a very composed state of mind. The hangman proceeded to pinion the arms of Hannah, and the burial service was commenced by the chaplain. Immediately after the Castle clock had struck the hour of twelve, the door leading to the drop opened and the culprit, who walked with a firm step, accompanied by William Gray, Esq., the chaplain, Mr. Noble (the Governor), Mr. Green (the Deputy-Governor), Mr. Pears, Askren (the hangman), and the usual retinue of halberdmen, walked forward on to the scaffold. Here he knelt down and engaged in prayer fervently for a few moments.

The executioner then proceeded to cover the culprit's features with the white cap, to tie his legs, and to adjust the rope, which in the opinion of many, was not very satisfactorily executed.

The fatal bolt was then drawn, and after some protracted struggles the culprit ceased to exist. Before he died, a prayer-book which he held in his hand dropped from his grasp.

We may add that the convict made no further statement of any consequence relating to the murder, from the period he left the condemned cell to the hour of execution.

The crowd conducted themselves in a very orderly manner and if any expression of feeling was evinced, it was of sympathy with the culprit's untimely end, at so early an age.

The body after hanging until one o'clock was cut down, and buried within the precincts of the prison, pursuant to the sentence passed upon him.

He was by trade a tailor, and a native of Manchester, and has left a father and mother and eight brothers and sisters.

JOSEPH SHEPHERD.

Saturday, April 3rd, A.D. 1858.—Joseph Shepherd, of Holdsworth, near Halifax, aged 22, was executed at York Castle, for the wilful and deliberate murder of Bethel Parkinson, at Wadsworth Moor, on the 13th of January. He was a most hardened and impenitent wretch and blasphemed to the last.

On Tuesday last Shepherd said to one of the officers of the prison, "I don't mean to go to hell," whereupon the officer replied, "Don't you?" He then said, "I have done the best I know how," and this drew forth the rejoinder, "I don't think you have." Shepherd then observed, "In what way haven't I?" the answer was, "When one person has injured another in past life, if it lies in his power he has a right to make restitution; you cannot give life, but public justice demands a public confession." "Would you have me to confess what I never did?" was the question put by Shepherd, and the reply he received was, "No, but I believe you are guilty." He immediately said, "I am not."

Some idea may be formed of the hardihood of the culprit when we state that he has, within the last day or two, made observations to the effect that he hoped he could have a "blow-out" before he was hanged, as he should like a good dinner, that he should rather go to hell as he was (that is, die a natural death), than go to heaven with a halter round his neck; that he would rather be shot than hanged, that he was glad the weather was fine, as he would rather be "topped" (hanged) in summer than in winter, and that if he caught the watchman in the burial-ground (after the execution) he would give him a good thrashing. This and other conversation equally to be deplored, if not more so, he has indulged in, and we believe he has said that at such an hour on Saturday he should be dancing on nothing. During the present week he, in a jocose manner, made an inquiry if his coffin was made. The officer in charge remonstrated with him, telling him this was not the sort of conversation he ought to indulge in, and asked him if he believed there was a God. The culprit made a reply too irreverent and shocking to be repeated. On one occasion, after boasting of his innocence, and declaring he had never touched the murdered man, in reply to the interrogatory whether he meant to state that he did not know anything about the transaction, he said, "Oh, never mind that." It is rumoured that he has written to a companion, desiring him to be present at the execution.

Askren, the executioner, who resides near Rotherham, arrived at the Castle last night, and will remain there until after the execution.

This morning about four o'clock workmen commenced erecting the scaffold, and at a later hour groups of pedestrians, who had come apparently from a consideradle distance to witness the execution, were seen walking about in the streets of the city.

THE EXECUTION.

The Rev. J. Parkes, Wesleyan minister, attended upon the culprit at ten o'clock this morning, and remained with him up to the time of the execution. The criminal still manifested no change in his demeanour, and if anything was more callous and impenitent than ever, and he did not add anything to his former statement as to the murder.

At half-past eleven o'clock, William Gray, Esq., the under-sheriff, proceeded to the Castle, and made the usual formal demand of the body of the culprit, and precisely at twelve o'clock Shepherd made his appearance on the scaffold, his face, contrary to the usual custom, being already covered with the white cap.

This probably being a precautionary measure in consequence of the threat he had made against the executioner.

He was accompanied on to the scaffold by Mr. Gray (under-sheriff), Mr. Noble (the governor), the Rev. J. Parkes, Mr. Green (the deputy-governor), and other officers. The culprit knelt down for about a minute, during which the minister engaged in prayer with him, the criminal making the response, "Lord have mercy upon me, Christ have mercy upon me." These were the last words he uttered and he then nimbly sprang to his feet, and submitted to the operation of having his feet secured. The rope was then adjusted by Askren, the bolt was drawn and the criminal soon afterwards ceased to exist, but not without a considerable amount of struggling.

The crowd was one of the largest ever assembled on a similar occasion, and numbered from 10,000 to 15,000 persons, a large proportion of whom were women and boys.

The whole of the people conducted themselves with more decorum than is frequently observed on such occasions and several robust-looking men, apparently strangers, actually fainted away during the execution.

We may state that, contrary to the practice hitherto observed on such occasions, the sacrament was not administered, nor was the burial service read on his way to the scaffold.

The body, after having been suspended until one o'clock, was cut down and buried within the precincts of the prison, in accordance with the sentence which was passed upon him.

The father and mother of the culprit and his wife were present at the execution ; and also the poor widow of the murdered man Bethel Parkinson, and his father.

JOHN RILEY.

Saturday, August 6th, A.D. 1859.—John Riley was hanged behind York Castle for the wilful murder of his wife Alice Riley, at Kingston-upon-Hull.

On Monday, July 18th, John Riley, aged 36, was placed at the bar before Mr. Justice Hill, charged with the wilful murder of Alice Riley, at Kingston-upon-Hull. The prisoner, who is a thin sallow-looking man, dressed in fustian trousers and a short white smock, and has an obliquity of vision, pleaded " Not guilty."

The prisoner and his victim were man and wife, and had lived together for about twelve years, and they had children nearly that age. They had resided for some time in Lincoln-shire, where they had a serious quarrel, when, in consequence of the prisoner taking a knife, and threatening his wife's life, she left him and went to reside in Hull. Her husband visited her from time to time while she was living there, and finally went to reside with her altogether.

The prisoner now seemed to be very indolent, doing nothing for the support of his wife and family, but depending entirely upon the exertions of his wife for his sustenance. Mrs. Riley seems to have been very clever as a sempstress, and she earned in this way money sufficient to keep her and her family and her wretched husband for some time, and the latter, when all honest means failed, forced his unfortunate victim to prostitution to acquire money to satisfy their daily wants. They had frequent quarrels, the husband ill-using the wife for not earning money enough to keep him in idle-ness, and she on the other hand resorting to drink to drown her sorrow.

In May last they had another quarrel, and the neighbours, on going into the room, found that the poor woman had been very badly used, and was with some difficulty recovered. The prisoner was brought before the magistrate for the assault, when he was sent to prison for one month. On being liberated in June last, he returned to his wife, but did not seem to have had any affray with deceased up to the time of the murder. The eldest boy had gone out for the day, and in his absence the prisoner and his wife had breakfast together, and in the course of the morning had some drink, both husband and wife seeming to be in very good tempers. The woman, it appears, always went to bed when she had got any drink to sleep off the effect, and having had some on the Sunday morning, in the afternoon she had retired to bed, previously, however, telling a woman who kept the lodging-house to call her up at five o'clock, as she wanted to go out to take tea with a friend.

Soon after this the prisoner told his little boy to go out and play, and he did so, not returning until three o'clock. The prisoner being now alone, locked the door, and it is presumed to commit the dreadful act of cutting his wife's throat, for within a short period from this time, a neighbour wanted to borrow a saucepan, and she, finding the prisoner's room door locked, shouted, "Alice, Alice," but received no answer. She then went round to the room window, and called out the woman's name again, but with no better success. Just at this time, however, the woman heard a crack inside the room, and she then opened the window and looked in. To her horror she saw the prisoner hanging by the neck. She immediately alarmed the neighbours, and a man named Richardson proceeded into the room, and quickly cut him down. Life was not extinct, and so he left him in the care of some other persons, while he and a man named Balgarno went to the bed to awaken the wife, whom they found with her throat cut. On a table near the bed, but out of reach of the deceased, was found a common table knife covered with blood. The prisoner on being charged with the crime said nothing.

On being searched and examined at the station-house, some spots of blood were found on his clothes, and he said they had been the result of accident a few days before. Riley afterwards asked another policeman named Pearson where his little boys would be sent to, and afterwards added, "The knife I cut her throat with was the same she attempted to cut my throat with some time before." The prisoner further explained that the blood on his smock and shirt sleeves was from a cut in his head sometime before and was there when the row commenced. The prisoner also at the time added, " It's no use saying I'm innocent when I'm not."

His lordship summed up the evidence, and the jury found the prisoner guilty of murder, and he pronounced sentence of death in the usual manner.

THE EXECUTION.

After his conviction the unfortunate man was regularly attended by the Rev. J. C. Thompson, the chaplain of the Castle, and under that gentleman's Christian exhortations, Riley seems to have been brought to a proper appreciation of the awful position in which he stood. His aged father, from Louth, and his brother and sister, from Hull, paid him a visit a few days ago, and the unfortunate man then expressed his contrition and sorrow for the dreadful offence he had committed, and expressed the hope that he would be forgiven by his Maker. The scene which was presented was of a most heart-rending description ; but it may easily be supposed that even this did not bear comparison with the agonizing scene that took place last Saturday, when the criminal's two sons, both of whom gave evidence against their father upon his trial, took their last leave of their parent. The expenses of their journey were humanely defrayed by the high sheriff of the county.

At an early hour this morning, the workmen commenced erecting the drop in front of St. George's Field, and the solemn preparations for the awful ceremony were speedily completed. At the usual hour the wretched man, with his arms pinioned, appeared on the scaffold, attended by the regular officials ; after spending a few minutes in prayer, the executioner proceeded to perform the duties of his office, by drawing the cap over his eyes, and adjusting the rope ; when the fatal bolt was withdrawn, the drop fell, a momentary thrill of horror ran through the assembled multitude, a convulsive struggle ensued, and the unhappy man ceased to exist. There was a large concourse of people assembled to witness the last moments of the miserable man.

Charles Normington.

Saturday, December 31st, A.D. 1859.—Charles Normington, aged 17, was executed at the drop behind the Castle for the wilful murder of Mr. Richard Broughton, aged 67, of Roundhay, near Leeds, on Saturday, the 6th day of August of the same year.

The prisoner, who is a very diminutive person, and of boyish appearance, was only 4 feet 8¾ inches in height. With one exception, he is the youngest condemned criminal that has been in the Castle for many years. His trial lasted from nine o'clock in the morning till five o'clock in the afternoon.

The jury found him Guilty.

Mr. Justice Wightman then passed sentence of death upon the prisoner. A shriek was heard from a woman (said to be the prisoner's mother), in the gallery, which was repeated after sentence had been passed.

CONFESSION OF NORMINGTON.

It will be very satisfactory to the public to learn that Normington has made a full confession of his guilt, and in publishing that confession, we insert a dash in four or five instances, in order that we may not be the means of defeating justice. He made the statement in the evening of the day on which he was tried, and almost immediately after his removal to the condemned cell. He then appeared very much depressed, and began crying. Mr. Green, the deputy-governor, advised him, whatever he did, to make good use of the short period of time allotted to him, and not to tell another lie. Normington then said, "I will not ; it was me that did it, and the other man stood by, and it was me that got his (deceased's) watch ; I gave it to him (the other man), and he kept it while we got to Leeds. I went to pawn it ; I had not been in his company before that day ; we met that morning near the Marsh Lane Station ; he told me his name was ——, and he lived near —— ; a fair was held there, but I cannot tell the name just now ; it was about four miles from —— ; he was about —— years of age, and —— in height. I went to two or three pawnshops, and after I had pawned it (the watch),

I gave him 3s. of the money, and kept the other myself, and then we parted; I have not seen him since; he pulled his (deceased's) waistcoat open, but it was me that took his watch."

This confession confirms the statement Mr. Broughton made before he died, that two men attacked him, although the hypothesis of the prosecution at the trial was, that Normington alone committed the murder. The morning after he had made the above confession, he was visited by his mother, and during the interview that took place between them, she begged of him to tell the truth. He replied, "I have; I have told Mr. Green all about it." Mr. Green (who was present at this interview), then asked Normington if it was at —— where the other man lived. He said, in answer, "Yes, that's the place; it is about four miles from ——."

We understand that the culprit has since stated that he gave the deceased several blows with the bludgeon, and felled him to the ground; that the other man tore open the deceased's waistcoat, and kicked him whilst he was on the ground, and that he (Normington) took his watch. It has been rumoured that the culprit has only been five weeks out of prison since he was ten years of age, but from what we hear, he has only been once in prison before, and that for fourteen days.

THE EXECUTION.

At about eleven o'clock in the morning, the Rev. Thomas Myers, the Thursday-afternoon lecturer to the prisoners, arrived at the Castle, and, along with the Chaplain, spent the last hour of the unfortunate criminal's brief existence, in exhorting him to look up for succour in his hour of tribulation to Him who first gave him life which was about to be sacrificed.

The sacrament was also administered by the rev. gentleman, and during the whole of the morning, Normington was remarkably firm and composed. He prayed fervently, and repeatedly made use of quotations from the Scriptures, which had been read to him since his condemnation. In fact he appeared to be in a very proper frame of mind, and fully prepared to meet his dreadful fate.

Shortly before twelve o'clock, W. Gray, Esq. (the under-sheriff), arrived at the Castle, and formally demanded the body of Normington, who was thereupon delivered into the hands of the executioner.

The process of pinioning then commenced, and by the time this was concluded, the clock denoted the fatal hour. The solemn procession was then formed, and consisted of W. Gray, Esq., the Governor and Under-Governor of the Castle, the Rev. J. C. Thompson, and the Rev. T. Myers (who both appeared in their robes), and the usual complement of officials. Having proceeded slowly on to the scaffold, which the criminal reached with a firm step, he knelt down whilst prayer by the Chaplain was offered up in his behalf; Normington called out audibly, "Lord have mercy on my soul," and having arisen, the executioner adjusted the fatal noose, drew the bolt, and the unfortunate man was launched into eternity. His struggles were not severe, and before the lapse of two minutes the prisoner hung a lifeless corpse.

After hanging the usual time, the body of the unfortunate man was cut down, and will be interred this afternoon within the precincts of the Castle, in accordance with the terms of the sentence passed upon him by Mr. Justice Wightman. The crowd collected opposite the scaffold at the time the execution took place, could not be less than from 9,000 to 10,000 persons—a number considerably over that which witnessed the last execution.

During the whole of the morning the weather was dull and overcast, and about eleven o'clock a drizzling rain set in, which continued to fall during the time of the execution.

Askren, from Maltby, near Rotherham, was the executioner.

NORMINGTON'S LETTERS.

The following letters have been written at Normington's dictation :—

York Castle, 20th December, 1859.

MY DEAR MOTHER,

I send you these few lines, and I sincerely hope they will find you in good health. I am glad to tell you that I am quite well, and my mind is quite easy; and I can assure you that I do not fear my fate, for I put all my trust in the Lord Jesus Christ. In Him I hope to find rest and pardon for all my sins. I hope, dear mother, that you will not fret, but pray for me, and believe me I have quite resigned myself, and do not dread the hour so fast approaching. I pray the Lord to give strength here and peace hereafter. I believe in His promise to pardon the greatest sinner, and I believe He will forgive me, and grant me the rest I pray for. Therefore, dear mother, do not fret for me. I can assure you I feel very happy in my mind, and hope and believe that I shall soon be in everlasting happiness and rest, for believe me I fear nothing, trusting entirely in the Lord. I hope you will pray unto Him, and that you will be saved, and enjoy eternal happiness. This, dear mother, is my sincere prayer for you, and it is hoped we shall meet again in the Kingdom of Heaven, where we shall be far happier than here in the world of trouble. I think of all my friends, and pray for you all, and hope you will all do the same for me.

I remain, Dear Mother,

Your affectionate Son,

CHARLES NORMINGTON.

York Castle, December 28th, 1859.

DEAR FATHER,

I have had my mother here to see me this morning, and I have taken my last farewell of her in this world. It is very hard to part with you, my dear parents, but it is the providence of God, which I hope will be beneficial to you and all my friends, and I pray to God that my fate may be a warning to everybody, and be the means of bringing you to a saving knowledge of the truth as it is in Christ Jesus. Dear Father, if it be God's will that we should not meet again on earth, I hope that we shall meet in Heaven. I have one wish to express to you, which I hope you will grant me. I am, perhaps, going a little too far in dictating to you, but I hope you will consider my last, and I may say my dying wish, that is, I hope you will be again reconciled to my mother, and I hope you will live together again and be happy. I don't want to hurt your feelings, nor yet to upbraid you with anything, but I wish to say that things might have been different if you and mother had lived in the fear of God ; but I pray that you will begin now, when I shall have a hope of meeting you again in Heaven. Unless you do, there will be no hope for you.

Dear Father, I hope you will take these things into consideration. You know what a great sin you have committed by leaving my mother and your family to the wide world in the way you do. Dear Father, I could die now content if I thought you and mother would live together again. I pray for you, and I forgive you, and I hope God will forgive you.

I now must conclude, with kind love to all, hoping to meet you all in Heaven. I must now bid you an eternal farewell, and may God bless you and all my friends.

I remain,

Your affectionate Son,

CHARLES NORMINGTON.

The culprit caused two other letters to be written, one to his mother and the other to his uncle and aunt. He entreated the former to pray for him and for herself, and stated that he was at peace with the world.

The following is an extract from the letter to the uncle and aunt :—

I do not despair, but the Lord will pardon me. I own I do not deserve pardon, but I hope and trust in Him and in His mercy, for He delighteth not in the death of a sinner, but that he should turn from his wickedness and live. I expect to receive the Sacrament next Sunday. I hope I shall not receive it unworthily, and I expect to die on Saturday week. [The letter was written on the 21st inst.] I hope you will all pray for me that I may not despair in my last moments. Mr. Thompson, the chaplain, is very attentive to me. He visits me twice a day, and prays with me, and I attend divine service every morning, and I pray for forgiveness. I humbly implore your forgiveness for the distress I have brought upon you, and I hope you will forget and forgive. Indeed, I praise God when I think of His goodness in permitting me to live so long a time to repent when He might have let me go off, all at once, so many times I have rejected His call. I have great fortitude, and do not fear to meet death, for God is with me.

JAMES WALLER.

Saturday, January 4th, A.D. 1862.—James Waller, aged 31, a woolcomber by trade, was executed at York Castle, for the wilful murder of William Smith, on Tuesday, the 5th of November, 1861 (Smith was a gamekeeper in the employ of Timothy Horsfall, Esq., of Hawksworth Hall, near Otley, in the parish of Bingley, in the West Riding), by shooting him with a double-barrelled gun, loaded with shot.

The prisoner pleaded " Not Guilty," in a firm tone of voice.

After the trial, the jury retired for twenty minutes, and brought in a verdict of guilty.

Proclamation for silence having been made, the prisoner was asked if he had anything to say why sentence of death should not be passed upon him. He made no reply. Mr. Justice Wightman assumed the black cap, and said :—
" James Waller, the jury, who are the proper judges of the facts, have come to the conclusion, after a careful deliberation of your case, upon the evidence before them, that you are guilty of the fearful crime of murder ; and judging from the

whole case, as it has been presented before the Court in evidence, and judging from the expressions which you on several occasions had used, there seems to me to be no reason to doubt, that no other conclusion can exist in the minds of any one who has heard this case, that without any adequate motive, without any such reason as might justify the jury to reduce the crime of which you have been guilty to that of manslaughter; you wilfully took away the life of this unfortunate man. I do not wish to aggravate, by any observations of mine, the terror and horror of the situation in which you stand, but I am bound to tell you that this is one of those cases to which is annexed the fearful penalty of death by the law both of God and man. I can hold out no hope of mercy to you for such a crime as this. You have deprived this unfortunate man of life, and I earnestly exhort you to prepare for that great account which you will have to give hereafter. I can hold out no mercy to you, and I therefore entreat you to endeavour to prepare for eternity. The sentence I now pass upon you is, that you be taken to the place from whence you came, and thence to the place of execution, and there be hanged by the neck until you are dead, and that your body be buried within the precincts of the jail in which you have been confined, and may the Lord have mercy on you."

The prisoner, who was very neatly attired, evinced only a slight emotion at the conclusion of the learned judge's address.

CONFESSION OF THE CULPRIT.

If there was the slightest lingering doubt existing in the mind of any person as to Waller having committed the crime of murder, it is satisfactory to be enabled to dissipate such doubt, he having confessed his guilt to the high sheriff, without any qualification or reservation whatever, and fully acknowledged the justice of his sentence. He was visited by the chaplain at seven o'clock in the evening, and from nine until eleven the officers who had charge of him read to him various portions of Scripture. The culprit then joined in singing psalms and hymns, and at ten minutes past eleven o'clock he retired to rest, and fell asleep. He slept

till half-past four in the morning. A little before seven
o'clock, he was visited by Mr. Green, the deputy-governor
of the prison, and the culprit's own clothing was substituted
for the prison dress he had been wearing since his conviction. He was then removed to the small room connected
with the Assize Courts, where prisoners sentenced to death
are usually placed, and where they remain during the last
few hours of their existence. He was accompanied by Mr.
Green, to whom he said whilst crossing the Castle-yard,
that he had no doubt that he should soon be in heaven.
In fact he appeared more cheerful and resigned, than he
had done during the last fortnight, and partook of a hearty
breakfast. He was visited by the chaplain shortly before
eight o'clock, and again between nine and ten. The sacrament was administered to him at eleven, by the chaplain
and the Rev. T. Myers.

THE EXECUTION.

From a very early hour in the morning the desire to witness the consummation of the dread penalty of death upon a
fellow-creature was evinced by the group of persons who
collected in front of the black dismal instrument which
stood out in all its grimness, as a contrast to the brightness
of a resplendent sun-lit day. The bulk of the persons,
forming these groups, however, evidenced the fact that they
were from the sister riding, of which the criminal Waller
was a native, not a few of whom had taken the advantage of
a nocturnal walk in order to arrive at the scene of the execution which they had come to witness. Indeed the fatigues
suffered by some few in thus reaching the city, induced them
to seek rest in sleep in the field opposite the drop. In
the coolness with which the people discussed circumstances
of the criminal's offence, the easy jaunty manner in which
some perched themselves upon the rails, skirting St. George's
Field, and the ribald and disgusting expressions which came
from others in reference to the unfortunate man's approaching end, one failed to find the working of that great moral
lesson which the public strangling of a criminal was designed
to effect. As the mid-day hour approached, the number of
spectators gradually increased until the crowd might be

counted by its thousands. Not an inconsiderable portion of these were juveniles, assembled, probably, to gain their first experience of the rigorous character of the fate which is the murderer's lot. Some, however, by their careless and rude demeanour, might lead to the impression that the occasion was not one of rare occurrence to them, and that it was taken advantage of rather as an opportunity of indulging in fun, than as the serious reflections of the dreadful consequences of guilt; auxiliaries common to such gatherings as the one just referred to, present in the shape of vendors of nuts and oranges, the character and cheapness of the article they offered ringing in stentorian voice upon the ears of the assembled crowd. Thimble-rigging formed one of the amusements of the crowd. As a serious set-off to this feature of the scene, however, those useful members of our community, the city missionaries, were engaged in the philanthropic task of distributing tracts, the contents of which were designed to warn their readers of the fickleness of human life, and the necessity of preparing for death. Within a few minutes of twelve, the road, to the eye of a spectator, presented a busy and bustling appearance, which, but for the knowledge of the fact, could scarcely have led to the impression that the rush was to witness a human life, which had been guilty of one of the blackest crimes, launched into eternity. At the hour of execution there could not have been less than 8,000 or 10,000 people present.

A few minutes before twelve o'clock, the Under-Sheriff arrived at the Castle, and formally demanded the body of Waller, which was thereupon delivered into the hands of the executioner. The process of pinioning then commenced, and by the time this was concluded the clock of the Castle denoted the fatal hour which had been fixed for the criminal's death. A procession was then formed in the usual order, and consisted of William Gray, Esq., the Governor and Under-Governor of the Castle, the Chaplain and the Rev. T. Myers (both of whom appeared in their robes), and the usual complement of halberdmen and other officials. The procession arrived slowly upon the drop, the criminal walking with a firm step. Before his execution, he fell upon his knees whilst the usual prayers were read, and he responded to the Lord's Prayer in the most earnest manner. At the conclusion, Waller arose and submitted himself to the executioner, who at once adjusted the fatal noose, secured his legs, and, by drawing the fatal bolt, launched the unfortunate man into eternity. During the latter process, he prayed in the most fervent manner, and when the fatal drop took place he was supplicating the Lord to receive his soul. His struggles were rather severe, but life was extinct in less than a couple of minutes. After hanging the usual time, the body was cut down and interred within the precincts of the Castle, in accordance with the terms of the sentence passed upon him by the judge.

It is satisfactory to know that Waller, at nine o'clock on the morning of the execution, again acknowledged his guilt of the crime for which he was about to suffer. While speaking of Smith, the murdered man, he said, " I had my revenge, and this is my reward, but I hope that he (Smith) is in heaven, and I hope to meet him there soon. There is no bad feeling between us now." Some time after, whilst talking to his family, who had occupied a large amount of his anxiety since his trial, he said, " I have two children in heaven, and I hope to meet them there." The state of the criminal's mind immediately before his death was of the most satisfactory character, and he died full of hope of salvation through the merits of Christ.

We have been particular in describing all the process of this notable public execution, being the last we have to record for the present, and it may be taken as a fair representation of what executions generally are at the Castle of York.

Frederick Parker.

Saturday, April 4th, A.D. 1868—Frederick Parker was executed at York Castle, for the murder of Daniel Driscoll, at South Duffield, near Selby, on Saturday, the 29th of February, 1868.

The leading facts in connection with the murder may be stated as follows:—The deceased was 27 years of age, and a journeyman bricklayer. He lived with his mother at Tottenham, Middlesex, but in January last he left his home in search of work, and found his way into Yorkshire. A short time ago he was committed to Beverley House of Correction, having "got into trouble," and the term of his imprisonment coming to an end on Saturday, the 29th Feb., he was liberated from goal on the morning of that day. A farm labourer, named Frederick Parker, living at Hemingbrough, who had undergone two months' imprisonment at Beverley, was released at the same time as Driscoll, and both of them left the prison in company together shortly before half-past nine o'clock. Driscoll had on his departure £4 11s. in a purse, and he had also a silver watch and silver Albert chain with a long key attached to it. Parker, when he left, had only 1s. 4½d. and a letter containing some postage stamps. In about an hour after leaving the goal they were at the Red Lion public house at Beverley, where they stayed but a short time. About seven o'clock in the evening they were at Bubwith, where they called for a glass of ale each, after drinking which they went away, stating that they were going to Hemingbrough. This was the last time that the deceased was seen alive, and he was found murdered three miles from Bubwith, in the neighbourhood of South Duffield. His body was found in a ditch by the road side, and his head was severely wounded, a thick hedgestake lying by his side, the weapon no doubt used by the murderer in taking away the life of his victim. The deceased's watch and money were gone with the exception of 2d.; a fact leading to the conclusion that the murder had been committed for the purposes of plunder.

On Sunday morning, the 1st of March, Parker was at Brind, and called at the house of a labourer named Bentley, where he had some breakfast. He produced the deceased's watch and chain, and also a purse containing gold and silver, being nearly the same amount of money that had belonged to deceased, He said that the watch was his, and that the glass, which was cracked, had been broken by the officers of the goal at Beverley. On leaving that prison he stated that in addition to the watch he had £4 0s. 11½d., and that finding he was ten shillings short he returned to the goal and applied for the money. Whilst at Bentley's he appeared to be very restless, frequently looked out of the window, and inquired if police-officers were in the habit of coming that way. He took his departure at half-past two o'clock in the afternoon, saying he was going to his uncle's house at Hemingbrough. In the evening Parker was at Newland, where he saw a labouring man named David Dillcock, with whom he was acquainted. He showed Dillcock the deceased's watch and offered to make him a present of it, but he would not have it, upon which Parker said that he would throw it into the river. He then took out of his pocket four sovereigns and 4s. 6d. in silver, which he handed to Dillcock, and he accepted it. Parker then departed and went along a lane in the direction of Airmyn. On the following night, Parker saw Wm. Dillcock another labourer, at Newland, to whom he offered the watch stating that he had "planted it" but this man also declined to take the present. David Dillcock had an interview with Superintendent Green, at Howden, and that officer returned with him to Newland. They made a search in the hedge bottom of the lane along which Parker had walked, and eventually they found the watch and chain wrapped up in some tow and straw, and this watch was identified as that which belonged to the deceased. Parker was apprehended at the house of his uncle, at Hemingbrough, by Mr. Gibson, Deputy Chief Constable of the East Riding, at an early hour in the morning of the 5th instant, on the charge of being the murderer of the deceased.

Parker was tried before Mr. Justice Smith, at York

Castle, on Thursday, the 12th of March, 1868, and the jury found him guilty of murder, the learned Judge passing sentence of death upon him.

The execution took place on the 4th of April following as already stated. At half-past eleven o'clock Parker, after having fallen upon his knees and prayed aloud, was removed from his quarters in the condemned cell to the pinioning room, having been previously attired in his own dress. He walked firmly, and on his way cried repeatedly for Jesus to have mercy on his soul, and saying in a few moments he should be with his Jesus, and how joyful and happy a thing it was to be able to say he should so soon be with Him. When he got in the pinioning room he again commenced praying earnestly, and constantly ejaculated such sentences as those given above. Just before the time for the execution he handed the Governor of the Castle a letter he had written, and which for the benefit of others he wished should be published. This was addressed to the band-master of the village of Hemingbrough, who was asked to read it to the rest of his friends. Some he mentioned individually, calling upon them to note and benefit by his fate, and in one instance he freely forgave one of them for some past injury he had done. He warned them against drink, which he said had brought him to his present position. At its conclusion, he bade his friends good bye for ever, and after hoping they might meet in heaven, signed himself their " unfortunate friend, F. Parker." The whole document was written in the happiest spirit, and from its terms must be a source of satisfaction to those who have anxiously tendered their christian ministrations to the culprit since his condemnation. At five minutes to 12 o'clock Mr. Gray, the Under-Sheriff, entered the pinioning-room, and formally demanded the body of the culprit from the Governor, and then pinioning commenced. This occupied but a minute or two, after which the procession for the scaffold was formed. This consisted of four halberdmen, W. Gray, Esq., the Governor (W. F. Lowrie, Esq.), the Chaplain, (Rev. J. C. Thompson), the culprit, the Under Governor, (Mr. Webster), three warders, and several of the Sheriff's attendants.

A few moments after the Castle clock struck twelve the procession appeared on the scaffold, when the murmur of the vast crowd immediately became hushed. The first act of the culprit was to turn his back to the assemblage and shake hands with the governor, the under-governor (Mr. Webster), and the head warders who had him in charge, wishing them "Good bye," and hoping they might meet in Heaven. Then he fell on his knees and responded to the prayers of the chaplain, whom he in conclusion followed earnestly in the Lord's Prayer. Immediately after, Askern came forward, and placing a white cap over his head, adjusted the noose of the dangling rope round his neck. Then tying his legs the culprit was ready for the last act of drawing the bolt. This was promptly done, and the body fell with a loud thud which could be heard in the crowd, and was lost to the sight of the spectators. A slight convulsive twitching was all that could be seen by those on the scaffold, and the murderer was dead. During the whole of the process of pinioning, Parker had remained firm and thus maintained himself to the end, his last words being "Lord Jesus receive my spirit." An hour after the execution, the body was cut down and buried within the precincts of the prison.

INDEX.

—•◦•—

THE END